GLOBAL
MEDIA

Menace or Messiah?

Revised Edition

THE HAMPTON PRESS COMMUNICATION SERIES

Mass Communications and Journalism
Lee B. Becker, supervisory editor

Magazine-Made America: The Cultural Transformation of the Postwar Periodical
David Abrahamson

It's Not Only Rock & Roll: Popular Music in the Lives of Adolescents
Peter G. Christenson and Donald F. Roberts

Global Media: Menace or Messiah?
David Demers

American Heroes in the Media Age
Susan F. Drucker and Robert S. Cathcart (eds.)

The Ultimate Assist: The Relationship and Broadcast Strategies of the NBA
and Television Networks
John A. Fortunato

Media, Sex and the Adolescent
Bradley S. Greenberg, Jane D. Brown, and Nancy Buerkel-Rothfuss

Community Media in the Information Age: Perspectives and Prospects
Nicholas W. Jankowski with Ole Prehn (eds.)

forthcoming

China's Window on the World: TV News, Social Knowledge and
International Spectacles
Tsan-Kuo Chang with Jian Wang and Yanru Chen

Journalism Education in Europe and North America
Christina Holtz-Bacha and Romy Frölich (eds.)

Newspapers and Social Change: Community Structure and Coverage of
Critical Events
John C. Pollock

The Impact of Gender on Journalism: Canadian, U.S. and European Experiences
Gertrude J. Robinson

GLOBAL
MEDIA

Menace or Messiah?

Revised Edition

David Demers

With a Foreword by
Melvin DeFleur

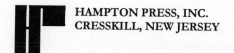

HAMPTON PRESS, INC.
CRESSKILL, NEW JERSEY

Printed in the United States of America

Library of Congress Cataloging-in-Publication Data

Demers, David
    Global media : menace or messiah? / David Demers, with a foreword
by Melvin DeFleur. --Rev. ed.
        p. cm. -- (The Hampton Press communication series)
    Includes bibliographical references and index.
    ISBN 1-57273-431-0 (ppb)
        1. Mass media--Ownership.   2. Communication, International.
    3. Mass media--Social aspects.   I. Title.   II. Series.

P96.E25 D46   2001
302.23--dc21   2001039953

Hampton Press Inc.
23 Broadway
Cresskill, NJ 07626

TO DEB

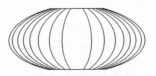

CONTENTS

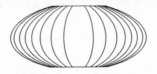

FOREWORD

David Demers has made an important contribution to all who study mass communication, whether they are students, professors, researchers or professionals.

Global Media: Menace or Messiah? provides an easy-to-follow road map through what, for many of us, can be a complex and often confusing intellectual territory. It guides the reader through that terrain by explaining the issues in simple language and by presenting the views of a broad range of scholars, many of whom hold controversial views. In its eleven chapters, the book focuses on much more than how global media corporations are organized and how they are changing. It also discusses the nature of their goals, how they are controlled, controversies over their assumed power, and the implications of their continued growth for the future.

Professor Demers analyzes these issues with solid scholarship, citing both classical and contemporary sources for many of the positions discussed. He also reviews findings from relevant research that shed light on many of the claims advanced by both critics and supporters. He has an impressive command of the nature of global media and the positions taken by both their antagonists and defenders. That command is based on his own long-term dedication to conducting and interpreting research on media ownership. It is revealed in his analytical thinking about the consolidation of ownership and control over many decades. This expertise has enabled him to assess objectively what is likely to take place in the future.

Simply put, this book describes and assesses the nature and consequences of the ever-increasing number of mergers among corporations in control of media that deliver content to audiences world-wide. Those mergers, resulting in the growth of transnational media organizations, have been widely criticized by an increasing number of social scientists and communication scholars in recent years. Professor Demers lays out systematically the nature of the various positions taken in an objective way. He then examines each analytically in terms of its ideological foundations, the type of evidence that exists regarding the assertions that its advocates have made, and whether there is, or is not, objective evidence to make a judgment about whether their conclusions can be supported.

As the discussion points out, the issue of consolidation of ownership and control of global media organizations cannot be separated from the broader contexts within which it has been occurring — specifically within both capitalism and democracy. As an economic system, Demers notes, capitalism is presumed to promote competition, which in turn leads to greater efficiency in the production of goods and services.

Since Adam Smith, the fundamental rule of capitalism has been to maximize profits and minimize costs. Increasing efficiency can help accomplish those goals. But if producers have competition, whatever is being produced must be sold at lower prices. This benefits customers because they get what they want cheaper. However, this outcome produces a classic dilemma: Profits decrease as competition increases, because costs usually remain the same. Although increasing efficiency can help up to a point, the most effective way to lower costs is through economies of scale. That is, producers can achieve this through mergers. Such consolidations can reduce costs and thereby increase profits by purchasing on a larger scale, by "downsizing" employees, and by eliminating duplications in management and other functions.

That is exactly what has happened in the media industries over many decades. Chain ownership of newspapers began in the 1800s. That trend continued through the twentieth century. Today, the daily newspapers that have survived are very profitable because mergers and economies of scale have reduced their costs. Exactly the same trend has consolidated ownership of magazines, radio and television stations, motion picture studios and book publishers. Looked at in this way, the forces behind consolidation among media producers and distributors are no different economically than those related to supermarket retailing, health insurance, home repair supplies, auto production or fried chicken restaurants. Those who consolidate and provide their customers with attractive products or services at a lower cost will prosper.

Consolidation of media ownership, therefore, is an inevitable outcome of mature capitalism. It need not be seen as an insidious plot on the part of greedy owners, or as a conspiracy between producers and a government intent on dominating the minds of the world. The fact that there are now 12 huge corporations that control a very large share of the enterprises that produce entertainment and information for a global audience reveals nothing more sinister than does the fact that most of the hamburgers consumed world-wide are produced by three major chains.

Professor Demers points out that the embedding of media consolidation within the political system of democracy is more controversial. The basis of concern for many scholars and critics is the assumption that media content can control minds. There are grounds for these concerns. It is widely understood that what people read, hear and view in mass communication content plays a central role in what they think about objects, situations and events in their social and physical world. Simply put, people interpret reality within a structure of beliefs derived from the communications that they receive — whether from media, from school, the church or from personal word-of-mouth transmissions.

The principle of the social construction of reality was first laid out in the colorful Allegory of the Cave three centuries before the birth of Christ, and it has been a recurring theme in philosophy, the social sciences and media theory ever since. Thus, many critics maintain, if the media consistently present to their audiences deliberately designed and carefully selected news, entertainment and other information that supports and champions a particular set of political values, then it is likely that this will be what the majority of audiences accept as truth in their interpretations of reality. They point to the fact that people like Adolph Hitler, Joseph Stalin, Fidel Castro and Saadam Hussein all were able to remain in power in part because they rigidly controlled the content of their media.

As *Global Media: Menace or Messiah?* points out, many of those who decry global media consolidation fear that this change will narrow the diversity of what the controlling organizations offer. The charge is that they will concentrate on embedding themes and values in their content that help them maintain their positions of power in order to protect their profits. At first glance, this does seem an ominous possibility. However, it does not hold up under closer inspection. Perhaps the main flaw in such a thesis is the factor of audience selectivity. The earliest mass communication theory (Magic Bullet) was based on the idea that people passively attend to whatever content is offered by the media and are immediately, directly and unthinkingly influenced by what is presented.

The modern critics appear to accept something like this idea. However, by the time of World War II that theory began to be replaced by the realization that the audience was active rather than passive. Research began to accumulate showing that people sought from the media the kinds of content that pleased them — content that was consistent with their interests and that they could use to gratify various kinds of needs. They simply ignored that which did not interest them. That principle does not fit well with the claim that contemporary media corporations, whether large or small, local or global, have captive audiences that mindlessly attend to whatever those who control them want to present.

Furthermore, a claim that contemporary media systems offer content that is less diverse than was the case earlier would be difficult to support. Anyone who visits a modern magazine store where hundreds of specialized periodicals are displayed, who turns to her or his cable or satellite TV to select from up to a hundred or more channels, many of which offer very specialized content, or who tours through a large chain bookstore with hundreds of thousands of publications on display, would dismiss the claim of limited diversity. The sheer number of choices in whatever area of content is simply staggering.

But there is more.

There is the issue of world domination by the global media organizations, which are said to champion the political system that insures their profits. Some critics feel that movies, television shows and other media content produced in the United States, or at least in Western democracies, are designed deliberately or unwittingly to displace the values, customs and authority systems in less developed parts of the world. Some go so far as to say that there is an implicit conspiracy between media organizations and those in political control to disseminate Western media content as widely as possible. The goal, say some critics, is to replace local cultures with those more favorable to Western capitalists so that American and European political power and profits can expand.

At first glance this argument seems to have intuitive validity. When poor subsistence farmers in a remote part of the world see the way of life and the abundant material culture of Western societies on TV or in a movie, they can be motivated to obtain some of the goods and benefits. This clearly could have an influence on their willingness to change their way of life — to obtain better food, health care, housing, or even freedom from repressive political domination. Negative influences can occur also. When people see media depictions of behavior that they would like to emulate, but which are regarded as deviant by their indigenous cultural norms, dissatisfaction with traditional ways of life can be the result.

The problem is not with the idea that innovations may be adopted — that can and does happen. It is with the assumption that there is some sort of vast conspiracy to dominate traditional societies, or to replace political systems different from democracy and capitalism by the dissemination of media content designed to motivate people to abandon what they now have. A more likely assumption, as Professor Demers reminds us, is that many countries are too poor to produce media content consistent with their own indigenous culture — so they simply import movies, television programming and other mass communication content that their citizens like. The global media corporations obviously profit from this and encourage it — not to consolidate someone's political power, or to reshape local economies, but simply to make money. The same system prevails in marketing automobiles, pharmaceuticals, airliners, fast foods and computer software.

Global Media: Menace or Messiah? does an outstanding job of setting forth these various arguments and positions, identifying their ideological foundations, assembling research evidence that is relevant to the issues and discussing the implications of each. Professor Demers does not present a case that is aggressively hostile to any of the thoughtful arguments that have been advanced by serious scholars devoted to such conceptual frameworks as critical cultural analysis, cultural imperialism or the other challenges to the trends that have been occurring. However, he does insist upon looking analytically at all of the evidence, including factual information about what the media organizations are doing and what the accumulation of trustworthy research indicates. He rejects the belief that conclusions can be based solely on anecdotes, selected cases or predetermined pronouncements based on ideological assumptions.

Finally, building on the sociological theories developed by August Comte, Emile Durkheim, Ferdinand Tönnies and Herbert Spencer, Professor Demers analyzes a major form of social change that has been, is now, and will continue to characterize not only media organizations operating globally but societies as a whole. The central idea is diversity. That is, as urbanization, migration, industrialization and the adoption of complex technologies continue in the world, individuals become less and less alike and social life becomes increasingly complex. Populations become more heterogeneous in terms of what tasks people perform as the work force becomes more specialized and as they are located at different positions in an expanding socioeconomic class structure.

Increasing diversity is found among the inhabitants of contemporary societies in terms of culture of origin, educational attainment, religion, political preference, recreational interests and a hundred other characteristics. Increasingly, such a society is held together by the principle of mutual dependence that Durkheim called "organic solidarity." That is, people may not know each other, or even care about each other, but each makes some contribution to the overall social order that helps maintain its stability.

As the final chapter explains, this characteristic of structural differentiation is clearly in evidence among large media organizations, and their complexity will continue to develop into the future. This is inevitable if they want to remain profitable. As more and more mergers take place, and the number of organizations providing media content to the world grows smaller, each will have to serve the interests of more and more diverse sub-segments of increasingly complex societies. This trend is clearly in evidence in American domestic television as well as in the magazine industry. Specialized content designed around every interest and hobby can be found in these media. Currently, viewers can select a channel devoted solely to history, to world news or to direct marketing. Soon, as technology continues to advance, there will be channels (rather then mere programs) devoted solely to such topics as golf, gourmet cooking, archery, animal training, and home vegetable gardening, to mention only a few.

This type of "narrowcasting" has for some years characterized the magazine and book industries. In other words, in increasingly heterogeneous populations each member will actively make decisions based on personal interests as to what media content to select. The result will provide an even more complex spectrum of niche markets than exists now. These will have to be served with widely varying media content. Global media organizations will become more and more structurally differentiated in order to supply those markets. As they do this, they will be less and less able to concentrate on some central set of themes and values that are designed to influence and sway large numbers of people to adopt a particular set of economic or political systems. Structural differentiation, in other words, leads to less concentrated power, not more. If profits are to be maintained, their supposed persuasive power will be reduced.

It would appear, then, that global media organizations are neither menace nor messiah. They are like other businesses that have had to consolidate to become more efficient in order to reduce costs and maximize profits. If Adam Smith were alive today, he would recognize that they are acting within the basic principles of mature capitalism. They are unlikely to control the thoughts and beliefs of nations in order to dominate or destroy indigenous cultures. They are equally unlikely to elevate the tastes, values and ideals of humankind beyond their present levels.

Melvin L. DeFleur
Boston University
Summer 1999

ACKNOWLEDGMENTS

The first edition of this book was published in December 1999. At that time, I expected the contents of Chapter 3 — which examine the world's leading global media corporations — would become outdated within several years. But it happened in less than a year.

In 2000, AOL acquired Time Warner, making the world's largest media corporation even larger. Vivendi of France purchased Seagram's Universal film and recording businesses, pushing The Walt Disney Company out of second place. Viacom purchased CBS, which would have moved that film and television company up to fourth spot except that Bertelsmann's revenues rose dramatically. The News Corporation's revenues also rose but it slipped from fourth into sixth place because of the gains by Vivendi and Viacom.

Needless to say, I am very pleased to have had the opportunity to update Chapter 3 as well as to make corrections and minor changes to other portions of this book. But the major themes and issues remain unchanged.

As always, I am grateful to those who assisted me in the first and second editions. During many of the weeks I spent writing this book, Debra L. Merskin would often send me newspaper and magazine clippings about global media. "Thought you could use this," she would often write. She was right. Her thoughtfulness, support and constructive comments on earlier drafts of this manuscript are deeply appreciated.

A special word of thanks also must be extended to Melvin DeFleur, who graciously agreed to take time from his busy schedule to write the FOREWORD. Professor DeFleur is one of the most prolific writers in the social and communication sciences, and his numerous books and writings have been influencing my thinking and thousands of other scholars for many years.

I am also indebted to professors Lee B. Becker, K. "Vish" Viswanath, Julia Corbett, Mark Neuzil and Jim Upshaw. Dr. Becker, who is a communication series editor at Hampton, provided sound advice for improving the manuscript and, in several instances, saved me from embarrassing mistakes. Dr. Viswanath diligently read and critiqued earlier drafts of the manuscript and, as always, provided many insightful and useful suggestions. I am also grateful to him for the many enjoyable conversations and debates we have had about the structure and function of mass media systems. Drs. Corbett and Neuzil's comments and suggestions on early drafts of the manuscript played a crucial role in securing a publisher. Their critiques were most thoughtful and appreciated. And Professor Upshaw, a former international television news correspondent, provided a unique and fresh critique of the manuscript.

I am also grateful to Hampton Press's Barbara Bernstein, who offered a good contract, a good attitude and sound editorial advice; professor Phillip J. Tichenor, who has played the single most important role in shaping my personal intellectual history; Washington State University student Jennifer Richardson, who edited the final manuscript with a punctilious eye; Washington State University student Allison Parker and Ohio State University students Melissa Tell and Heath Weber, who read portions of the manuscript and provided valuable feedback; Alex Tan, director of the Edward R. Murrow School of Communication at WSU, who also read portions of the manuscript and provided support and encouragement for this and many other projects; and to many other scholars out there whose research has enriched my own.

All errors, of course, are mine.

David Demers
Pullman, Washington
April 2001

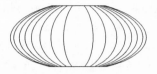

INTRODUCTION

W hen I was a kid during the 1950s and 1960s, it was hard to imagine a world with global media. Today it's hard to imagine one without them.

Global media corporations produce most of the news and entertainment we consume. This includes most of the films coming out of Hollywood, most of the programming on major U.S., European and Asian television networks, most of the programming on cable television and satellite television, much of the news and music programming on radio, and much of the content we see in major magazines, newspapers and popular books.

The modern world as we know it would come to a screeching halt without access to the information and products generated by global media. Corporations depend on global media to make good business decisions. Governments depend on them to make good political decisions. And individuals depend on them to make good personal decisions. In fact, data compiled by Hoover's Business Press shows that the average U.S. adult spends more time per day consuming media content (10 hours) than she or he does working or sleeping (eight hours each).

Yet, despite this dependence, most people know very little about global media. Who runs them? What do they control? What impact do global media have on people and societies? Will global media help democratize the world? Or will they promote consumerism and centralize political decision-making? In short, are global media a menace or messiah? These are some of the key questions that *Global Media: Menace or Messiah?* seeks to answer.

This book is written for a broad audience — one that includes not only undergraduate and graduate students taking courses in communications, journalism, political science, sociology, public administration, business, economics and history, *but also* concerned citizens, professional communicators (i.e., people who work in advertising, journalism, public relations, telecommunications), corporate executives, government officials and public policy makers.

These individuals and the organizations they represent have frequent contact with global media and, consequently, have a strong need for information about them — yet there are few palatable sources they can turn to. Virtually all of the books written on the topic are geared for graduate-level courses. Most are difficult to read and are full of jargon and technical terms.

In contrast, *Global Media: Menace or Messiah?* is designed to be reader-friendly. Numerous anecdotes and examples are used to tell the story. Technical jargon is avoided or explained. References and notes are relegated to the end of the book. And it's concise.

Of course, to be reader-friendly and concise, this book cannot address every issue related to global communications. For example, this book cannot explore changes in communication technology in any depth. Whole volumes have been written on just that topic. Instead, the purpose here is to focus on media organization as the unit of analysis, and on the impact that changes in media organization and content are having on people and society. For additional reading, please consult the references provided in the NOTES at the end of this book.

Why This Book?

The idea for this book came to me several years ago after I read an article about global media in a magazine targeted to a general audience. The author, a neo-Marxist, or "leftist," scholar, argued that Time Warner, Disney and other "global media" threaten democratic ideals and good journalism because they are driven by profits, not by the desire to produce high-quality news and entertainment programming.

This is not a new criticism. Large-scale media organizations have been criticized since the late 1800s. What is relatively new, however, are leftist critiques in the popular press. Historically, critical media scholars tended to publish in scholarly journals and books narrowly targeted to college students and faculty. But now one can easily find the works of scholars like Noam Chomsky in popular magazines and film documentaries.

The appearance of left-wing critiques in the popular press has both good and bad consequences for the globalization debate. On the one hand, the public gets access to information that traditionally was restricted to an elite, academic audience. Neo-Marxist scholars have many good arguments, to be sure.

On the other hand, though, a great deal of scientific research fails to support many of the more radical leftist claims, and the citizen who seeks to be fully informed will have a difficult time finding summaries of that research in the popular press. The proponents of media globalization, who largely consist of economists and corporate executives, have ignored much of the criticism from the left, placing their faith in the idea that the market will produce the most socially responsible media system.

While the free-market perspective is naive, the lack of response to antimedia criticism has created a void — that is, the public and policy makers have virtually no access to more balanced accounts of the organizational changes taking place in the communications industry. As a media scholar and citizen, this concerns me greatly, since the popular press and public opinion may influence public policy decisions, oftentimes more than scholarly reflection and logic.

This book is not a defense of global media. Like all mainstream media, global media often publish or broadcast content that has adverse consequences for the poor and other disadvantaged groups. Mainstream media generally serve the interests of those in power. But this book is not a full-blown attack on media globalization. Large-scale news media corporations can and have often exposed injustice and wrong-doing in the most powerful elite groups in society. They are not simply lap dogs of the rich and powerful.

Global Media: Menace or Messiah? is designed to be a corrective to the extremist positions that currently dominate the intellectual landscape. The perspective I offer is based in part on research I have conducted over the past decade on the corporate form of organization in the U.S. newspaper industry. Global media are simply the most "corporatized" of all media forms (see formal definition in the next section). Although many readers no doubt will disagree with some (or perhaps all) of my arguments, my main desire is that this book will bring more reason and balance to the debate about the origins and consequences of global media systems.

There is little question that neo-Marxist scholars will be the strongest critics of this book. They will charge that, in an attempt to reach a broad audience, I have oversimplified their arguments, which are summarized in Chapter 6. Although space prevents a detailed accounting of their many writings, I believe that my synthesis accurately summarizes the strengths and weaknesses of their work. Where it does not, I welcome a critical response.

What Is a Global Medium?

Most professionals and scholars agree that a *global medium* is a media organization that generates print or electronic messages or programs for dissemination to large numbers of people around the world. Some analysts prefer the term *transnational media corporation,* meaning an organization that has operations in more than one nation. But in either case total sales or revenues is usually used to rank-order the leading global or transnational media organizations.

This definition is useful in many contexts (see, e.g., Chapter 3). However, total sales does not tell us much about that organizational form. To understand the effects of global media structure on people and society, key features or characteristics of organizational structure that are producing those effects need to be identified. In other words, what aspects of global media organization are producing the effects that people interpret as good or bad?

As logical as this question may seem, few researchers and virtually none of the critics have bothered to provide a formal definition of organizational structure. Although *size* is certainly an important feature of organizational structure, size is not the only important factor. Global media also are characterized by a *complex hierarchy of authority,* a *complex division of labor,* a *large number of rules and procedures, rationality in decision-making* (i.e., searching for the most efficient means to achieve a goal), and, very importantly, a heavy reliance upon *highly trained and educated professionals for day-to-day decision-making.* The owners of global media corporations are either absentee stockholders or they tend to deal with long-term rather than day-to-day decisions.

More formally, these characteristics and others can be grouped together under the rubric of what is now commonly called the *corporate form of organization.* A detailed discussion of this concept, which has a long and illustrative history in sociology, is contained in the Appendix at the end of the book. For most of our needs, however, global media may be conceptualized as transnational corporations that have a complex organizational structure. The polar opposite of the global or corporate form of media organization is the *entrepreneurial media organization,* which has a simple organizational structure (the simplest is a one-person operation) and has operations in only one country.

Although professionals and scholars often talk in terms of these dichotomies (corporate versus entrepreneurial, global versus nonglobal), in the real world these *ideal types** are better conceptualized on a continuum, in which all media organizations may be ranked as higher or lower than each other. Global media represent one extreme end of the continuum — they are the largest, most complex corporations in the mass communication industry. At the other end of the continuum are the smallest locally owned and managed media organizations.

---

*An ideal type is any conceptualization that represents a phenomenon only in its abstract or pure (idealized) form. Ideal type definitions are useful for understanding and studying social phenomena.

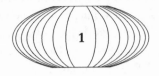

THE GOOD, THE BAD
AND THE GLOBAL

It's the stuff fairy tales are made of.

A military ambulance driver returns from World War I and starts up an animated film company with a friend. The company goes bankrupt, but he and his brother form a new company that eventually succeeds. They produce several short animated films during the late 1920s, including the first cartoon with a soundtrack. It becomes a classic. The company grows.

During the 1930s, the brothers produce several full-length animated films that draw critical acclaim. A decade later they add several live-action films to their list of successes. And during the 1950s, they produce several television shows, one of which attracts four million viewers per week. The brothers pioneer the marketing tactic of creating and selling products tied to their films and television shows. In 1955, they also open the world's first amusement theme park, which lures thousands of visitors a day.

One of the brothers dies during the 1960s and the other dies in the early 1970s, but the company — now a multimillion-dollar corporation — survives and begins construction of a second, much larger amusement theme park at a cost of $400 million (U.S. dollars). The park opens in 1971 and eventually becomes one of the largest tourist attractions in the United States.

During the late 1970s and early 1980s, revenues and profits decline after the failure of several films. But in 1984, a nephew of the founders and some major investors install a new management team headed by two former Hollywood film executives. They raise admission prices at the two amusement parks and begin production of several new films that are hits at the box office. In four years the company goes from last to first place among the top eight U.S. film studios, generating revenues of more than $2 billion and an average annual after tax profit of 20 percent.

During the 1990s, the company undergoes several management crises, but in 1995 it buys the ABC television network, some newspapers, and the ESPN sports network. The $19 billion acquisition represents one of the largest mergers in U.S. corporate history, and for a short time the company is the largest communications organization in the world.

Today, the company generates more than $23 billion a year in revenues, making it the third largest media company in the world. The company is so big, in fact, that its yearly sales exceed the gross domestic product of more than half of the countries in the world.

The story of this company's rise from entrepreneurial brotherhood to global corporation may sound like a fairly tale. But it isn't. As you might have guessed by now, the company is Walt Disney, founded by brothers Walt and Roy.

Disney has produced some of the most successful films in history. The list includes the first animated film with sound, *Steamboat Willie*, which starred Mickey Mouse, *Snow White & the Seven Dwarfs*, *Fantasia*, *Flubber*, *Beauty and the Beast*, *The Lion King*, *Pocahontas*, *Toy Story*, *A Bug's Life*, *The Love Bug*, *Who Framed Roger Rabbit?*, *Old Yeller*, *The Great Locomotive Chase*, *20,000 Leagues Under the Sea*, *Dumbo*, *Bambi*, *Pinocchio*, *The Reluctant Dragon*, *Song of the South*, *The Living Desert*, *The Little Mermaid*, *Aladdin*, *Three Men and a Baby*, *Good Morning Vietnam*, *101 Dalmatians* (animated and live action), and *Pretty Woman*.

In 1999, the Disney kingdom included investments in (or ownership of):

- television (10 U.S. stations, including five in the top five markets — WABC in New York, KABC in Los Angeles, WLS in Chicago, WPVI in Philadelphia and KGO in San Francisco);
- television production companies (Buena Vista Television, Walt Disney Television);
- cable television channels (Disney, ESPN, ESPN2, ESPNews, Lifetime, A & E and History);

- radio (40 stations);
- film studios (Disney, Touchstone, Miramax, Hollywood Pictures, Caravan Pictures);
- record labels (Hollywood Records, Disney Records, Mammoth Records);
- online services (part ownership of American Online);
- retailing (more than 400 Disney Stores);
- magazines (*Disney Adventures, FamilyFun, FamilyPC*);
- publishing companies (Hyperion Books, Chilton Publications, Disney Press, Hachette Presse);
- theme parks and resorts (Walt Disney World, Tokyo Disneyland, Epcot, Disneyland Paris, Disney-MGM Studios Theme Park, Disneyland Park, Magic Kingdom);
- a cruise line (Disney Cruise Line).

In 1998, Disney sold the newspapers it acquired through the ABC/Capital Cities buyout.

Without question, Disney enjoys one of the best corporate images in the world. People around the world love Mickey Mouse, Donald Duck, Bambi, Snow White and hundreds of other charming and funny characters. Disney films, goods and services are widely perceived to promote prosocial values, including love, obedience, parental respect, independence, honesty, humility, integrity, courage, sacrifice, compassion, kindness, good citizenship, equality and democracy. As Newsweek put it:

> *What is the Walt Disney Co. but a dream machine, a teller and seller of fairy tales? And at the heart of every Disney saga are some of life's most basic themes: friendship, family and the struggle for independence. The Little Mermaid defies her father for love. Simba the lion cub flees home, finds friendly refuge amid the wilderness and overcomes an evil uncle to assume his rightful place as king. Always, the young hero breaks away, triumphs over great dangers and returns to the fold. All is forgiven, there's always a happy ending.*

Needless to say, a lot of people believe that if more media companies were like Disney, the world would be a better place.

But not everyone shares this imagination.

Global Media as Menace

To many scholars and critics around the world, Disney and other media that exhibit the characteristics of the corporate form of organization are the stuff nightmares are made of (see "Introduction" and "Appendix" for definitions of global/corporate media).

Global media don't really care about promoting a diversity of ideas, democratic principles or equality, the critics argue. All they care about is profits. Global media are greedy organizations that are destroying good journalism and democratic values. News and entertainment programming are trivial and do more to encourage consumerism and materialism than a robust debate about social inequities and injustices. And most Disney children's films, such as *The Lion King,* help reinforce a patriarchal value system that discriminates against women and other groups.

Global media have too much power, the critics argue. They point out that at the beginning of the 20th century most privately owned newspapers, magazines and book publishing companies were small and were owned and operated by individuals or families. There was a lot of competition, and few were large enough to control national or even local markets.

But today, on the dawn of the 21st century, 10 media corporations alone account for more than half of the $300 billion (U.S. dollars) in yearly worldwide revenues generated by the communications industry, which now includes radio, television, cable, satellite and on-line services. AOL Time Warner and Vivendi Universal, the two largest corporations, alone account for one-fifth of all sales.

This power, the critics argue, represents a major threat to good journalism and democratic principles. The assumption underlying most Western political systems is that a diversity of ideas is crucial for good decision making. But global media, the critics contend, are less likely to publish information that offends powerful groups and elites, because that kind of content could alienate advertisers, news sources or consumers and sink the bottom line. In fact, many critics argue that the news and entertainment content becomes less critical of dominant ideas and institutions as media become more "corporatized." And, according to the critics, the end result is less diversity in the so-called *marketplace of ideas.*

In short, critics argue that global media are a menace to good journalism and democracy. As mass communication scholar Robert W. McChesney sums it up:

A specter now haunts the world: a global commercial media system dominated by a small number of super-powerful, mostly U.S.-based transnational media corporations. It is a system that works to advance the cause of the global market and promote commercial values, while denigrating journalism and culture not conducive to the immediate bottom line or long-run corporate interests. It is a disaster for anything but the most superficial notion of democracy — a democracy where, to paraphrase John Jay's maxim, those who own the world ought to govern in it.

This *critical model*, as I call it, is extremely popular among academics around the world. In fact, the overwhelming majority of materials written by scholars is critical of corporate media, especially global corporate media.

But not all scholars agree.

Global Media as Messiah

Some free-market media economists and media executives tell a different story. Global corporate media like Disney, they argue, are the organizational solution to inefficiencies and poor productivity in the marketplace. Global media emerge because national media are incapable of satisfying the information and entertainment needs of an increasingly complex and interdependent world. Furthermore, global media enhance democracy because they have the resources to produce higher quality, more content-diverse products and services.

Because global media are products of or are heavily influenced by Western culture, they help spread values like representative democracy, free speech, equality for women and minorities, and the notion that a diversity of ideas is important. Global media also are more tolerant of nonmainstream or unorthodox ideas than are entrepreneurial media, which tend to reinforce traditional value systems. And global media have the potential to help integrate disparate countries and cultures into a global village, reducing the potential for war or social conflict and increasing understanding across cultures.

In short, global media have the potential to play the role of messiah, or at a minimum, to do some good for society and people. As telecommunications professor Richard A. Gershon argues:

A ... myth concerning TNMCs [transnational media corporations] is that the consolidation of media companies into the hands of a select few has had an adverse effect on the marketplace of ideas. There is no evidence to support this claim. In fact, just the opposite has occurred. Since 1984, there has been a proliferation of new media technologies and services. ...

In assessing the potential dangers of media concentration, the TNMC is unlikely to use its creative and/or editorial facilities to promote a corporate agenda. TNMCs like Time Warner or Bertelsmann are far too diverse in their media holdings to succumb to a single corporate ideology. ... The combination of worldwide privatization trends coupled with advancements in new media technologies precludes any one company or person from dominating the marketplace of ideas.

And, according to Time Warner's chairman and CEO Gerald M. Levin,

Underlying both our journalistic and creative mission is diversity. For us, the inclusion of people of different races, genders, beliefs, ethnic backgrounds and sexual orientations is as much a competitive necessity as a social ideal. We simply can't hope to understand or reach the widest possible range of global and local audiences unless that variety of human experience and perception is reflected — indeed, celebrated — throughout our company.

So, Who's Right?

Are global media a menace or a messiah?

This book takes the position that neither of these perspectives is completely right or wrong. The messiah perspective can be faulted for not placing enough emphasis on the social control function of media. Global media, like all mainstream media, produce content that is generally consistent with the interests of their stockholders as well as with dominant values and institutions in Western society. In the context of today's world, this means that the news and entertainment content of global media helps support and legitimize mainstream Western values, such as responsible capitalism and social order, and mainstream Western institutions like business corporations. In contrast, scientific research shows that groups or individuals who criticize these values or institutions or engage in social protest usually have great difficulty getting favorable news coverage in mainstream media.

The menace perspective, on the other hand, can be faulted for not placing enough emphasis on social change. Although scientific research clearly shows that mainstream media content provides broad-based support for the status quo, research on newspapers also shows that content becomes more critical of mainstream values and groups as media grow and become more structurally complex. Such criticism is not always translated into social change. But it often increases the probability of change. In fact, this book will argue that corporate media in general and global media in particular have promoted or legitimized many of the social changes that have taken place in Western countries during the 20th century. This includes expanded political and economic rights for minorities, women, environmentalists, and for people with alternative lifestyles.

In short, this book contends that both critics and proponents of global media have misunderstood that trend. Global media like Disney are agents of social control, to be sure. All media serve a master. But, it will be argued, global media also have a greater capacity than nonglobal or entrepreneurial media to generate content that is critical of traditional authorities and ways of doing things. One factor making this possible is the managerial revolution. For the last 80 years or so, power within media organizations has been shifting from owners — who are increasingly becoming absentee stockholders — to professional managers, who pursue goals other than just profits, especially product quality. This shift in power has important consequences in the communications industry, especially for global media corporations.

Overview

Misunderstandings about the consequences of global media content in large part stem from a failure to consider the historical origins of the corporate form of organization, which can be traced to the Middle Ages. This topic is addressed in Chapters 2 and 4. Specifically, Chapter 2 (*The World Is Shrinking*) focuses on the history of mass communication from a broad context. This chapter will show that the growth of Disney is not an isolated incident. It is the outcome of a number of complex historical, social, economic and political events and factors.

Chapter 3 (*The Global Media Playing Field*) turns to the present and examines the 10 largest global media organizations. The focus here is on describing the structure and goals of the organizations. Because the media industry is constantly changing, some of the material in this revised chapter is likely to become outdated. However, the important issue in this book is not the specifics of each company, but rather more general processes that characterize global media companies and the impact they are having on people and societies.

In Chapter 4 (*The Paradox of Capitalism*), we begin examining these processes by providing an explanation for the growth of global media. And the explanation takes us straight to a paradox of capitalism itself — that competition, over the long run, can actually produce less competition. Basically, it boils down to economies of scale. Large-scale organizations generally have lower operating costs, and this makes it difficult to maintain many smaller companies.

The arguments and views of free-market economists and supporters are presented in Chapter 5 (*The Global Villagers*). The notion that global media have the capacity to integrate the world and reduce social conflict is their strongest argument. But later, in Chapter 8, it will be argued that global media have a limited capacity to promote social change. They help reinforce dominant institutions and value systems.

Then, in Chapter 6 (*The Global Media Critics*), the views of the critics are presented. The critical literature is vast, and many theories and arguments are out there. However, most *critical corporate models* contend that global media seek to maximize profits, and that this emphasis on profits leads to less diversity in the *marketplace of ideas*. Some critics even believe that the problem can only be solved by abolishing capitalism as an economic system.

I begin presenting my views in the chapters that follow. In Chapter 7 (*Are the Critics Right?*), I show why the neo-Marxist and critical models are inadequate. Basically, I argue that these models have failed to address the origins of ideas themselves — that ideas are the products of social interaction, which has increased substantially as societies have become more structurally complex. Critics have failed to resolve an important paradox: How can the diversity of ideas be decreasing when there is more criticism of capitalism and Western values than ever before?

In Chapter 8 (*Global Media and Social Control*), I explain how all mainstream media play a role in maintaining social systems. Here I share ground with critical scholars and I am critical of the free-market model, which has naive assumptions about the benign nature of news and information.

However, in contrast to the neo-Marxist models of media organization, Chapter 9 (*Global Media and Social Change*) shows how corporate media in general and global media in particular have a greater capacity to promote social change. One of the major reasons for this is the managerial revolution, which is outlined in Chapter 10 (*The Global Managerial Revolution*).

In the final chapter (*Global Media in the 21ˢᵗ Century*), I offer trends and predictions about the future of global media systems and their long-term effects on people, the communications industry, and the nation-state. Although some of these trends and predictions are controversial, I hope they serve as a starting point for further discussion about the impact of global media.

But to understand the future of mass communication, we first need to delve into the past.

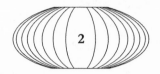

THE WORLD
IS SHRINKING

The Walt Disney Company wasn't built in a day. Indeed, it took more than a half-century for the entrepreneurial firm to evolve into a global media corporation.

But the history of this corporate giant, like all the others, reaches back much farther than the 20th century. None of these corporations would be here today were it not for a number of other social, economic and political changes. For example, without literacy, a money economy, advanced technology and capitalism, there would be no global media corporations. Another important factor is the division of labor — a topic so important that I devote Chapter 4 to it.

For now, though, my purpose is briefly to review the history of mass communication around the world. A general theme is that the pace of social change has quickened, especially in the last century. Today, even the passage of one year can bring many changes in the structure of a media industry. And the more we understand the history of mass communication, the more we can understand the growth and development of the largest global media, which are discussed in the next chapter.

So, for a moment, let's go back in time to study the history of mass communication.

The Origins of Communication

The year is 50,000 B.C., or thereabouts. Needless to say, there are no mass media. Even the idea of mass communication is inconceivable to people of that era, who are known as Neanderthalers. They have large faces with big teeth and little or no forehead. They are about to become extinct (fossil records disappear about 35,000 B.C.). But for the time being they are doing quite well. They hunt and gather food and live in temporary shelters and caves.

Anthropologists do not know the origins of human communication. But bones and artifacts from this period indicate that Neanderthalers communicate primarily through word of mouth and through gesture. They also make rudimentary carvings in stone and on cave walls. But the alphabet and paper haven't even been invented yet. That is another 45,000 years off.

Let's go forward 25,000 years, to the year 25,000 B.C. The Neanderthalers are extinct, or that's what contemporary research seems to suggest. Now there are the Cro-Magnons, who look a lot like modern humans, but their sudden appearance is a mystery to contemporary anthropologists. Language and art are more refined. But writing is still limited to symbols and icons, and story-telling remains the most important source of news and entertainment. Knowledge continues to be an oral tradition, passed down from generation to generation. Older people are valued in part because they carry with them knowledge of the past.

Once again, let's move forward. Now it's the year 5,000 B.C. Despite the passage of 20,000 years, not much has changed in terms of communication systems. Egyptian hieroglyphics are perfected, but alphabetic writing and full writing systems are another two millennia away. Also, there is no easy way to transport information in writing. The Egyptians won't begin using papyrus, a tall reed from which a paper-like material is constructed, until about 3,000 B.C.

Communication continues to be a face-to-face affair, and knowledge continues to be primarily an oral tradition. Because ideas and knowledge cannot be easily stored, societies are unable to accumulate elaborate technologies or culture (e.g., arts, theater). It is also difficult to get accurate information about events. Memories are not always very good and stories change as they are passed on from person to person. Rumors spread easily. Nevertheless, agricultural methods are improving. People are less nomadic, and more towns and cities are springing up across Europe, Africa and Asia.

Change Is Coming

Let's advance 4,000 years, to about the time of Jesus Christ. Change is now much more evident.

In about the first century A.D., the Chinese invented paper. Prior to that time, they used bamboo and silk, but the former was heavy and the latter was expensive. Between 59 B.C. and A.D. 222, the Romans publish a hand-lettered "daily gazette." This forerunner to the modern newspaper provides information about the Empire. However, literacy is limited primarily to the clergy, political elites and those who serve them. Knowledge is highly centralized in the church and state. There are no newspapers or book publishers. The books that do exist are handwritten — a slow, expensive process that often results in inaccuracies.

News and ideas also travel slowly — generally no faster than a horse or a sailboat. The local church is the medieval equivalent of today's encyclopedia, and most news of the world comes from the pulpit. Literacy is not necessary to earn a living. And, needless to say, when word of mouth is the primary means of communication, rumors abound. It is difficult to get accurate information about events and political matters.

Please advance another thousand years, to A.D. 1000. The Chinese had invented and refined block printing during the last four centuries, and now they are publishing weekly reports called Tching-pao. Crude forms of newspapers called flysheets, made from wood blocks, begin to appear in Europe. France establishes one of the first postal systems. Other postal systems appear in England and Denmark during the early 1600s.

But there still are no mass media. Gutenberg's printing press is still another 450 years in the future. Perhaps more important, literacy remains limited. Most people cannot read or write and still have no need for such skills. They farm, fish or trade goods. Interpersonal communication is all they need to get through daily life. The church and state continue to control information. In England, the Stationers' Company is created to regulate all printed material. Criticism of the government and the monarchy is punishable by imprisonment or death.

The Print Revolution

Time to move on, but this time let's slow down even more, to a 500-year leap. The year is
1500. The first printing press in the Western Hemisphere is set up in Mexico
City in 1535. The second arrives in Lima, Peru, in 1581. The first modern
newspapers begin to appear in Germany and France in the early 1600s. The first
newspaper in Italy emerges in 1645. And in London from 1640 and 1660 (just
prior to the restoration of the monarchy), more than 30,000 news publications
and pamphlets roll off the printing presses.

Printing houses are now springing up all over Europe and the Americas.
Books, newsletters and crude newspapers are being mass produced and are
becoming available to the populace. The first book publisher in the United
States, Cambridge Press, is established in 1638. The first continuously published
newspaper in the United States begins publishing in 1704. The first English-
language magazine also appeared in London in that year. The first newspaper
in Latin America, the *Gaceta de México,* a monthly, begins publishing in 1722 in
Mexico City. In 1750, London has five daily newspapers, six tri-weeklies, five
weeklies and several other publications, for a combined circulation of 100,000.

Literacy is growing in many nations around the world. In the New England
colonies, male literacy is about 60 percent; in England about 40 percent. The
church and state are losing their monopolies over information and knowledge.
The idea that the earth revolves around the sun — theorized by Copernicus and
mathematically verified by Galileo — can no longer be suppressed. (It would
be another three centuries, however, before the Roman Catholic church would
apologize for persecuting Galileo.)

Let's slow our time travel to a 300-year interval. The year is now 1800. Book and
magazine publishers are much more common in the Western world. Many are
publishing novels in serial form, such as Daniel Defoe's *Robinson Crusoe.* In 1741,
Ben Franklin wrote and published *General Magazine,* which contains poems,
book reviews, sermons and news.

Newspapers also are part of the commercial and political landscape in most
large cities throughout the world. The first English language newspaper in
Africa began publishing in 1800; the first periodical devoted to issues and
concerns facing black Africans appeared in 1801. The first modern Chinese-
language newspaper in China begins publishing in 1833 in Canton. An English
language newspaper is founded in Thailand in 1844. The *Times of India* traces its
history to 1838. The Singapore *Straits Times* begins publishing in 1834. And the

first newspaper in Nigeria is founded in 1859. They, like other newspapers of the time, are small by today's standards. Most, for example, publish fewer than 1,000 copies a day. But they are growing in power and importance.

Politicians and business people around the world are becoming more and more dependent upon them. News is becoming crucial for making good decisions. And the newspaper publisher is becoming a powerful person in the community. Most newspapers are owned and operated by an entrepreneur or a family, or in some cases a self-interested religious, political or economic group. In many non-Western countries, some newspapers are owned by the government. Large cities usually have more than one newspaper. Advertising is growing. The number of newspapers will increase dramatically in the next 50 years.

The Telegraph and Silent Pictures

It's time to slow our rate of time travel once again — to 50-year intervals. The year is now 1850. The changes in communication are now amazing. At the beginning of the century, news and information traveled at the speed of a horse or boat, as it had for thousands of years. But thanks to the telegraph, messages are now being transmitted across large distances in the United States and Europe in fractions of a second.

The world's first wire news services is established in France (Havas). Others follow in the United States (Associated Press) and Great Britain (Reuters). Newspapers in Mexico begin receiving information via telegraph from Texas in 1885. Trains and steamships also are transporting news, information, goods and services at a much faster pace. Most moderately sized cities now have more than one newspaper. And the newspapers are growing. In big cities, some are selling more than 30,000 copies a day. The cost has dropped dramatically, so much that even working-class people can afford to buy one. In New York, for example, a newspaper costs just one cent. They call it the "penny press."

Still, many areas of the world are without any newspapers. In fact, even today, the vast majority of people in Africa, South America and some parts of Asia do not subscribe to or read a newspaper daily. Radio dominates as a mass medium in many of these areas.

The year is now 1900. A transatlantic telegraph cable connects Europe and the Americas. Guglielmo Marconi sends the first wireless sound across the

Atlantic Ocean. The telephone, phonograph, wireless radio and photography have all been invented and are changing people's lives.

A motion picture industry also is emerging. A Paris café begins projecting motion pictures in 1895. The public quickly acquires a seemingly insatiable appetite for the nickelodeon, a coin-operated phonograph. For five cents, the nickelodeon produces a two-minute recording through a pair of stethoscope-like earphones. In 1915, D. W. Griffith releases *Birth of a Nation*, the first full-length film to have an impact on culture. (However, the film has been strongly criticized for its sympathetic portrayal of the Ku Klux Klan and stereotypes of African Americans.)

The first Russian news agency, ROSTA, begins operating in 1918 and is renamed TASS (Telegrafnoie Agenstvo Sovetskavo Soiuza) in 1925. TASS becomes the main source of news for nations aligned with Russia and is government-controlled until the dissolution of the Soviet Union in 1991.

Because of the large capital investment, the telegraph industry is dominated by governments and large private companies. Entrepreneurs still operate most newspapers, but this also is changing. Many of these companies, especially those in large cities, are acquiring the characteristics of the modern corporation (see "Introduction" for formal definition). They have a highly complex division of labor and role specialization. A typical metropolitan newspaper, for example, is staffed with a chief editor, a managing editor or night editor, a city editor, two dozen reporters, a telegraph editor, a financial editor, a drama critic, a literary editor and editorial writers. The production side of the business included printers, pressmen, typographers, and photoengravers. Some publishers have accumulated so much cash that they are opening or purchasing newspapers in other cities. The seeds of chain ownership have been sown.

Around the world, newspapers, magazines and book publishers continue to grow in number as well as size. In the United States alone, there are 2,000 daily newspapers and 1,800 magazines. Canada has more than 100 dailies. And the United Kingdom has more than 156 dailies. Circulations of some newspapers exceed 200,000.

Talking Pictures, Radio and Music

Once again, let's slow our rate of travel, this time to 25-year increments. The year is 1925, just two years after Walt and Roy Disney have established their new company. In most large cities, you find dozens of daily newspapers and book and magazine publishers. Most are still locally owned and operated by individuals, families or small corporations. None is large enough to control the local or national markets, much less the world. The telegraph industry is in decline; its functions are being replaced by wireless communications, the telephone and radio.

Silent movies are at their peak. About 700 are produced in the United States that year. Average weekly movie attendance approaches 50 million. Hundreds of millions of people around the world are going to the movies. By the 1930s, however, the silent movie is gone, replaced by "talking pictures." The film-making industry is big business and is dominated by fewer than a dozen Hollywood companies.

In 1921, five radio stations are licensed in the United States; five years later there are 528. Two million radios are sold in 1925. In 1926, the National Broadcasting Company (NBC) becomes the first radio network. Meanwhile, the U.S. music recording industry is manufacturing and selling more than 100 million records a year. Radio provides a big boost for sales. The jazz, swing and blues styles of African-American musicians also help the recording industry expand its sales.

Radio Argentina begins broadcasting music, literary readings and civic announcements in 1920. By 1926, every major city and every nation in Latin America has a radio station. The first radio station in Africa begins broadcasting from Johannesburg in 1920. In Japan, three privately owned stations begin operating in 1925. They consolidate under government order in 1926, and eventually become the powerful NHK and the nation's leading broadcasting system. Experimental radio stations begin broadcasting in Australia, China, Indonesia and the Philippines during the 1920s.

In 1936, Great Britain becomes the first country to begin regular television broadcasting. Television stations begin broadcasting on a limited basis in other Western countries, but the commercial use of television is put on hold during World War II.

Television and Satellites

The year is 1950. The first television station in Latin America begins broadcasting. Although few people own a television, within the next decade most homes in Western countries will have one. NHK introduces television to Japan in 1953. In 1954, the British government sets up a second broadcast service, the Independent Television Authority (later renamed the Independent Broadcast Authority), to offer programming alternatives to the BBC. Three major networks emerge in the United States.

However, from a sociological perspective, what's more interesting (but most people at the time fail to notice) are the changes taking place in the structure of media organizations. The small entrepreneur is disappearing. Economies of scale in production make it hard for smaller companies to compete. They are being bought out or merged with larger companies. Many cities are now served by only one newspaper. The newspaper industry is increasingly being dominated by the corporate form of organization, in which professional managers run the day-to-day business and most owners are absentee stockholders.

The radio, book, film and recording industries are also becoming "corporatized." This includes CBS (radio), Penguin (books), MGM (movies), Gannett (newspapers) and Columbia (records). Also disappearing is the one-industry business. Now there is cross-media ownership — newspaper companies own television and radio stations, and vice-versa. As these corporations grow, the trend is to branch out even more into nonmedia businesses. They become "conglomerates."

Meanwhile, consumption of all forms of mass media continues to increase. Margaret Mitchell's *Gone With the Wind*, for example, is selling 40,000 hardcover and 250,000 paperback copies a year. Millions of people in the United States and other Western nations spend their evenings, especially Sunday evenings, huddled around the radio, listening to their favorite programs. In 1946, average weekly movie attendance in the United States reaches an all-time high — 90 million. The number of television stations increases from eight in 1945 to 98 in 1950. By 1955, more than 35 million households own a television. Newspaper household circulation in the United States is at an all-time high. In fact, for every household, more than 1.3 newspapers are sold.

Time for a leap — to 1975. In the Western world, television is now playing a major role in people's lives. The typical U.S. citizen spends an average of more than 25 hours a week watching the "boob tube." Viewing is heavy in other Western nations as well, but it doesn't match the U.S. level because much of the programming in those countries is controlled by the government and is not geared to popular tastes. Nevertheless, the most popular programs tend to be from Hollywood.

Television is much slower to develop in Africa and other areas of world, partly because the cost of a television is far beyond the means of the average family. By 1982, only 60 percent of the countries in Africa had a television station. All television stations there are owned by the governments. But the number of radio stations has grown substantially. By 1975, there were more than 350 radio transmitters in Africa. Asia had more than 1,300.

In 1960, only five million TV sets exist in the Soviet Union, but this number jumps to 55 million by 1975. Moscow offers viewers a choice among six channels. The Russians are watching educational programming, quiz and game shows, crime series, films, children's programming, variety shows, plays and soap operas. And there are 3,000 radio and 1,460 television transmitters in operation.

Guatemala has three television stations and 75 radio stations. In the Netherlands, there are two television services, three national radio services and a system of regional FM stations. The entire country has access to these broadcast services, thanks to 17 radio transmitters and 13 television transmitters.

In the United States alone there are nearly a thousand television stations. Programming is dominated by three national networks (ABC, CBS and NBC), but cable television is growing. Originally designed for remote areas difficult to reach with over-the-air television signals, cable companies are now aggressively marketing in metropolitan areas, where cable is less costly to install and much more profitable. The first commercial satellite is launched in 1965, relaying TV, radio, telephone and data communication signals to member countries.

Consolidation and Specialization

Meanwhile, the entire mass media industry is caught up in growth consolidation and specialization. In the U.S. book publishing industry alone, more than 300 mergers take place between 1958 and 1970. There are still more than 50,000 publishers in the United States, but they are becoming more specialized. Some publishers target the college textbook market, others the trade book market. And within those two general groups, they specialize even more — natural science, social science, cookbooks, self-help, and so on.

The magazine industry follows the same trend. General circulation magazines such as *Look, Life* and *Saturday Evening Post* go out of business, partly because of competition from television. However, advertisers are also seeking to target prospective customers more efficiently and less expensively. Increasing *differentiation* in goods and services is driving the trend. Basically, this means that

businesses and factories are producing a greater number and variety of goods
and services in response to a market that is becoming increasingly specialized.
Businesses seek to identify and serve specialized *niches* (see Chapter 11 for more
details).

Although the number of U.S. daily newspapers remained roughly the same
during that time period (about 1,750), the number of individuals or corporations
who owned them declined from about 1,400 to 850. Nearly two-thirds are
owned by chains or groups.

The growth of large-scale media organizations is even faster in the film
industry. Seven companies — Columbia, MCA (Universal), MGM, Paramount,
Twentieth Century-Fox, United Artists, and Warner Brothers — dominate. At
the same time, the market reach of these media corporations becomes
increasingly global. In fact, film exports are growing so much that some film
companies are making more money from foreign than domestic box office
receipts.

Other U.S. media companies, especially those with investments in
television, also begin pursuing overseas investment opportunities. Much of the
content broadcast on television stations around the world is from America.
Despite complaints about cultural imperialism, foreign countries continue to
broadcast American programming, partly because it is popular and much less
expensive than original productions.

The dramatic changes taking place in mass media industries generate new
theories and ideas about what is happening. Many social scientists believe
society is shifting from the age of industrialization to the age of information.
Mass communication scholar Marshall McLuhan and his followers talk about
a "global village" — the idea that everyone in the world can be connected to
each other through electronic information systems. The multinational
corporation becomes the new model for business. Many economists begin
talking about economic globalization, or the idea that the entire world is
increasingly becoming linked into one large market.

Today's Global Village

Welcome back to the present. Needless to say, over-the-air television seems a bit old-
fashioned in this age of cable and satellite television transmission. In theory, the
limits on the number of channels are gone. Cable lines and satellites can
transmit hundreds and even thousands of channels. More than 120

communication satellites currently beam TV pictures to earth. Satellite subscribers can now order first-run movies from home.

One consequence of the growth of cable and satellite television is that the three major U.S. networks have lost substantial viewership. In 1960, 90 percent of those watching television at any point in time were tuned to one of the three major networks. Today, less than 40 percent are watching the big three and the figure is dropping every year. People are turning to newer networks (e.g., Fox, UPN) and to specialized cable programming. They like movies, self-help shows, reruns of old television shows, sports, 24-hour news, nature/science channels, and business/stock market news. Cable News Network (CNN) is now the broadcast news industry model. It has 90 million viewers in more than 200 countries.

Contrary to some predictions, newspapers haven't died. To be sure, their numbers have fallen in many countries. In France, for example, the number of dailies declined from 26 in 1945 to 10 in 1997. However, their profit rates remain high. In the United States, they are three to four times higher than the typical large corporation. Most major newspapers also now have Web pages. Although they are not making a great deal of money from them, the amount of money people are spending on products and services offered through the Internet is exploding rapidly. And for the first time in history, almost anyone can be a publisher or producer of information and ideas and reach millions around the world.

Yet, there is little evidence to suggest that the Internet will threaten the economic vitality of major media corporations. In fact, just the opposite appears to be happening. Corporations are getting bigger, and they're harnessing the Internet as a mechanism for reaching audiences and consumers. Today's buzz term is *transnational media corporation* (TNMC), or, more simply, global media. In fact, U.S. media scholar Robert McChesney points out that the

> *most striking development in the 1990s has been the emergence of a global commercial media market, utilizing new technologies and the global trend toward deregulation. This global commercial media market is a result of aggressive maneuvering by the dominant firms, new technologies that make global systems cost efficient, and neoliberal economic policies encouraged by the World Bank, IMF, World Trade Organization, and the U.S. government to break down regulatory barriers to a global commercial media and telecommunication market.*

In fact, just 12 media corporations account for more than half of the $250 billion (U.S.) in worldwide revenues generated yearly in the communications industry. All of these companies have operations in three or more media, most often television, newspapers and radio. The mom-and-pop media company is disappearing rapidly. Even small weeklies are now being gobbled up by chains and corporations. The modern corporate media organization is controlled and managed by a new breed — the highly educated, skilled professional. Most owners are absentee stockholders who have little control over day-to-day operations.

Historical Conditions Favoring Corporate Growth

Numerous historical conditions contributed to the growth and development of the corporate form of organization in general and the global medium in particular. But following the lead of the famous German sociologist Max Weber, who wrote during the early part of the 20th century, three in particular are worth further discussion.

The first is the development of money economies. A money economy, which allows quantitative calculation of income and expenditures, gives permanence and predictability in social organization. Cash salaries, rather than other rewards, are used to compensate individuals. This, according to Weber, creates just the right balance of dependence and independence for the faithful execution of responsibilities in the organization. In contrast, unpaid volunteers are too independent of the organization to submit unfailingly to its rules, and slaves are too dependent upon their masters to have the initiative to assume many of the responsibilities necessary for proper functioning of the organization.

The second condition promoting the development of the corporate media is education. Literacy is essential for print media. But education and literacy are also crucial for corporate organizations to function effectively and to achieve their goals. In contrast to other forms of organization, corporations rely heavily on written records and documents. Schools, which themselves have a complex organizational structure, also socialize individuals into corporate procedures and methods. Historically, schools also have played an important role in breaking down traditional forms of knowledge and in ushering in the principles of rationalization of modern life.

The third condition that encourages the development of corporate structure is capitalism. Capitalism brought with it the rational estimation of economic risks, which required that the regular processes of the competitive market not be interrupted by external forces in unpredictable ways. Interference with free trade, such as banditry, piracy and social upheaval, threatens capital, and the development of a strong government is necessary to maintain social order. Capitalist enterprises, Weber argued, seek to make and accumulate profits, and do this through the rationalization of work and production (i.e., finding the most efficient means to achieve a goal or solve a problem). Weber saw the mass media as performing an important role in this process.

> *Business management throughout rests on increasing precision, steadiness, and above all, the speed of operations. This, in turn, is determined by the peculiar nature of the modern means of communication, including, among other things, the news service of the press. The extraordinary increase in the speed by which public announcements, as well as economic and political facts, are transmitted exerts a steady and sharp pressure in the direction of speeding up the tempo of administrative reaction toward various situations. The optimum of such reaction time is normally attained only by a strictly bureaucratic (or corporate) organization.* [parenthetical added]

Reducing Social Distance

Although our journey through the past shows that the trend toward globalization of the communication industry has been gradual and underway for hundreds of years, it is also clear that the pace has quickened considerably in the last two decades or so. And the trend toward globalization is likely to continue. In fact, many analysts predict that during the next decade fewer than five companies will account for more than half of all industry revenues.

Although it is difficult to predict with any certainty what will happen in the field of global communications, one thing is certain: Global communications has made the social world a smaller place. It has obliterated distance as a barrier to communication across space and time. In doing so, social distance is reduced, enabling people of different cultures and beliefs to communicate with greater ease and more frequency. And playing the lead role in this new information order is a handful of media corporations that have operations all over the world. The global media.

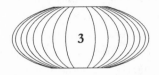

THE GLOBAL MEDIA
PLAYING FIELD

Call it coincidence, or call it fate.

In 1923 — the same year Walt and Roy Disney created their animated film company — Henry Luce and Briton Hadden began publishing a weekly news magazine that would eventually grow into the world's largest media corporation. AOL Time Warner, as that company is now called, is expected to earn more than $36 billion (U.S.) in 2001 — more than one of every $10 spent in the communications industry.

In terms of total revenues, The Walt Disney Company is ranked third, with expected sales of $26 billion in 2001. In second place is Vivendi Universal, with expected sales of $30 billion. Vivendi Universal was created in 2000 after the French conglomerate Vivendi purchased the Seagram Company, which owned Universal (film) Studios and Polygram Records.

There are seven other major global media companies and several dozen smaller, potential world players. But none can match the influence of AOL Time Warner. Every day Americans and hundreds of millions of other people around the globe are bombarded with AOL Time Warner news and entertainment programming. AOL Time Warner is the most diversified media company in the world, operating more than 200 subsidiaries in every medium except newspapers. The company employs more than 80,000 people in 75 countries. The corporation is so big, in fact, that even Bugs Bunny works for it.

This chapter provides a brief summary of the 10 largest global media corporations. All of the corporations own or operate mass media companies (e.g., newspapers, radio stations, television and cable TV stations, motion picture studios, music recording studios, book publishing and online services) in many countries around the world. The list excludes communications companies like Microsoft, IBM, and the telephone companies whose products or services facilitate communication (e.g., telephone, computers, beepers) but do not involve the production of symbolic images and information for consumption by large audiences.

Following the lead of other analysts, this chapter uses total sales or revenues (U.S. dollars) to identify the top global media companies. However, it should be emphasized that this criterion is not necessarily the best indicator of the power of a corporation. The quality of the products they produce may also play an important role.

The information presented in this chapter is the latest available (updated in 2001), much of which is gathered from the company's web sites and other recently published secondary sources (see chapter notes for more details). Of course, the reader is cautioned that the global media field is constantly changing, and the relative position of these companies may already be changed by the time this edition is published. The content here is meant to be illustrative — to provide a general overview of the scope and reach of these companies. From a public policy perspective, the more important issue is the impact these global media are having on people and societies — a topic I address in Chapters 5 through 11.

#1 — *AOL Time Warner Inc.* *(2001 expected sales = $36 billion)*

AOL Time Warner began with *Time* magazine and this philosophy:

> *Although daily journalism has been more highly developed in the United States than in any other country in the world ... People in America are, for the most part, poorly informed. ... People are uninformed because no publication has adapted itself to the time which busy men* [sic] *are able to spend on simply keeping informed.*

That statement is taken from the prospectus that Luce and Hadden wrote for the first issue of *Time* in 1923. Prior to that, the two friends had been editors of their college newspaper at Yale and had worked briefly as reporters. Although they didn't have much news experience, they had a good idea — to publish a magazine for busy middle-class people who need an efficient way to get public affairs news. So, they condensed and compartmentalized national and international news each week under the headings of business, science, religion, education, art and the press. They focused heavily on human interest. And they wrote their stories using a narrative approach, rather than the "colder" inverted-pyramid summary-lead approach. The end result was a staggering success. By 1929, the magazine had a circulation of 200,000.

Hadden died that year and never saw the magazine reach its peak. But Luce carried on and founded several other very successful publications, including *Fortune, Life* and *Sports Illustrated*. In 1962, when *Time* reached a circulation of three million, Luce moved Time Inc. into its own 48-story building at the Rockefeller Center. It earned $270 million that year. Luce ceded power in 1964 and died in 1967.

Luce was a very colorful and controversial publisher. It was no secret that his politics were conservative, and *Time* did not adhere to the traditional standard of objectivity in reporting. It was staunchly anticommunist and often altered its own reporters' copy to reflect that bias. During the McCarthy era, *Time* also attacked President Truman, Secretary of State Dean Acheson and Adlai Stevenson. Later, *Time* criticized President Kennedy. In the early 1960s, when nationally prominent U.S. reporters were sending back reports of corruption in the South Vietnamese government, *Time* attacked the reporters, accusing them of plotting to overthrow the South Vietnamese government. Two *Time* correspondents in Saigon resigned in protest.

Despite the death of Luce, the Time Inc. empire continued to grow. In 1972, it launched HBO, a pay channel offering movies and sports entertainment. Two years later HBO was the largest pay cable program supplier in the United States. HBO was the first to use satellite communications for transmitting TV programming. In 1976, Time Inc. became the first publishing firm to earn $1 billion in one year. By 1978, HBO and the cable television operations of Time Inc. were generating nearly half of its revenues — quite incredible given that the company for 50 years had been oriented solely to print journalism.

During the early 1980s, Time Inc. faced a number of challenges. Revenues from the magazine division and HBO had leveled off and the company lost $47 million in a cable venture. Only 10 percent of its income was derived from overseas ventures — an undertapped source of revenue. The company began searching for another company that might help it tap foreign markets.

In 1989, under threat of a takeover bid, Time Inc. purchased Warner Communications Inc. for $15 billion. Warner was a highly diversified entertainment company that included television and film studios, music, publishing and cable television. Time's management tried to convince stockholders that the short-term gains of accepting the takeover bid could not match the long-term gains under the proposed merger. However, they never got an opportunity to vote on the deal (see Chapter 10 for more details), and it took many years before the company turned a profit. After the acquisition was announced, the value of Time's stock dropped from $182 to $70 a share. The only people who profited from the merger were top executives at Time Inc. and Warner, most of whom walked away with millions, and Warner stockholders, whose stock increased about a third in value.

In 1996, Congress deregulated the telecommunications industry, which allowed Time Warner to purchase Turner Broadcasting (CNN and other cable networks). To get government approval for the purchase, however, Time Warner had to agree to broadcast cable channel MSNBC (Microsoft NBC, owned by General Electric), a competitor of CNN, on half of its cable systems.

Time Warner began to turn a profit in the late 1990s. In 1999, the company had $27.3 billion in sales and earned about $2 billion.

In January 2000, Time Warner and America Online, which was the largest Internet service provider in the United States with 20 million customers, announced their intent to merge. The deal was worth $160 billion, making it the biggest merger in history. More accurately, the deal was an acquisition rather than a merger. AOL, which had a lot of cash on hand because market speculation had driven its stock price up, purchased Time Warner. AOL stockholders own more than half of the new company.

But the "merger" was approved by the Federal Trade Commission only after AOL Time Warner agreed to open its cable television lines to Internet rivals. Basically, this turns the cable lines into a public channel for delivery of information on the Internet.

AOL Time Warner is expected to be profitable, because both AOL and Time Warner made money before the merger. Estimates are that the company will earn $2 billion to $4 billion on $36 billion in sales.

Time magazine continues to be very successful, with a circulation of four million. However, the revenue from this subsidiary now represents a small proportion of the total revenue that AOL Time Warner takes in. Time Inc., a subsidiary, operates the company's magazine, book, music and video businesses. Time Warner Entertainment runs the company's television, recording and movie production businesses. The company's holdings or investments include:

- **Cable Television:** Cable News Network (CNN), CNNfn (financial news), CNN Headline News, CNN-SI (*Sports Illustrated*), HBO (Home Box Office), TNT (Turner Network Television), The Cartoon Network, Cinemax, TBS (Turner Broadcasting Systems), WB Network (Warner Brothers Television Network), Comedy Central, CNN-SI (CNN Sports Illustrated), Court TV, TCM (Turner Classic Movies)
- **Satellite Television:** PrimeStar satellite television service
- **Television Networks:** Warner Brothers
- **Recording Industry:** Warner Music Group
- **Film/Movies:** Warner Brothers studios, New Line Cinema, Castle Rock Entertainment, 1,000 movie screens outside the United States
- **Magazines:** *Time, People, Sports Illustrated, Fortune, Entertainment Weekly, Martha Stewart Living, Life,* DC Comics, and more than a dozen other magazines
- **Books:** Time-Life Books, Book-of-the-Month Club, Little, Brown & Company; Warner Books, Oxmoor House, Sunset Books
- **Cable Television Systems:** 22 cable television systems serving 13 million household subscribers (20% of the U.S. market)
- **Online Services:** America Online, CompuServe, Netscape, ICQ (youth oriented messaging network), Digital City, Moviefone, AOL Instant Messenger, Roadrunner (jointly owned with Advance/Newhouse), Spinner Networks and NullSoft, Inc.
- **Other holdings:** Hughes Electronics (part ownership), Six Flags theme park chain, Atlanta Hawks, Atlanta Thrashers, Atlanta Braves, 150 Warner Brothers retail stores, World Championship Wrestling, Goodwill Games

AOL Time Warner also has joint ventures or equity investments with a number of other competitors, including Viacom, AT&T Broadband Services, Sony, Advance/Newhouse, News Corporation, Bertelsmann and NBC. About two-thirds of AOL Time Warner's income is generated in the United States, but overseas revenues are expected to climb to 50 percent within a decade. AOL

Time Warner is focusing heavily on global television and the Internet, especially broadband services (high speed Internet services).

When the merger was announced, AOL Time Warner Chairman Steve Case told reporters, "This merger will launch the next Internet revolution. We're still just scratching the surface." In a press release, he said, "We're kicking off the new century with a unique new company that has unparalleled assets and the ability to have a profoundly positive impact on society. By joining forces with Time Warner, we will fundamentally change the way people get information, communicate with others, buy products and are entertained — providing far-reaching benefits to our customers and shareholders."

Gerald Levin, former chairman of Time Warner, is AOL Time Warner chief executive officer. Ted Turner, who founded CNN, is vice chairman of the new company.

#2 — *Vivendi Universal* (2001 *expected sales* = *$30 billion*)

Vivendi Universal is a French company that was created in 2000 by the acquisition of Seagram Company, which owned Universal (film) Studios and Universal Music Group. Vivendi, the parent company, is the world's leading water company, with 100 million customers in 100 countries. It also offers wastewater services and employs 275,000 people worldwide. The company entered the communications field in the 1980s, when it purchased a 15 percent stake in European pay-TV provider Canal Plus and created a mobile phone unit.

Since then, it has gradually increased its media holdings. Vivendi now owns all of Canal Plus and Havas S.A., one of Europe's largest media companies. Havas was founded in 1832 by Charles Louis Havas, a former French banker and newspaper publisher. Havas published a bulletin that provided French newspapers with translations of foreign publications. In 1835, it became the world's first news agency and operated the first wire service.

Havas owns partial interest in Europe's number one advertising agency, which has 220 affiliates in 65 countries. Havas' CLT subsidiary is Europe's top commercial television and radio company, and it controls 30 TV and radio stations. Havas also is France's leading publisher of directories and circulars and billboard advertising. The corporation publishes several leading French magazines, including *L'express* and *Le Point*, and also has investments in tourism and recreation.

Since the buyout, Havas has been refocusing its core business on the written word, which includes stepping up its presence in multimedia. Havas Interactive is a leading producer of interactive resources for knowledge and references. Havas employs 23,000 workers.

The history of Universal Film studios goes back to the early 20th century, but it had fallen on tough times in the 1990s. Universal was given new life in 1995 when Canadian-based Seagram purchased it from the Japanese electronics company Matsushita for $5.7 billion. Since then, however, Universal has sold its television production studio and two cable networks, USA and Sci-Fi, to Home Shopping Network, Inc., a $1 billion corporation controlled by Hollywood mogul Barry Diller. The deal was complicated. But, basically, Seagram got a 45 percent interest in the new HSN, which has been renamed USA Networks Inc.

In summer 2000, Vivendi announced that it was purchasing the Seagram Company for $43.3 billion and would put its media operations under the name, Vivendi Universal. This is expected to create the world's second largest global media corporation with revenues of about $30 billion. Vivendi Universal will be based in Paris.

The Vivendi-Seagram deal brings an end to the Bronfman family's control over Seagram, which has ruled for three generations. However, Edgar Bronfman Jr. is now vice-chairman of Vivendi Universal, with the Internet and music business reporting to him. The Bronfman family also will remain the largest shareholder in the combined company. Vivendi executive Jean-Marie Messier continues as the chairman.

The Vivendi-Seagram deal was approved by the European Union's executive commission on the condition that Vivendi sell its 24.5 percent stake in British Sky Broadcasting, a satellite venture whose largest investor is Rupert Murdoch's News Corporation (see discussion below). The decision by Vivendi to sacrifice BSkyB for the Seagram deal reflects its strong desire to gain greater access to music and films in order to compete with AOL Time Warner and Disney.

To get approval for the Seagram acquisition, Vivendi also agreed to open access to its new mobile Internet portal "Vizzavi" to all rivals for two years. The company also promised to allow competing distributors access to Universal Music and agreed to limit the number of Vivendi Universal films distributed through European outlets that the merged company will control. Vivendi plans to sell off Seagram's alcoholic beverage business.

Although analysts are skeptical about whether the purchase of Universal assets will deliver returns to Vivendi, Messier said he sees an opportunity because the distribution technology will be the Internet, and through the Vizzavi venture, his company could establish an early stronghold in Europe, where wireless Internet access is growing much faster than in the United States. The deal will also give Vivendi substantial access to North American markets, which it had heretofore lacked.

#3 — The Walt Disney Company (2001 expected sales = $26 billion)

Disney already has been discussed extensively in the first chapter. We should add here, however, that for a short time in 1996 — before the merger of Time and Warner — it was the largest media company in the world in terms of total sales. Disney was propelled into first place with the $19 billion acquisition of Capital Cities/ABC.

In terms of number of employees, Disney is also one of the top two largest companies, with more than 120,000 on its payroll. It is widely agreed that Disney also has the best brand and name recognition in the world, even though some leftist scholars and some conservative religious organizations are critical of the company (a topic that we'll address in later chapters).

Nearly half of Disney's income comes from movies, publishing and merchandising. Nearly a third comes from broadcasting. The rest of its income comes from its theme parks. Disney's goal is to expand its overseas revenues from about a fourth of its total income to half by the year 2000. Disney plans to launch Disney Channels in a number of overseas markets, including China, France, Italy, Germany, and the Middle East. Disney also has a number of joint ventures with other companies, including three "baby bells."

Disney has been criticized for having too many members on its board of directors who do not own stock in the company. Many Wall Street investors believe that vested directors are more responsible to stockholders. However, stockholders have little to complain about. The company has returned profits of 20 percent per year for the last decade. In January 1998 the company's stock jumped six percent in one day on news of fourth quarter profits. However, in late 1998 the value of the stock had dropped more than 25 percent, partly because of lower earnings.

Disney's ABC television network also continues to struggle in the face of increased competition from cable stations. The network has placed a moratorium on new hiring and cut 300 jobs in 1997 and 1998. Several years earlier ABC made $500 million in profit. That figure is expected to drop to $150 million in 1998. In 2000, the ABC network was No. 1 in ratings, but the stock price of Disney has remained flat since 1998.

In addition to the properties mentioned above, Disney owns or has major investments in 10 U.S. television stations, Buena Vista Television, Walt Disney Television, several cable television channels (Disney, ESPN, ESPN2, ESPNews, Lifetime, A&E and History), 40 radio stations, several film studios (Disney, Touchstone, Miramax, Hollywood Pictures, Caravan Pictures), several record labels (Hollywood Records, Disney Records, Mammoth Records), America Online (partial ownership), 400 Disney Stores, magazines (*Disney Adventures, FamilyFun, FamilyPC*), Hyperion Books, Chilton Publications, Disney Press, Hachette Presse, theme parks and resorts (Walt Disney World, Tokyo Disneyland, Epcot, Disneyland Paris, Disney-MGM Studios Theme Park, Disneyland Park, Magic Kingdom), Disney Cruise Line and a chain of high-tech arcade game stores.

In April 1998, Disney opened the Animal Kingdom Park near Orlando. The park is a zoo but, unlike other zoos, attempts to recreate as much as possible the natural surroundings of the wild animals on display. In 1999, Disney created the Walt Disney Internet Group, formerly GO.com, which oversees its Internet operations, including Disney Online, ESPN.com and ABC.com. The sites attract 23 million surfers a month. Disney Internet took in $51 million in 1999 and only lost $6 million. In 1999, Disney company as a whole earned $23.4 billion and generated a modest 5.6 percent profit.

In July 2001, Disney purchased Fox Family Worldwide Inc. from the News Corporation and Saban Entertainment Inc. for $5.3 billion. Fox Family Channel, which reaches 81 million U.S. households, was renamed ABC Family.

The Disney Chairman and CEO is Michael D. Eisner, says the company will rebound. "It is true that the ladder doesn't go infinitely to the sky. A year of very modest growth is not the end of the world. ... It simply means that this was a year of investment, reinvigoration and in some cases cost containment in our main businesses."

#4 — Bertelsmann AG *(1999 sales = $16.5 billion)*

Bertelsmann is a privately held German firm that was founded in 1835, making it the oldest company in the top global media group. The original company

primarily published religious materials until it shut down temporarily during
World War II. A relative of the original founder who had spent most of the war
in a Kansas POW camp rebuilt the plant after the war.

Bertelsmann started the first book club in Germany in 1950 and invested
heavily in German television during the 1960s. However, most of its income
continues to come from book sales. In the 1970s and 1980s, the company added
U.S.-based Bantam Books and Doubleday Publishing to its operations.
Bertelsmann publishes fiction books, reference books, how-to books and
religious publications. Its book club is now one of the largest in the world, with
25 million members. Bertelsmann also publishes *McCall's* and *Family Circle* and
owns the Arista and RCA record companies.

In 1994, Bertelsmann teamed with America Online to set up a European
online venture, in which it had a 50 percent stake until selling its share back to
AOL (now AOL Time Warner) in 2000. In 1998, the company purchased
Random House, the largest book publisher in the English-speaking world, from
Advance Publications (see #10 below). The $1.5 billion deal means that
Bertelsmann accounts for nearly one-third of all trade books sold in the United
States and 10 percent of all books sold.

In 1999, Bertelsmann purchased more than four-fifths of scientific
publisher Springer Verlag. In 2000, Bertelsmann sold its half interest in AOL
Europe back to AOL and spun off Lycos Europe, a joint venture with Lycos.
It also launched Bol.com, its online book retailer, purchased online music
retailer CDNOW, and entered into an agreement with online music service
Napster, which will offer Bertelsmann music products.

Altogether, Bertelsmann operates more than 600 companies in 53 countries
around the world. It employees nearly 65,000 people.

Bertelsmann has been consistently profitable. About a third of its income
is generated in Germany, a third in the United States, and a third in all other
countries. In addition to the holdings mentioned above, Bertelsmann owns or
has major investments in four German television channels, Premier pay TV,
British, French and Dutch TV channels, 18 European radio stations, 50 percent
ownership of CLT-Ufa, which owns 19 European television channels and 23
European radio stations, and more than 150 newspapers, magazines and
publishing houses.

Bertelsmann's Chairman and CEO is Dr. Thomas Middelhoff. Although
Bertelsmann is expanding operations in the United States, it believes multimedia
growth lies in international, not just U.S., markets.

#5 — Viacom (2001 expected sales = $16 billion)

Viacom was created in 1970 by CBS after the Federal Communications Commission ruled that television networks could not own cable systems and television stations in the same market. Viacom emerged as a global company in 1994 with the acquisition of Paramount Pictures and Blockbuster Video and Music. Before the deal, it was (only) a $2 billion company. The acquisition was orchestrated by CEO Sumner Redstone, who controls more than half of its stock and made Viacom one of the most successful media companies in the world.

In 1995, Viacom launched United Paramount (Television) Network (UPN) with Chris-Craft Industries. In 2000 Viacom attempted to purchase Chris-Craft, but Rupert Murdoch and New Corporation made a better offer. However, Viacom purchased CBS for $45 billion, which is expected to catapult it into the fourth place in terms of total media revenues. Redstone will remain chairman and chief executive officer of Viacom and Mel Karmazin, president and CEO of CBS, will become president and chief operating officer.

Viacom owns or has major investments in:

- **Cable Television:** MTV, Nickelodeon, VH1, TNN, Country Music Television, MTV2, TV Land, Home Team Sports, Midwest Sports Channel and an interest in Comedy Central
- **Pay TV Channels:** Showtime, The Movie Channel, FLIX and an interest in Sundance and Noggin Channel
- **Radio:** Infinity Broadcasting Corporation, which owns 160 radio stations
- **Television:** CBS Television Network, Paramount Television (production and syndication); television stations (16 CBS and 19 UPN), CBS Productions, Eyemark Entertainment, Viacom Productions, Spelling Television, Big Ticket Television and King World Productions Inc.
- **Film and Theaters:** Paramount Pictures (production and distribution), 100 theaters in Canada, 104 theaters in Asia, Europe and South America, United Cinemas International (joint venture with Universal)
- **Books:** Simon & Schuster, The Free Press, Pocket Books
- **Video:** Blockbuster Video with 6,000 stores in 27 countries

- **Internet and Web Sites:** mtv.com, vh1.com, cbs.sportsline.com, cbs.marketwatch.com, SonicNet.com, and Nick.com
- **Other:** Five theme parks, outdoor advertising

In 1999, Viacom had $12.9 billion in sales and earned a modest 2.9 percent profit. About a third of Viacom's income is generated from films, a third from music, video rentals and theme parks, and a third from broadcasting and publishing. Like many other large-scale media organizations, Viacom implements company-wide cross-promotions to improve sales. A good example of the former is its heavy promotion on MTV of the hit movie "Clueless" in 1995.

Viacom also seeks to expand its foreign markets. It has invested nearly a billion dollars since 1992 in international expansion, and the goal is to increase earnings from outside the United States to 40 percent by the year 2000. Nickelodeon and MTV are its main weapons. MTV is already available in 250 million homes around the world.

#6 — *The News Corporation* (2000 sales = $14.2 billion)

News Corporation traces its roots to 1952, when Keith Rupert Murdoch, current head of the company, inherited two Australia newspapers from his father. Murdoch launched the first national daily in Australia in 1964. Four years later he purchased *News of the World,* a London Sunday paper. In 1969, he purchased another London newspaper and turned it into a tabloid that published sensationalist stories and pictures of bare-breasted women. He began purchasing newspapers in the United States during the 1970s, including the *New York Post.* Using sensationalism once again to boost circulation, Murdoch has acquired a world-wide reputation as a "yellow journalist" — a derogatory term used to describe the newspaper sensationalism of Joseph Pulitzer and William Randolph Hearst at the turn of the century.

However, Murdoch is not entirely deserving of that title. That's because he and his family also own or have investments in what most people consider to be very respectable media, including *The* (London) *Times, TV Guide* (and 25 other magazines), Twentieth Century Fox Film Corporation and HarperCollins Publishers. Top executives of Disney, Time Warner, and Viacom have all commented that Murdoch is the media executive they respect or fear most. And it's easy to see why.

News Corporation operates companies on six continents in every major medium except music. It owns more than 100 newspapers, making it one of the largest three newspaper companies in world. In 1986, the company launched Fox Broadcasting, the first new U.S. television network since 1948. News Corporation also owns 30 television stations that reach more than 40 percent of the households in the United States. It has major investments in cable television — including Fox News Channel and Fox Sports Net — and satellite television (British Sky Broadcasting and Star TV, an Asian satellite television system). In 1995, the company teamed up with TCI (now AT&T Broadband Services) and two other companies to provide satellite TV service to Latin America. The company also owns the Los Angeles Dodgers baseball team.

In 1999, News Corp. and Japan's SOFTBANK teamed up to establish eVentures and epartners, companies that invest in international and U.S. Web companies. Responding to AOL Time Warner's merger, News Corporation announced in 2000 that it was placing all of its satellite holdings into a new company, called Sky Global Networks. In 2000, News Corp. also purchased Chris-Craft Industries, which owned eight United Paramount Network (UPN) affiliated television stations. In July 2001, News Corp. sold its 49.5 percent investment in Fox Family Worldwide Inc. to Disney for $5.3 billion. News Corp. plans to use the cash to purchase DirecTV, a satellite broadcaster.

About a fourth of the company's income is generated from film entertainment, a fourth from newspapers, a fifth from television and 30 percent from magazines and books. News Corporation is investing heavily in satellite television communications systems — a risky but potentially very profitable enterprise. Murdoch's family owns about 30 percent of News Corporation's stock. Murdoch became a U.S. citizen in the 1980s, which enabled him to comply with FCC regulations governing ownership of U.S. broadcast media.

News Corporation reported record profits during the 1998 fiscal year, earning $1.2 billion ("profit before abnormal items"), which represented a 21 percent increase over the year before. Profits in 1999 were $700 million.

#7 — *Sony (2000 media sales only = $11.3 billion)*

Sony emerged in the 1950s as one of Japan's most innovative electronics companies. In 1950, it produced the first Japanese tape recorder. This was followed by one of the first transistor radios and the pocket-sized radio. The

"Sony" name, which is derived from the Latin word for "sound," was adopted in 1958.

Since then, Sony has had a number of other successes in the retail electronics market and some failures (such as the Betamax VCR tape technology, which was out-distanced by Matsushita's VHS technology). The company has recently entered the competitive computer market, teaming up with Intel to make a new line of personal computers.

Sony is one of the world's largest corporations, grossing nearly $50 billion yearly. However, it did not become a global media player until the late 1980s, when it purchased CBS records and Columbia Pictures.

The entertainment side of Sony is divided into two major divisions. Sony Music Entertainment Inc. includes the labels Columbia, Epic and Tri-Star Music Group, among others. Artists include Michael Bolton, Pearl Jam, Mariah Carey, Billy Joel, Michael Jackson and Japanese artists Kome, Yutaka Ozaki and Dreams Come True. Sony Music is the second largest recording company in the world, behind Universal Music.

Sony Pictures Entertainment Inc. includes Columbia Pictures, Tri-Star Pictures, Sony Pictures Classics, Loews Theatre Management Corporation and Sony Pictures Studios. To date, the music entertainment side of the business has been profitable, but the television and film industry portion has done poorly. However, it has no plans to leave the entertainment field, partly because it believes the film business provides leverage for the technical side.

#8 — National Broadcasting Company (2000 sales = $6.8 billion)

NBC was created in 1926 by the Radio Corporation of America (RCA), a subsidiary of General Electric, to develop radio programming. Today, NBC, a wholly owned subsidiary of GE, has major investments outside the United States in cable and satellite. This includes CNBC Asia and CNBC Europe, both 24-hour business channels.

The company is also planning to broadcast NBC Asia, a general entertainment channel. In addition to the NBC television and radio networks, NBC owns and operates 13 television stations, the CNBC cable financial news channel, the MSNBC cable news channel (a joint-investment with Microsoft), and has a partial interest in A&E, Court TV, American Movie Classics and more than a dozen other cable channels. NBC is launching a new football league with

World Wrestling Federation Entertainment in 2001 and is focusing on the Internet as a source of future revenues.

#9 — The Thomson Corporation (2000 media sales = $5.9 billion)

The Thomson Corporation traces its origins to Canadian Roy Thomson who started a radio station in 1930 in Ontario. Later he began purchasing newspapers in Canada, the United States and Great Britain. Today, Thompson Corp. is one of the world's leading publishers of legal, reference and specialized information. Nearly three-fourths of the company's stock is owned by the Thomson family. According to company documents, Thomson's goal is to become "the world's foremost information and publishing house."

The company owns or had investments in 130 daily newspapers in Canada and the United States, including *The* (Toronto) *Globe and Mail,* but in 2000 it sold its community newspaper assets for $2.5 billion (excluding the flagship newspaper) to concentrate on electronically delivered products and services, especially those that can be delivered through the Internet.

Thomson also owns or has investments in

- Wadsworth Publishing Company and more than a dozen other publishing houses in Asia, Central America, Europe, Africa and the United Kingdom
- Gale Research and a number of other companies (e.g., Primark) providing broad-based reference and database services in print, microform and electronic formats
- West Group, which publishes legal and regulatory information for law firms, libraries and the government, primarily in the United States, and a number of other legal and reference publishing groups located in Canada, Australia, New Zealand, Sweden, Denmark, the United Kingdom and Asia

#10 — Advance Publications (2000 sales = $4.5 billion)

Advance traces its roots to Samuel Newhouse, who purchased the *Staten Island Advance* in 1922. Newhouse used profits from that paper to purchase others in the United States during the 1940s to 1960s. During the late 1950s and 1960s, he expanded into magazines and cable television. When he died in 1979, his two sons, Samuel I. "Si" Newhouse Jr. and Donald E. Newhouse, took over. They purchased Random House in 1980, the largest general interest book publisher in the United States, and sold it to Bertelsmann (see #6 above) in 1998.

Today, Advance Publications is one of the largest privately held media companies in the world. It owns more than a dozen magazines, including *The New Yorker, Glamour, Condé Nast Traveler, Architectural Digest, Vogue, Vanity Fair* and *Bride's*. Advance also owns or has interest in 41 local weekly business newspapers; three auto racing magazines; cable television (1.4 million subscribers); Advance Internet Inc., which operates nine major news and information web sites; and Newhouse Newspapers, which operates 26 daily newspapers in the United States, including *The* (Cleveland) *Plain Dealer,* The (New Orleans) *Times Picayune,* the *Newark Star-Ledger,* and *The* (Portland) *Oregonian*. In 1999, Advance joined forces with four other media companies to purchase AdOne, an online classified advertising network.

Other Potential Global Media Players

Other firms vying for a global presence but having less international reach than the companies above are NHK of Japan; Reed Elsevier of Britain/Netherlands; EMI of Britain; Hachette of France; AT&T Broadband and Advance Publications of the United States; and Cisneros Group of Venezuela. The world's major news wire services, including Reuters of Britain, The Associated Press of the United States and Agence France Presse, also provide a substantial amount of the news and information about world political and economic matters. And the BBC, which launched the World Service Television in 1994, has a substantial presence. These agencies have bureaus and reporters throughout the world, but they are not as highly diversified or as large as the other corporations.

Although there is disagreement about the long-term impact these global media companies are having on people and societies, researchers generally agree on the reason why these media companies tend to grow. Ironically, the trend toward large-scale organization is a byproduct of free-market capitalism itself — a contradiction of capitalism, as Karl Marx presciently pointed out more than a century ago.

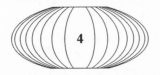

THE PARADOX
OF CAPITALISM

I call it the "great paradox of capitalism."

In principle, free-market competition is supposed to be the engine of capitalism. It's supposed to keep prices low and product quality high. And no competitor is supposed to get large enough to control prices or the market.

Yet, in the "real world," competition tends to set in motion "forces" that, over time, reduce the number of competitors in an industry. In fact, the history of most industries in so-called free-market economies is the history of the growth of oligopolies, where a few large companies eventually come to dominate. The first examples occurred during the late 1800s in the oil, steel and railroad industries. All of them eventually became dominated by a handful of "robber barons" — Rockefeller, Carnegie, Gould, Vanderbilt. Antitrust laws eventually were used to break up many of these companies, but oligopolistic tendencies continue in these and most other industries. The communications industry is no exception.

In the early 1900s, for example, most medium-to-large cities in the United States, Great Britain and Europe had two or more daily newspapers. At one point, New York City had more than 15. Today, however, fewer than a dozen U.S. cities have daily newspaper competition. The rest have only one daily. New

York has three major dailies. The decline in competition has occurred even though the population and number of businesses in these cities have grown dramatically. At the same time, the number of individuals or companies that own U.S. newspapers has declined from about 2,000 in the year 1910 to less than 450 today. More than 85 percent of all dailies are owned by chains or groups.

The U.S. broadcasting industry has experienced similar trends since the Federal Communications Commission lifted restrictions on ownership. In 1984, the FCC raised the number of television stations a person or organization could own from seven to 12, provided they reach no more than 25 percent of the country's TV viewing households. This, along with changes in the tax law, sparked a trend toward consolidation in 1985 and 1986. A total of 227 TV stations changed hands. In 1995, for example, 190 groups owned more than three-fourths of the television stations in the 100 largest markets. Restrictions on ownership were also relaxed in the radio industry. As a result, from 1987 to 1995, the percentage of radio advertising revenue captured by the top four groups increased from eight to 12 percent.

But it doesn't stop there. In 1996, the U.S. Congress enacted a law that lifted all restrictions on television station ownership as long as a company's holdings reached no more than 35 percent of the national audience. The 1996 Telecommunications Act also lifted all restrictions on radio station ownership. As a result, there were 185 acquisitions and mergers in the broadcasting industry in 1996. Experts predict that the 1996 Telecommunication Act also will promote many more mergers and acquisitions in the future. Moreover, whereas newspaper companies historically tended to own just newspapers and broadcast companies just radio and television companies, today the trend is cross-media ownership — meaning one company may own many different broadcasting and print media. Most global media corporations, for example, own a wide variety of media formats.

Around the world, the trend generally has been one of less governmental interference in the private sector, and the result in many industries has been more concentration of ownership. But if the rules of capitalism are supposed to encourage competition and discourage concentration of ownership, then why are these trends taking place? Is there something wrong with the system? Or does this mean the end of capitalism and free-market economics?

Where's the Invisible Hand?

It may seem strange to ask these questions at a time when many people are proclaiming the victory of capitalism over communism. Yet, with the growth of global media corporations as well as transnational corporations of all kinds, those questions are more relevant today than at any time in history. And, ironically, to get the answers we must turn in part to the ideas of Karl Marx, whose ghost still haunts Wall Street.

Marx was an intellectual who lived during the 1800s. He wrote a great deal about capitalism and its problems. Although often dismissed by conservative free-market analysts, many of his insights and predictions have withstood the test of time. Among the most important is his predication that competition promotes centralization of ownership. This is quite amazing given that during his lifetime there were no large-scale corporations. But capitalism, he argued, contained the seeds of its own destruction. Indeed, the paradox is very real. However, to fully appreciate Marx's theory, we must first take a look at the writings of one of his predecessors — Adam Smith, who is considered by many to be Marx's nemesis and the greatest champion of capitalism.

Smith's ideas about business organization are contained in his classic book, *An Inquiry into the Nature and Causes of the Wealth of Nations* (often shortened to *Wealth of Nations*). Published in 1776, the book challenged two major schools of thought that dominated economic theory at the time. One of those schools, which was advanced by the Mercantilists in England, argued that gold was the basis of wealth and that gold was to be obtained by selling goods and services to foreign nations. Conversely, Mercantilists believed that a nation should prohibit the transfer of gold to other nations. The other school of thought, which reigned in France, praised the virtues of the farmer, not the merchant. The Physiocrats argued that all wealth came from agriculture and food production.

Smith rejected both positions. Wealth is in the productivity of labor, he argued. Increase the productive capacity of a nation, and wealth will follow. And how does a nation increase its productivity? Through the division of labor.

On the first page of the *Wealth of Nations*, Smith cleverly illustrates his theory with the example of a pin factory. Ten laborers working independently can scarcely produce 10 stick pins in a day, he says. But when the work tasks are broken down and the work is coordinated, 10 men can produce as many as 48,000 pins a day.

One man draws out the wire, another straights it, a third cuts it, a fourth points it, a fifth grinds it at the top for receiving the head; to make the head requires two or three distinct operations ... and the important business of making a pin is, in this manner, divided into about eighteen distinct operations, which, in some manufactories, are all performed by distinct hands ... .

Smith argued that three factors explain why the division of labor increases human production. First, specialization increases dexterity. When production is separated into simple tasks, a laborer becomes more proficient in performing that task. Second, the division of labor saves time that would normally be lost in passing from one job to another. "It is impossible to pass very quickly from one kind of work to another that is carried on in a different place and with quite different tools." And third, when production is separated into simpler tasks, machines can be constructed that enable one person to do the work of many. This, more than the other two, is primarily responsible for reducing costs and increasing the productive capacity of organizations and nations.

Smith was not specifically concerned with developing a theory of the organizational growth. But his theory incorporates the notion that organizations grow as the division of labor increases.

In order to increase output, capitalists must invest more and more money to pay for machinery and other equipment. This resulted in what Smith called accumulation, or capital investment. Although demand for labor and the cost of wages would increase as businesses grow, accumulation would not fizzle out because Smith believed increasing wages also would produce an increase in the number of laborers. Increasing wages would improve living conditions. This would reduce infant mortality (which was quite high in Smith's day) and, in turn, increase the supply of workmen. The accumulation process could proceed in cycles of greater and lesser production, but the process would continue basically until all of the earth's resources were consumed.

Although Smith's theory incorporates the notion of organizational growth, Smith did not believe concentration of ownership and large-scale organization would be the result, for two reasons. First, market forces would prevent any firm from becoming too large. Concentration of economic power, if it did occur, was only a temporary phenomenon. The growth of any particular firm would be checked by the emergence of other competitors.

Second, and perhaps more importantly, Smith rejected the notion that joint-stock companies (forerunner to the modern corporation) were an effective form of organization for most business ventures. Joint-stock companies could function relatively well in banking and insurance industries, where they could be used to fund large public works projects (e.g., canals, water supply). But the heart of capitalism, Smith believed, lay mainly in sole proprietorships and partnerships. The owners in these organizations usually managed day-to-day activities and, hence, only they could be expected to look after their investment very closely.

History has proved Smith wrong on this point. Indeed, today most of the large corporations that dominate many manufacturing and service industries, including global media corporations, are controlled by highly educated professionals, not the owners. The separation of ownership from control, in fact, appears to have facilitated, rather than diminished, the effectiveness of large-scale organization and its ability to adapt to changing economic, political and social conditions (see Chapter 10).

Nevertheless, despite this shortcoming, Smith's analysis offers at least two major insights for the study of global media: (1) *Larger, more complex media organizations generally are more efficient, productive and profitable because they have a more advanced division of labor;* and (2) *Media controlled by managers generally place less emphasis on profits because they typically do not benefit as directly from profits as the owners.* The latter topic, which is quite controversial, is taken up in more depth in later chapters, especially Chapter 10.

Smith died in 1790. Marx wrote his major works on capitalism in the 1850s and 1860s, which was still a relatively early stage in the history of the industrial revolution.

The Ghost of Marx

Marx agreed with Smith that competition promotes the division of labor. He also agreed that the division of labor increases the productive capacity and wealth of a nation. But unlike Smith, Marx argued that competition would promote concentration of capital and ownership on a grand scale. One of the major problems with Smith's model, Marx analysis suggests, is that it failed to anticipate the effects that economies of scale would have on barriers to entry in the marketplace.

Marx also disagreed with Smith in terms of who would benefit from such wealth. Smith worried about the effects that the division of labor would have on workers. Tasks that are broken down into simpler motions become more monotonous, and work becomes more mundane. But he remained generally optimistic. Wages would increase as the productive capacity of a nation increases, and this would push human happiness beyond anything dreamed of before. But by the middle of the 19th century, this sanguine assessment was of dubious merit. Laborers in many of the factories in England and other nations worked long hours, were paid little and lived in extreme poverty. The wealth generated by the division of labor went not to the laborers but, rather, as Marx observed, to the capitalists.

In Volume I of his famous book, *Capital*, Marx argued that competition drives capitalists to search incessantly for ways to increase productivity. Capitalists innovate in one of two ways. The first is by increasing the division of labor. The second is through the use of machinery. In either case, the end result is that innovation allows capitalists to produce more units at a lower per unit cost and, thus, to reap increased profits — at least until other competitors adopt the innovation. When that happens, the supply of the product increases, prices fall, and "surplus profits" are eliminated. The price remains relatively stable until another innovation comes along, and then the cycle starts over again.

Marx argued that the major consequences of innovation were concentration and centralization of capital. Marx defined concentration as growth in capital, or an increase in the size of companies. Capitalists must continually reinvest profits in order to remain competitive. Most of the reinvestment goes to production and development of new machines and methods for reducing labor costs. This increases the size and scope of mass production and the ratio of capital to the labor process. However, Marx argued that concentration of capital leads to an increase, not a decrease, in the number of owners. This occurs because, over time, capital is divided among family members, often through inheritance, and earmarked for new ventures.

Although ownership tends to become decentralized as a firm grows, this process is slow and is more than offset by centralization of capital. He defined centralization as the combining of capitals already formed — that is, a reduction in the number of competitive firms in a particular sector of industry. Centralization occurs in one of two ways. The first is when larger, more successful companies purchase the assets of weaker, less competitive and innovative firms. Economies of scale are primarily responsible for this. Marx writes:

The battle of competition is fought by cheapening of commodities. The cheapness of commodities depends, ceteris paribus, on the productiveness of labor, and this again on the scale of production. Therefore the larger capitals beat the smaller.

The second method of centralization occurs through the formation of joint-stock companies (forerunner to the modern business corporation), which, he argued, often pool large amounts of capital together for the purpose of gaining greater control over a particular market. The credit and banking system plays an important role in funding such ventures.

In the broader context, Marx argued that concentration and centralization of economic power leads to increasing polarization of the classes and, eventually, revolution. Declining rates of profit will force many companies out of business. To remain competitive, others will have to lay off workers and replace them with machinery or lengthen the working day and cut wages. Over time, private enterprise as a whole becomes increasingly oligopolized and monopolized. Class consciousness will emerge as the ranks of the working and unemployed classes increase, and they eventually will revolt and overthrow the bourgeoisie.

Scholars widely agree that history generally has failed to support Marx's predictions about the declining rate of profit and polarization of the classes. The passage of antitrust laws and the growth of labor unions and the middle class helped diffuse the tension. There also is conflicting evidence about whether ownership of capital is becoming increasingly centralized. Some researchers claim that despite variations across industries, the trend toward centralization has continued unabated since the 19th century. Others contend that the degree of centralization has changed little since the 19th century — maybe even declined since World War II — and that even in highly concentrated industries there is a great deal of competition. The debate continues, but few scholars dispute the general observation that concentration of capital exists in many industries, especially the manufacturing sector. For example, the four largest U.S. firms in the automobile, computer, cigarette, detergent and metal products industries account for 50 to 100 percent of total production and sales, and the 200 largest firms in the entire U.S. business world account for most corporate wealth and income.

Despite these shortcomings, Marx's analysis offers two major implications for the analysis of global media systems: (1) *Unfettered competition tends to promote the growth of large-scale media organizations because it stimulates innovation, reduces prices and runs less efficient media organizations out of business;* and (2) *The death of entrepreneurial media owners tends to promote dispersion of ownership as capital is divided among heirs, even though capital still tends to concentrate via centralization of ownership* (i.e., chain ownership).

Thus, the trend toward global media companies stems in part from the paradox of competition — that is, competition promotes innovation and economies of scale that run less competitive firms out of business. As a rule of thumb, bigger companies can produce products and services for less cost. In fact, the decision by Disney to purchase ABC was motivated in part by the belief that the network would complement Disney's film and television production studios as well as its library of films and shows. The end result is that the new, bigger companies typically can produce and market their media services less expensively than competitors. According to U.S. media scholar Robert McChesney:

> *Why exactly do firms like Disney, Bertelsmann, and Time Warner feel the need to get so large? ... When Disney produces a film for example, it can also guarantee the film showings on pay cable television and commercial network television, it can produce and sell soundtracks based on the film, it can create spin-off television series, it can produce related amusement park rides, CD-ROMs, books, comics, and merchandise to be sold in Disney retail stories. Moreover, Disney can promote the film and related material incessantly across all its media properties. In this climate, even films that do poorly at the box office can become profitable.*

Although there are variations across media industries, as a general rule of thumb the trend toward large-scale organization can be characterized as a three-stage process. In the first stage, which occurs soon after a new medium is introduced, many different firms spring up vying for part of the profit-pie. As they get larger and competition increases, some companies go out of business or are purchased by other companies. In the second stage, the number of competitors begins to decline. Large companies begin to emerge as market leaders. In the third stage, oligopolies rule. The industry stabilizes and the trend toward large-scale organization and concentration of ownership continues to the extent that economies of scale are possible and there are incentives to sell or buy.

Competition and Global Media

The competition paradox generally rules wherever free-market economics has been allowed to operate. Because of the collapse of the Soviet system and because many developing countries have relaxed restrictions on private ownership of television and radio stations, this means a substantially greater part of the world is now subject to the paradox of competition. Of course, the trend toward globalization can be halted with government intervention. Even the United States, which arguably has the most laissez-faire economic system in the world, prohibits any one corporation from owning television stations that reach more than 35 percent of the households.

The growth of large-scale media organizations may also be checked by a new technology that makes an older technology obsolete. This is what happened to the telegraph, which was replaced rather quickly by telephone and wireless communications. Many analysts today believe the newspaper industry is also a dinosaur facing extinction. However, more often than not an industry will adapt to changing conditions. For example, Western Union, the original telegraph company, just announced that it is merging with a major U.S. bank (Norwest). Similarly, newspapers are also adapting to changing conditions. Almost all major newspapers in developed countries, for example, are now offering news online. Although newspapers have yet to turn a significant profit from such ventures, rumors of that industry's death have been greatly exaggerated. It may take a generation or two, but consumers will eventually adapt to online news and information, partly because it will cost less to deliver news in that manner and partly because young people are growing up on computers (see Chapter 11 for more details and more predictions).

In short, the historical trend around the world has been toward less government intervention and more private enterprise, even if it means concentration of media power. As long as free-market economics reign, global media empires can be expected to expand and consolidate. This is particularly true when a local market becomes saturated. Large corporations then search for new markets around the world in order to maintain or increase profits.

But is the pursuit of profits and the growth of large-scale media corporations good or bad for people and society? Many critics argue that the trend is destroying good journalism, democratic principles and diversity in the marketplace of ideas. Yet others believe that competition in the media marketplace is still very strong and may actually be increasing, not decreasing, despite the emergence of global media. They even argue that global media are creating a "global village" — one which can reduce social conflict and war and bring greater peace and harmony to the world.

Who's right? Neither, I argue in Chapter 7. But first let's look at what the proponents and the critics have to say in Chapters 5 and 6, respectively.

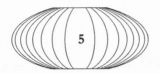

THE GLOBAL
VILLAGERS

On January 8, 1815, a British force of 7,500 soldiers confronted 6,500 American troops under the command of Gen. Andrew Jackson in the famous Battle of New Orleans. The British plan was to capture New Orleans and thereby gain access to the entire Mississippi Valley. Jackson's job was to stop the British. Both sides believed a great deal was at stake, perhaps even control of the United States.

Both were wrong.

A treaty had already been signed in England two weeks before, bringing the War of 1812 to an end. A ship carrying the news would not arrive in Washington, D.C., for five more weeks, and the news would take several more weeks to reach New Orleans.

The consequences of slow communications are sometimes devastating. The British suffered more than 2,000 casualties, including 289 dead. The British general-in-command, Sir Edward Pakenham, was among those killed. The Americans suffered 71 casualties. (By the way, although the Americans won the battle, there was no clear victor in the war.)

Faster methods of communication do not always produce beneficial results. Take, for example, the scandal surrounding the sexual relationship between

51

President Clinton and former White House intern Monica Lewinsky. Early in the controversy, a major U.S. newspaper posted a story on the Internet that contained incorrect information about the affair. The report was picked up by several other media before being corrected. Technology doesn't distinguish between truth and falsehood, and lies and hoaxes can be spread very quickly. Political communication scholar Steven Livingston also points out that some observers take a negative view of the "CNN effect" — that is, instantaneous global news media reports — because they believe it can jeopardize national security or force political elites into making bad decisions. Many military and political elites, for example, were displeased with the CNN news reports that came out of Bagdad during the 1991 Gulf War.

However, there is little doubt that prior news of the War of 1812 treaty would have saved lives at the Battle of New Orleans, and today there is little public controversy about the benefits of instantaneous communication. Millions of lives and billions of dollars in property are saved every year because of advance notice of adverse weather conditions and natural disasters (remember El Niño of 1998?). And even some harsh critics of global media will concede that the "CNN effect," at a minium, makes it more difficult for political and military elites to control the news in their own interest. In fact, it is reasonable to argue that the power of global media is growing in relation to national political and social institutions.

McLuhan's World

Speedy transmission is one of the first things that proponents of global media cite to back up their position. Indeed, global media have the power to transmit messages to virtually every place in the world within milliseconds. When Princess Diana died in a car crash in September 1997, within minutes CNN and other television networks were broadcasting live reports from Paris to hundreds of millions of people around the world. Within hours, billions were aware. No event in the history of the world has been transmitted so quickly to so many people.

But speed is not necessarily the most important advantage of global media. Even more important, proponents can argue, is the potential power of global media to integrate the world. In other words, global media have the potential to create a *global village* that can improve relations between countries and reduce the potential for war and social conflict.

The global village concept was exploited during the 1960s by communication scholar Marshall McLuhan, who believed that electronic media, especially television, could tie the entire world into one social system or society. McLuhan argued that print media, such as newspapers, alienate people from each other, because reading is a solitary activity. According to McLuhan, before the printed word, people learned about the world through personal experience and word of mouth (see Chapter 2). They experienced the world through their senses — sight, sound, smell, taste and touch. Story-telling was a primary means of transmitting knowledge and ideas, and this face-to-face form of communication bonded people together socially.

But written documents and books made people less dependent upon personal experience and interpersonal communication, McLuhan argued. With books and newspapers, they could learn about the world in isolation from each other. There was no need to socialize. The written word engages the mind, not the senses. Reading is linear, rational, solitary and individualistic. The written word "detribalizes" society. Thus, according to McLuhan, much of the alienation that people experience in modern society has its basis not in the content of ideas, but rather in the way they consume them. This is what he meant by oft-cited phrase, "the medium is the message." The content of the messages is much less important for social integration than the medium itself.

The implication of McLuhan's argument is that alienation reached its peak during the early 1900s, before the appearance of movies, radio and television. However, things allegedly are now changing. Electronic media are "retribalizing" modern society, he argued. People are increasingly experiencing the world through the senses again (sight and sound, at least). Music videos, in particular, would be considered particularly powerful in this regard, because they excite the senses. The world is becoming a global village.

Or is it?

Is McLuhan Right?

McLuhan's theory has many shortcomings. Empirical research on reading the local newspaper, for example, shows that print media are very effective at making people feel connected to a community. Although reading is a solitary activity, people often discuss what they read with others. To wit, book clubs are very effective at making people feel part of a group.

The notion that an electronic global village can integrate people as strongly as a face-to-face one is also overdrawn. Television is a one-way medium (at least at the present). The Internet is a two-way medium, but this, too, is no substitute for personal interaction and human intimacy. And if people are supposed to be less alienated in today's electronic world than they were at the turn of the century (when print media were at their peak), then why haven't suicide rates decreased? The causes of alienation are not just communication — they are also tied to how meaningful people find their personal and professional lives.

Media scholar James Grunig also argues that McLuhan is wrong because increasing specialization of media systems is fragmenting the world rather than turning it into a global village. He writes:

> *The important value question is not what the media do to people but how people themselves choose to use the media. Specialized media will allow many more individuals a wider choice of the media they use. This individual freedom should increase, and the manipulative power of the media should decline.*

Grunig is correct that people have a greater choice of media today than in the past, and that this generally decreases the power of any particular medium (see Chapter 11 for elaboration of this idea). However, the notion that global media are incapable of creating a global village — at least in a crude sense — is off the mark. In fact, I shall argue in more depth later that increasing political and economic specialization actually promotes globalization of media systems. That's because specialization increases the dependence that people and organizations have on each other to achieve their goals. These inter-dependencies, in turn, create a greater need for information and news.

Media and Social Integration

Thus, despite many shortcomings to McLuhan's global village thesis, there is some merit to the idea that global media are helping to integrate people from different cultures and perspectives into one global system. Many examples can be cited. Take, for example, the death of Princess Diana. Her funeral was watched by hundreds of millions of people around the world (30 million in the United States alone). Metaphorically, the media's role may be likened to that of a funeral director, who provides a place where mourners may grieve over the loss of a loved one. In Diana's case, the space was electronic (television), but the coverage sounded very much like a funeral service. Television news commentators spoke in subdued voices. The words "tragedy," "loss" and "sorrow" were mentioned repeatedly, giving viewers the feeling that their "global family" had lost a dearly beloved relative.

Another good example of the integrating power of global media was coverage of the Asian economic crisis that began in late 1997. Business news channels such as CNNfn, CNBC, MSNBC and Bloomberg provided constant updates on the crisis. This information, in turn, helped executives around the world assess the impact of the crisis on their companies and investments. Although the decisions that come from this news and information do not always produce desired results for people, the main point is that global media help link people around the world into one economic system.

The power of global media to integrate is not limited to tragic events or economic disasters, however. Entertainment programming plays an extremely powerful role in relaxing (some people say pacifying or narcotizing) people while at the same time reinforcing dominant values and norms in a society. Virtually all entertainment programming, in fact, has some moral lesson for the viewer. Sociologist Herbert Gans points out that mainstream media (which includes global media) promote a number of social values (see Chapter 8 for more discussion of news values).

One of the most important is social order, or the idea that people should not use violence to achieve their goals. If people are upset about something, they should use nonviolent means to seek change. After a riot breaks out, for example, news media always call for calm and a cessation to the violence. This is always the case, except when the government uses force. In times of emergency, the military and police may use force or threat of force to restore order. Even when the military or police use excessive force, they are almost always supported by the media or public. During the 1968 Democratic National Convention in Chicago, for example, a national commission found that police were the ones who instigated violence against peaceful anti-Vietnam War protestors. However, media coverage of the event portrayed the protestors as spoiled brats who needed old-fashioned discipline. Interestingly, opinion polls showed that the public supported the police, not the protestors.

Needless to say, entertainment programming (especially television) almost always advances the theme that "crime doesn't pay." Police are usually the "good guys," and when they aren't they are always the exception to the rule. In the end, truth and justice almost always win out. Family values are also emphasized in entertainment programming, even though alternative lifestyles (e.g., single family homes) often become the foundation for a comedy (after all, it's easier to make jokes when the relationships are kooky). Cowardice is bad. Patriotism is good. And loyalty, honesty, sincerity, compassion, devotion and love are frequent themes of entertainment programming. These values, of course, are important for social order in most societies, regardless of political or economic conditions.

The fact that most programming, especially on television, reinforces certain values and norms does not mean that all programming supports peace and harmony. Mass communication researcher George Gerbner has found, for instance, that people who watch a lot of television tend to develop what he calls a "mean world syndrome." That is, they tend to see the world as a meaner and scarier place than it really is, because television is so heavily laden with violence and crime. This can be viewed as having adverse psychological effects, because people might become afraid to leave their homes. However, it may also have adverse effects for civil rights. Gerbner shows that people who harbor these views also tend to be strong supporters of the police. Thus, high levels of television viewing may help maintain public support for authoritarian police practices.

Global news media agencies, such as CNN, also play an important role integrating the world. Without the news media, many governments, businesses and individuals could not achieve their personal and professional goals. People depend heavily on the news media for information to help them through everyday life. Shoppers monitor ads for the best grocery prices. Financial consultants follow stock market reports on television all day long. Public officials read newspapers to keep up on the latest political developments. Business people read newspapers and specialized magazines to follow their investments and keep up with trends in their industry.

Although mass media are not necessary for societies to exist (see Chapter 2), without them the modern world as we know it could not exist.

Cultural and Functional Integration

More formally, the social integration effects of the media can be classified into two general categories. One is cultural integration. Here the media play a role in reinforcing certain ideas, values or norms (rules). Social order is one value we've already talked about. Another is responsible capitalism. This is the idea that a "free-market" economy is the best way to distribute goods and services in the world and that capitalists should play by the rules.

For example, the blame for the economic crisis in Asia was largely placed on policies, laws and practices that restricted trade, favored relatives of a dictator, supported monopolies or placed huge tariffs on imported goods. From a broader perspective, this criticism can be seen as playing a role, however small, in forcing those countries into a global free-market economic system, despite the consequences such economic globalization may have for national economies. In a sense, global media are saying, "Play by the rules, or else the world will exclude you from the market."

Because global media depend heavily upon Western political and economic elites for news, they will, of course, tend to reinforce the dominant values of those countries. In addition to social order and responsible capitalism, this includes support for representative democracy (the notion that a handful of elected elites rule), freedom of speech and the press (which does not include citizen right of access to the press), freedom of association (except when national security is at stake), education (as a means of social advancement) and equal rights for women and minorities (despite widespread discrimination).

To the extent that foreign nations embrace these values, greater global integration is likely to be the result. However, in countries that subscribe to a different set of values, there is also the potential for greater conflict rather than integration. Most notably, the growth of global media is likely to increase tension between the West and some Muslim countries in the Middle East, such as Iraq. Nevertheless, despite this potential, proponents of global media maintain that the long-term overall effects of global media will be to diminish rather than increase such conflict (see the next chapter for a different view).

The second way in which global media may help integrate the world is through "functional interdependence." Essentially, this means that, irrespective of most cultural values, global media help link people and organizations together so that they achieve their individual goals, especially economic goals.

For example, a large European grocery distributor depends heavily on mass media for information about commodity prices and markets from around the world. Asian businesses that purchase computer equipment, on the other hand, depend heavily on global media for information about the latest technology. American businesses that purchase textiles from overseas companies need to keep abreast of currency values. The mass media provide information that helps these businesses achieve their goals. Note, though, that in all of these cases, the people who control these businesses may subscribe to a different set of social and cultural values. But this doesn't matter. Their functional interdependence in the economic system integrates them into a global world. They depend heavily upon others, including the media, to achieve their own goals.

Free-Market Thinking

Like McLuhan, most contemporary free-market economists and global media executives see global media as having positive effects for most people and most countries. They believe global media reduce social distance, promote mutual understanding and reduce the potential for social conflict and war. For example, in January 1998, Gerald M. Levin, chairman and chief executive officer of Time Warner Inc., told an audience at Fudan University in Shanghai, China:

> *Although I was not a journalist, a major part of what drew me to Time Warner was its journalistic heritage. I believed — and still believe — that the dialogue of ideas which is at the heart of the journalistic enterprise is vital to the economic and social progress of people everywhere.*

> *I am a realist. The differences among cultures and nations that arise from varying economic circumstances, belief systems and historical experiences aren't about to disappear. To some extent, they are inevitable. What isn't inevitable, however, is that these differences become distorted and embittered by caricatures of simplifications. ...*

> *As I see it, global media and entertainment companies have an indispensable role in allowing us to see one another not as stereotypes or faceless adversaries, but as people who, for all their differences, share the same planet and the same destiny.*

Speaking before the Singapore Broadcasting Authority, Rupert Murdoch, CEO of The News Corporation, argues that

> *Consumers want choice and lots of it. They want to be empowered. It's our job to empower them. ... We cannot be cultural imperialists, imposing Western notions of decency and openness on countries that have different histories, totally different values and different cultures.*

Our news broadcasts seem unexceptional in countries with traditions of political openness, and destabilizing in countries that put a greater premium on stability than on dissent.

Walter Truett Anderson of Pacific News Service also argues that

The emerging global culture is not all T-shirts and fast foods, thank God. It is also a widening acceptance of principles of human rights. Such principles are becoming global norms, fragile ones to be sure, often honored in rhetoric and brutalized in practice, but nonetheless, understandable statements of what people all over the world can demand for themselves, and can expect to be demanded of them by others.

Logically, there is some merit to the notion that global media may help promote human rights, cross-cultural understanding and reduce social conflict. However, the integrating effects of global media do not necessarily benefit all groups or all societies, as the critics point out in the next chapter.

Social integration is no doubt the single most important "positive" effect that global media proponents may cite. But they also argue that a global media system is more economically efficient than a nation-based media system. This is extremely difficult to dispute. The previous chapter showed that a number of global media companies generate substantial economies of scale by selling their products and services through a global market system. Businesses that market products around the world will seek out global media for advertising because of economies of scale. Economic theory suggests that, as a general rule of thumb, this ultimately also means lower prices for media products and services.

In addition to less expensive good and services, most contemporary free-market economists believe media globalization leads to higher quality news and a greater diversity of ideas (see Chapters 7, 9 and 10 for more support of these arguments). They believe global media increase competition, despite many of the joint ventures among them (see Chapter 3). And when competition is strong, news media will work harder to report the news.

Proponents also point out that large-scale media have the resources to conduct in-depth investigations of corruption and wrong-doing. Furthermore, global news organizations such as CNN provide a less parochial or nation-centric account of the news because they have clients and viewers around the world. One visible sign of this is the fact that CNN avoids using the word "foreigner" in its newscasts. Needless to say, a global media risks alienating its international viewers and clients if its news coverage favors one country over another in a dispute.

Many media economists also believe there is little to fear from the size and power of global media, and that antitrust laws are sufficient for dealing with companies that threaten diversity in the marketplace of ideas. According to telecommunications professor Richard A. Gershon:

> In all areas of media and telecommunications, there has been a move toward consolidation of companies. The increase in group and cross-media ownership is the direct result of media corporations looking for ways to promote greater internal efficiencies. ... Ten MSOs [Multiple System Operators] control over 70% of the U.S. cable marketplace ... . The Disney Corporation has a virtual lock on children's animated films.

> Do such companies exhibit the classic forms of behavior of monopolies and/or oligopolies? Not exactly. It would be more accurate to say that most of these companies are market leaders within well-defined information boundaries. ... [A]dvancements in new media technologies including converging media formats and multiple distribution channels preclude the possibility of a few dominant media companies controlling the marketplace of ideas.

Indeed, many scholars believe new technologies, such as the Internet, will generate new opportunities and always hold the big companies in check. As the late Anne Wells Branscomb, a former Harvard professor, puts it,

> In this time of media mergers and communications conglomerates, the Internet — a loosely interconnected network of networks where each node operates independently without any centralized governing body — may be the most promising medium of communication that we can devise to maintain diversity of content, not only for U.S. residents but for users worldwide. Perhaps the Internet will provide an opportunity for small groups, even individuals, to sustain unfiltered access to the marketplace of ideas without going through a screening process directed by an advertiser-influenced conglomerate or a media mogul with his own views about politics and morality to be urged upon the world.

But not everyone agrees with the idea that global media will have beneficial effects or that the Internet can save us.

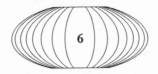

THE GLOBAL
MEDIA CRITICS

During the mid-1800s, Karl Marx predicted that growing alienation among factory laborers in capitalist countries would lead to revolution, the overthrow of capitalism and the emergence of the communist state, where everyone would have economic and political equality. This revolution was inevitable, Marx argued, because concentration of ownership would produce great disparities in income between the rich and the poor (see Chapter 4).

But by the 1920s, many of Marx's followers conceded that something had gone wrong. There had been no revolutions in capitalist countries. In fact, the only revolution to succeed had taken place in a quasi-feudalist state, Russia, where the Bolsheviks overthrew the Czar.

The theoretical crisis was "resolved" during the 1920s and 1930s with the emergence of the *Frankfurt School* of thought, which basically argued that the working classes failed to revolt because mass media and other cultural institutions fed them with false ideas (i.e., *ideology*) about capitalism. Without *class consciousness*, workers could not see how the system was exploiting them and why they should revolt.

Today, the descendants of the *Frankfurt School* are the most powerful and vocal critics of global media, which they see as an unwitting tool of political and economic institutions to keep ordinary citizens from recognizing the evils of capitalism. Moreover, according to the critics, if things continue on their present course, the 21st century will read like the plot line in a George Orwell or Aldous Huxley novel. More specifically:

The entire world will be converted into one big capitalist economic system dominated by a handful of global corporations. Only one or two media corporations will be left, and all decisions will be driven by profits and the bottom-line. Media will be filled with entertainment programming but there will be very little serious public affairs content. The emphasis will be on materialism, consumerism and commodification (i.e., turning all aspects of culture into items for sale). Ideas or beliefs critical of capitalism and global corporations will never appear in the media because they will be considered subversive. Groups that oppose the powerful corporations will have no medium through which to express their views. Diversity in the marketplace of ideas will be dead. But most people will be oblivious to these changes. They will be no longer interested in politics. They will spend most of their time watching virtual reality programming and living in a fantasy land. And political and economic elites will not mind. It's easier for them to control the populace.

Inside the Critical Mind

Although the scenario above is overly simplistic, it nonetheless captures the essence of what hundreds and perhaps thousands of scholars in the social sciences and humanities around the world, including many neo-Marxists, believe will happen if globalization in the communications industry continues unchecked. As the political economist Robert W. McChesney puts it:

> *The corporate media are carpet-bombing people with advertising and commercialism, whether they like it or not. Moreover, this is a market-driven system, one based upon one-dollar, one-vote rather than one-person, one-vote. In nations like Brazil or India, this means that a majority of the population will barely be franchised "citizens" in the new global media system. ...*
>
> *In short, the present course is one where much of the world's entertainment and journalism will be provided by a handful of enormous firms, each with distinct, but invariably pro-profit and pro-global market, political positions on the central social*

issues of our times. Even allowing for the presence of the occasional dissenting voice, the implications for political democracy, by any rudimentary standard, are troubling.

U.S. media critic Norman Solomon adds that:

> *In the future, will media coverage be diverse? Prospects are bleak. Consolidation of media ownership has been so rapid in recent years that now just 10 corporations control most of this country's news and information flow. ... Those conglomerates are in business to maximize profits. They're hardly inclined to provide much media space for advocates of curtailing their power.*

Ben H. Bagdikian, a former newspaper editor and university professor, writes that

> *The lords of the global village have their own political agenda. Together they exert a homogenizing power over ideas, culture and commerce that affects populations larger than any in history. Neither Caesar, nor Hitler, Franklin Roosevelt, nor any Pope, has commanded as much power to shape the information on which so many people depend on which to make decisions about everything from whom to vote for to what to eat.*

In their edited book on global media, British media studies scholar Annabelle Sreberny-Mohammadi and her co-editors argue that:

> *Simply put, in the drive for ratings and commercial success, public and private broadcasters have reduced their commitments — financially and ideologically — to news, public affairs and educational programming in favour of entertainment-based programming. In terms of internal diversity, then, commercialization and competition may have narrowed the range of what is on offer.*

For decades Noam Chomsky, a world-famous linguist and America's leading leftist dissident, has been criticizing the U.S. news media, which he and his colleague, Edward S. Herman, say

> *are effective and powerful ideological institutions that carry out a system-supportive propaganda function by reliance on market forces, internalized assumptions, and self-censorship, and without significant overt coercion. This propaganda system has become even more efficient in recent decades with the rise of national television*

networks, greater mass-media concentration, right-wing pressure on public radio and television, and the growth in scope and sophistication of public relations and news management.

British media theorist Nicholas Garnham adds that:

In assessing the likely impact of the new information technologies on broadcasting ... we need to remember that the actual history of the press is not one of developing freedoms, but on the contrary that the growth of an advertising-financed, commercial mass circulation press destroyed the independent working-class and radical press (as was the intention), steadily reduced the range of available views and information, incorporated nascent oppositional movements, helped to depoliticize our society and placed control of the channels of information in fewer and fewer hands.

And political economist Herbert I. Schiller, a vocal critic not only of global media but transnational corporations in general, writes:

What is happening in Europe and elsewhere represents far more than a continuation of heavy importation of Anglo-American media materials and the exposure of local audiences to this inflow. ... What is now happening is the creation of and global extension of a near-total corporate informational-cultural environment.

Scores of other critics could be cited. But I think you get the point.

These "critical" scholars come from a broad range of backgrounds and disciplines, but the bulk are in the social sciences, especially communication studies, journalism, sociology and political science. Many are sympathetic to neo-Marxist ideas. They go by a variety of names, including political economists, critical theorists, postmodernists, cultural theorists, media studies theorists and popular culture theorists. The list of critics also includes a substantial number of quantitative, nonleftist social scientists and professional journalists, who tend to agree with Bagdikian's more moderate perspective — that "bigness" is the problem, not capitalism per se.

The critics' goal is to convince students and the public that mass media, in their present form, are incapable of serving the needs and interests of the ordinary citizen, or the poor and disenfranchised. Although critics have many different perspectives, they all share the belief that global media are concerned more about profits than in helping people, especially the disadvantaged, and that a profit-oriented, market-driven medium is a threat to the public interest.

A Brief History of Criticism

Although scholarly criticism of global media is a relatively recent phenomenon, criticism of large-scale corporate media is not. In the early 1900s, Frank A. Munsey, a magazine and newspaper publisher, was widely despised for buying, merging and selling newspapers to make a profit and for proposing a national chain of newspapers. He believed there were too many newspapers in the United States and that this was inefficient. When Munsey died in 1925, newspaper publisher William Allen White wrote:

> Frank A. Munsey, the great publisher, is dead. Munsey contributed to the journalism of his day the great talent of a meat packer, the morals of a money changer and the manners of an undertaker. He and his kind have about succeeded in transforming a once noble profession into an eight percent security. May he rest in trust.

During the 1930s, magazine editor Oswald Garrison Villard and radical journalist George Seldes also wrote about the dangers of chain ownership. According to Villard, "Any tendency which makes toward restriction, standardization, or concentration of editorial power in one hand is to be watched with concern." Seldes was much more critical. He called the 21 members of the American Newspaper Publishers Association "the house of lords." He accused them of using their papers mainly to advance the commercial and political interests of themselves and big business.

During the 1940s, the Commission on Freedom of the Press continued this line of criticism, questioning whether freedom and democracy could survive in a system where the communication channels are concentrated in the hands of a few. "Have the units of the press, by becoming big business, lost their representative character and developed a common bias — the bias of the large investor and employer?" Later, the commission added:

> Our society needs an accurate, truthful account of the day's events. ... These needs are not being met. The news is twisted by the emphasis on firstness, on the novel and sensational; by the personal interests of the owners; and by pressure groups. Too much of the regular output of the press consists of a miscellaneous succession of stories and images which have no relation to the typical lives of real people anywhere. Too often the result is meaninglessness, flatness, distortion, and the perpetuation of

misunderstanding among widely scattered groups whose only contact is through these media.

The phenomenal growth of chain ownership in the U.S. newspaper industry during the 1950s, 1960s and 1970s ensured that "the problem" of large-scale media organization would remain on the front burner. Bagdikian emerged as the best-known critic. In the late 1980s, he even predicted that "if mergers and acquisitions continue at the present rate, one massive firm will be in virtual control of all major media by the 1990s." Although this has not occurred, the pace has quickened in the last two decades or so. As noted before, the top 12 global media organizations account for more than half of all communication industry revenues worldwide. And many analysts now predict that during the next decade only five companies will account for half of all revenues.

Contemporary Criticisms

Contemporary critics of global media have many complaints about global media. For example, mass communication scholar Robert McChesney argues that corporate media impair the democratic process. According to McChesney, democracy functions best when (1) there are no significant disparities in economic wealth; (2) people have a sense of community well-being; and (3) there is an effective system of political communication. However, he adds,

> *The preponderance of U.S. mass communication is controlled by less than two dozen enormous profit-maximizing corporations, which receive much of their income from advertising placed largely by other huge corporations. ... In my view, private control over media and communication is not a neutral or necessarily a benevolent proposition. The commercial basis of U.S. media has negative implications for the exercise of political democracy: it encourages a weak political culture that make depoliticization, apathy and selfishness rational choices for the citizenry, and it permits the business and commercial interests that actually rule U.S. society to have inordinate influence over media content. In short, the nature of the U.S. media system undermines all three of the meaningful criteria necessary for self-government.*

From a public policy perspective, the most significant complaint is the allegation that global media are reducing diversity in the "marketplace of ideas." This criticism and other major criticisms — including the charge that global media are hindering social change, imposing Western ideas on other cultures (media imperialism), and alienating media workers — are examined below.

Reducing Diversity

During the last 20 years or so, the term "diversity" has entered the language of everyday life in most Western societies. In most cases, its usage refers to the extent to which companies, the government, or industry segments have employees representative of the racial diversity in their communities or society as a whole.

In the field of communication, the term "diversity" has a much longer history, and it refers not to racial diversity but to the diversity of ideas, particularly political ideas. One of the assumptions underlying most Western notions of political democracy is that voters have access to a broad range of ideas and opinions. Without such access, they presumably cannot make good decisions. As former Supreme Court Justice Oliver Wendall Holmes put it, "the ultimate good desired is better reached by free trade in ideas — that the best test of truth is the power of the thought to get itself accepted in the competition of market ... ."

The "marketplace of ideas" metaphor is not an assumption that all critical scholars find appealing. They point out, quite correctly, that truth does not always emerge when it competes with falsehood in a private or public forum. Oftentimes, the group or person that has more money, more resources or more power wins out. However, critical scholars generally do agree that no political system would be fair or just if it suppresses ideas that are critical of those in power or the status quo. As such, the key question becomes: Does the growth of corporate media organizations lead to suppression of such ideas and hinder the democratic process? And on this question, there is no doubt about how the critics answer it.

"The antidemocratic potential of this emerging corporate control is a black hole in the mainstream media universe," writes Bagdikian. He adds:

What the public learns is heavily weighted by what serves the economic and political interests of the corporations that own the media. Since media owners are now so large and deeply involved in the highest levels of the economy, the news and other public information become heavily weighted in favor of all corporate values.

More specifically, Bagdikian and other critics cite two major reasons or factors to explain why global and corporate media contribute to the loss of diversity. The first one is concentration of ownership. According to Anthony Smith, a media scholar,

> *The public interest, hard always to define, must lie in the provision of a diversity of information from a diversity of sources — and therefore in the limiting of concentration of ownership. Otherwise, the democratic process itself is placed in thrall to a company or individual that may be pursuing, albeit quite legitimately, ends that are at variance with other objectives of a society. Nonetheless, concentration is being driven forward by regulatory and technological forces.*

Bagdikian and many other critics argue that the growth of global media and loss of entrepreneurial media are prima facie evidence of a loss of diversity. In some industries, such as the newspaper sector, this charge is true if the criterion for diversity is the actual number of business entities (sole proprietorships, partnerships and corporations) that control the media. However, if actual ownership is the criterion, then media have actually become less concentrated throughout the 20th century. The primary reason is that more and more media organizations are public corporations that sell shares of stock to the public. Although no statistics exist on media corporations per se, an amazing 45 percent of all Americans own stock in some corporations, many through their pension or mutual funds. This is the highest level in the world. Stock ownership in Europe is about 25 percent.

Historically, concentration of ownership was greatest during the 19th century, when media (especially print media) were owned by a relatively small number of individuals and families. However, as those organizations grew and their original owners died, they increasingly became the property of a growing number of owners, for two reasons. First, as Karl Marx observed, the original owners would bequeath their property to multiple heirs, who in turn would bequeath their property to multiple heirs. Needless to say, over time ownership usually became dispersed. Most family-owned media today have dozens of major stockholders, although there are exceptions here and there. Ownership and control of The News Corporation, for example, is highly centralized in Rupert Murdoch and his family (see Chapter 3). But this is more the exception than the rule, and it becomes increasingly difficult over time for one individual to maintain control of a growing corporation because of the second factor — "going public."

During the 20th century, many media organizations began selling shares of stock to the public in part to generate capital for expansion purposes. Most global media — 8 of the top 10 in fact — are public corporations whose stock is owned by hundreds and, in some cases, thousands of investors. Although top executives at some global media still own or control a very large share of the stock in those companies (see Chapter 3), over time, as they die, ownership generally will continue to become more diffused or diluted. Also, each time a corporation issues more stock, it tends to have the effect of diluting the power of the outstanding shares.

To get around the problem of ownership diffusion and to support the notion that global media ownership is becoming more concentrated, critics must assume that control of those media is largely in the hands of a few individuals — such as the board of directors and/or top management. Furthermore, they must assume that these directors or managers are serving their own interests before those of the audience or public.

The first assumption is reasonable — most stockholders have little direct say in the day-to-day operations of media corporations. Only those with substantial holdings have much say. However, the second assumption — that directors and, particularly, professional managers are serving their own interests to the detriment of the public — is much less reasonable. Some research suggests, in fact, that even though publicly owned media organizations are more profitable than owner-managed media, they actually place less emphasis on profits as an organizational goal and more emphasis on product quality. Why? Because they are more likely to be controlled by editors and professional managers who (1) see their work as an occupation or "calling," not just a job; (2) earn most of their compensation through fixed salaries and, thus, *do not benefit as directly or as much* from profits as the owners (companies are increasingly offering stock options to top managers, but salaries are still the most important source of income for most top-level managers; see Chapter 10 for more in-depth discussion of compensation issues); and (3) place much more emphasis on growing the corporation than on paying profits to the owners, because companies that are too profitable are targets for takeovers and growth is one way to expand the power and salaries of professional managers (see Chapters 7 and 10 for elaboration of these issues).

Nevertheless, despite this shortcoming, critics continue to argue that corporate and global media are greedier and threaten democratic values, even though they have yet to specify why it should be that they are greedier. To support their argument about the dangers of concentration of ownership, they point to Bertelsmann's purchase of Random House from Advance Publications in spring 1998 (Bertelsmann is the sixth largest global media company; Advance is 10th — see Chapter 3). Shortly after the deal was announced, sociologist and media critic Todd Gitlin wrote that

> *There's no glossing over that, if this deal is permitted to go forward, authors will have fewer places to sell their books. ... Editors will be dumped — to cut overhead — and more books will be turned over to free-lancers. ... And if consolidation is bad for editors and authors, how can it be good for readers. ... In the longer run, ... when authors can't make a decent living writing necessary books, readers suffer. They may not know they are suffering, but they suffer.*

The second factor critics say contributes to the loss of diversity is, crudely put, greed. "The helm is firmly in the grip of commercial and corporate greed," writes British media scholar Peter Golding. More specifically, large, corporate media are believed to place more emphasis on profits than on product quality and information diversity than small, entrepreneurial media. According to Herman,

> *The dominant media companies are large profit-seeking corporations, owned and controlled by very wealthy boards and individuals. Many are run completely as money-making concerns, and for the others as well there are powerful pressures from stockholders, directors, and bankers to focus on the bottom line. These pressures intensified over the 1980s as media stocks became stock market favorites and actual or prospective owners of media properties were able to generate great wealth from increased audience size and advertising revenues (e.g., Rupert Murdoch, Time-Warner, and many others). This encouraged the entry of speculators and takeovers, and increased the pressure and temptation to focus more intensively on profitability.*

To support their case, for example, critics can point to an incident that occurred in fall 1998 at ABC News, which is owned by The Walt Disney Company. According to the *Washington Post*, ABC News President David Westin killed a segment produced for the network's *20/20* program because it focused on alleged hiring and safety problems at Disney World in Florida. The segment, which was based on the book *Disney: The Mouse Betrayed*, charged that Disney World fails to perform security checks that would prevent the hiring of sex offenders. ABC denied it killed the story because of the negative publicity for Disney World. Moreover, the company pointed out that its news reports are not soft on Disney. Earlier in the year, for example, another *20/20* segment cited Disney as among a group of American companies that pay very low wages to workers on a Pacific island.

Another example critics can use to support their case that global media are unwilling to report negative news about themselves involved CBS during the 1998 Winter Olympics. A major sponsor of the games was the sports-shoe giant, Nike. CBS reporter Roberta Baskin accused CBS of refusing to rebroadcast her 1997 *48 Hours* report that was critical of Nike's labor practices in Vietnam because, she claimed, CBS did not want to offend Nike. The reporter also said CBS prevented her from doing follow-up stories on Nike and from replying to a *Wall Street Journal* article that criticized her original report. The network denied the charges.

More formally, three major arguments or propositions are used to support the claim that global and corporate media are more profit-oriented than small-scale or entrepreneurial media.

First, global media have more market power, which allegedly enables them to crush the competition and control advertising and subscription rates. The assumption underlying this claim is that those who control the media are profit-maximizers and that competition is necessary to keep them from holding the community hostage. According to the critics, corporate media derive their market power in part from economies of scale, lack of competition at the local level, greater knowledge of the marketplace, tax laws that favor corporate enterprises, and more efficient operations and greater rationality in decision-making. In particular, chains and large-scale media organizations are perceived to be more profit-oriented because they have more market power than independently owned and small media, respectively.

The second argument supporting the notion that the corporate or global media are more profit-oriented revolves around ownership structure. Because corporate media are more likely to be publicly owned than entrepreneurial media, critics believe corporate media must be constantly oriented to the bottom line to keep stockholders happy and investment dollars flowing in. Competition under these conditions is not just a matter of producing a better and less expensive product than a competitor — it means generating a profit that is higher than at companies in other industries as well. According to sociologists Paul M. Hirsch and Tracy A. Thompson,

In this demanding environment, performance is continually assessed by analysts and investors using the quarterly report on earnings. Analysts use information about a

firm's operations to generate forecasts about the company's long-term productivity and performance, which are reflected in the stock price. "Working for the numbers" has several important consequences for how newspapers operate. Strategies and activities geared toward creating value in the long run that require heavy investment in the short run become less attractive to executives because they decrease earnings in the current period.

The third argument supporting the idea that corporate or global media are more profit-oriented is based on the belief that they are less responsive to the social and moral concerns of the community. They are believed to be less responsive because their owners and managers are not strongly involved in the local community. Research shows, in fact, that owners of chain newspapers rarely live in the communities their newspapers serve, and managers of chain papers are less involved in local community organizations, are oriented more toward the organization and change jobs more frequently. Without strong ties to the local community, the chain organization is believed to be more interested in pursuing profits than the goals or interests of readers or the community (e.g., moral development). The notion that corporate media are less oriented to the local community also is expected to diminish community identity and solidarity. One expectation here is that the corporate and global media will publish less local or national news, and more nonlocal or international news.

The critics' charges do not end with profit-making. Because global media are assumed to be profit-maximizers, they also are assumed to place less emphasis on product quality and a diversity of ideas. The logic here is zero-sum: If a media organization maximizes profits, then it has less money to spend on news-gathering, improving the product or serving the public. In particular, critics charge that corporate or global media often sacrifice good journalism for profits. According to Hirsch and Thompson, "the move to public ownership led to the emergence of not only a new set of stakeholders in newspapers but a new logic for managing newspapers. Performance that is measured more in terms of economic than editorial accomplishments undermines newspaper executives' autonomy to pursue nonfinancial goals."

Although the zero-sum argument has a certain amount of intuitive appeal, the paradox is that media which make more money theoretically have more money to spend on improving the operation. Thus, the question is not just one of maximizing profits but also one of how much and what proportion of profits are spent on improving the media product. Researchers know little about this, however, because information about profits and expenditures is often proprietary.

In addition to more emphasis on profits and less on product quality, critics have argued that corporate or global media rob journalists of their professional autonomy and publish fewer editorials about local issues and fewer editorials that are critical of powerful groups or the status quo. Global media are less vigorous editorially, the critics contend, because they are afraid of offending advertisers, readers or sources, who may pull their advertising, buy fewer newspapers or refuse to cooperate with reporters. The effect of this alleged editorial timidity is a loss of diversity in the marketplace of ideas, which in turn is expected to imperil the democratic process.

To back up their claims, critics primarily rely on case studies and personal stories from former journalists and scholars. Typically, these critics recall incidents in which their former media organizations allegedly placed profits above product quality. Some of the titles tell the story: *When MBAs Rule the Newsroom; Read All About It! The Corporate Takeover of America's Newspapers; Networks of Power: Corporate TV's Threat to Democracy; Spiked: How Chain Management Corrupted America's Oldest Newspaper;* and *The Chain Gang: One Newspaper Versus the Gannett Empire.*

Hindering Social Change

Critics say corporate and global media have a conservative bias that impedes social change, which means systematic discrimination against the poor (as well as poor countries), women, minorities, environmentalists, organized labor and people with alternative sexual orientations. For example, British sociologist Peter Golding writes that

> *broadcast news is, for historical and organizational reasons, inherently incapable of providing a portrayal of social change or of displaying the operation of power in and between societies. It thus portrays a world which is unchanging and unchangeable.*

U.S. communication scholar Celeste Condit concludes that

> *We can endlessly generate studies that demonstrate that clever readers can take pleasure in reconstructing texts, but this does not certify that mass communication in general functions as a force for positive social change.*

And Canadian scholars Marc Raboy and Bernard Dagenais argue that

As all social institutions, media thrive on stability and are threatened by change. But ... media thrive on "crisis" and are threatened by "normalcy."

The tendency is, therefore, for media to seek out crisis where it does not exist, and to obscure the actual forces of change that threaten media privilege along with entrenched social privilege in general. Paradoxically, this means that media will tend to pay even more attention to a fabricated crisis than to one that can stake a material claim to reality. For social actors, provoking a crisis thus becomes a form of empowerment or social control.

Of course, some media critics acknowledge that news content may, on some occasions, promote the goals or interests of social movements; or that audiences may interpret media messages in a manner that is contrary to the "preferred reading" (which is defined as content that supports the interests of political and economic elites); or that people may use that information to protest against the dominant culture or elite groups. However, the overwhelming focus of critical scholarship has been on how media ignore or criticize the goals of social movements (especially liberal movements), and how the media serve (unwittingly or not) as "social control agents" for powerful elites and the institutions they control. Corporate and global media are almost always portrayed as organizations that work to the disadvantage of all except a small group of political and economic elites. Critics believe they can do little to help the cause of social movements. As Gamson puts it:

Qualifications and nuances notwithstanding, the overall role of media discourse is clear: it often obstructs and only rarely and unevenly contributes to the development of collective action (i.e., social movement) frames. [parenthetical added]

These and other critics argue that mass media hinder social change largely because their content tends to have a conservative bias. Political scientist Michael Parenti writes that mass media favor

management over labor, corporations over corporate critics, affluent whites over inner-city poor, officialdom over protesters, the two-party monopoly over leftist third parties, privatization and free market "reforms" over public sector development,

U.S. dominance of the Third World over revolutionary or populist social change, nation-security policy over critics of that policy, and conservative commentators and columnists like Rush Limbaugh and George Will over progressive or populist ones like Jim Hightower and Ralph Nader (not to mention radical ones).

More formally, Golding argues that news is ideological. This is not a conspiracy. Rather, the news is ideological because news organizations must make money and they depend upon elites for the news. News reinforces dominant values and social institutions, which themselves often discriminate against various groups. In short, mass media are seen by most critics as playing more of a social control than a social change function.

In this respect, Disney has been a major target of critics, who argue that much of its programming perpetuates gender, age and racial stereotypes that hinder social progress. Indeed, many of its movies portray women as the weaker sex — as being in need of men who will save them (e.g., *A Bug's Life*). *The Lion King* and many other Disney movies also are criticized for perpetuating aristocratic, patriarchal values. Furthermore, the Disney company is frequently accused of being aloof and unresponsive to criticisms about its programming. One group of media theorists was angered when Disney refused to allow them to use the name of their company in their book title. (Disney has the legal authority to do this because it owns the trademark to the name. For what it's worth, I also called, wrote and faxed Disney's vice president for community relations to get a response to these criticisms, but I received no reply.)

More generally, critics argue that TV entertainment is inherently oppressive because it makes people forget about the inhumanity of capitalism and the "ruling social order." Some time ago, neo-Marxist theorists Theodore Adorno and Max Horkeimer wrote that

to be pleased means to say Yes, ... Pleasure always means not to think about anything, to forget suffering even where it is shown. Basically it is helplessness, it is flight; not, as is asserted, flight from a wretched reality, but from the last remaining thought of resistance.

Finally, it should be noted that most contemporary critics acknowledge that social control is never fully achieved — that many disadvantaged and "oppressed" groups fight for social change. However, in the final analysis, these critics see the global media and mass media as institutions that help maintain the authority, power and privilege of political and economic elites.

Media Imperialism

International communications scholar Chin-Chuan Lee defines "media imperialism" as consisting of four major elements: (1) television program exportation to foreign countries; (2) foreign ownership and control of media outlets; (3) the transfer of the dominant broadcasting norms and media commercialism; and (4) the invasion of capitalist worldviews and infringement upon the indigenous ways of life in the adopting societies. The United States, he points out, is clearly the leading supplier of global television programs.

Many critics believe the ideas and values promoted in global media are destroying indigenous cultures, especially those not founded on capitalism. This is because the content of global media provides strong support for corporate capitalism and representative democracy. According to Professor Lee:

> *The strong presence of sleek foreign media products may take away opportunities that could otherwise be accorded to native artists, writers, and performers. ... Traditional arts and culture (both elite culture and folk culture) may have been on the decline as a result of the social change process. ... It is feared that foreign media have distorted the shared symbolic meaning of society and culture in terms of (1) creating mass frustration, (2) strengthening a "conspicuous consumption" pattern, and (3) fostering a "false consciousness."*

To the extent that media promote nonindigenous Western values, critics believe local customs, traditions and authority are threatened. Less developed nations in Africa, South America and Asia are believed to be most vulnerable to Western media. According to Chilean literary critic Ariel Dorfman and former sociologist Armand Mattelart, the threat that The Walt Disney Company represents

> *derives not so much from their embodiment of the "American Way of Life," as that of the "American Dream of Life." It is the manner in which the U.S. dreams and redeems itself, and then imposes that dream upon others for its own salvation, which poses the danger for the dependent countries. It forces us Latin Americans to see ourselves as they see us.*

Ironically, although many Third World nations are very critical of Hollywood, many still broadcast a lot of its programming, partly because it's too expensive to generate original programming. But even Europe, with its own highly developed media systems, feels threatened by American global media. According to European media scholars Kim Christian Schrøder and Michael Skovmand:

> *It is impossible to discuss transnational media cultures without facing the spectre of Americanisation, as it is still widely believed that if the European countries do not react forcefully and mobilize their rich and diverse cultural potential, we shall be committing spiritual suicide in a flood of Donald Duck Americanisation.*

It also should be pointed out that many neo-Marxist scholars prefer the term *cultural imperialism* to *media imperialism*, because they see most institutions, not just media, as playing a role in reinforcing the Western status quo. Other critics, however, do not like the term *imperialism* because it implies force or a conspiracy. Instead, they prefer the term *hegemony*, which is usually defined as ideological domination of nonelite groups through control of cultural forms and institutions. But whatever term is used, there is widespread agreement even among mainstream social scientists that Western media are "Westernizing" the world. International communication scholar William Hachten writes:

> *Whether this trend toward fewer, bigger, and more like-minded media of global communication is good or bad usually depends on the critic's personal tastes and ideology. But the internationalization of mass communication is proceeding in response to the needs and economic opportunities of a shrinking world. The transnational media are doing more than seizing the chance for greater profits from new markets, albeit those factors are obviously important. Whether viewed as another example of Western "media imperialism" or as a significant contribution to global understanding and integration, the international media are becoming increasingly cosmopolitan, speaking English, and catering to an internationally minded audience concerned about world affairs.*

Alienating Workers

Critics accuse global and corporate media of alienating workers. This also may be seen as having an adverse impact on diversity, because media workers may feel less motivated to work and do a good job. But having satisfied, self-fulfilled employees may also be an end in itself.

The logic behind the alienation thesis can be traced in part to the writings of Adam Smith and Karl Marx. They argued that the division of labor associated with large-scale organization created work that is alienating because it involves breaking down complex tasks into a number of simpler, more discrete steps or tasks — tasks that can often be performed by machines and unskilled labor. Routinization of the production process, they argued, makes work more mundane and monotonous.

Although many jobs at corporate media organizations do not involve factory-like motions, corporate media are still believed to be alienating because they (1) have a more complex set of rules and regulations, which critics say gives workers less autonomy, and (2) place less emphasis on cultivating close, interpersonal relationships among employees and bosses. In short, corporate media organizations are "cold" bureaucratic environments that are less concerned about their employees.

Proposed Solutions

Critics have offered a number of different solutions to the problem of global and corporate media. Mass communication scholar Garrett W. Ray summarizes some of them. They include (1) strengthening and enforcing antitrust laws; (2) limiting the number of media outlets that a person or organization can own; (3) restricting ownership across various kinds of media; (4) providing government and private monies to encourage and support noncommercial media; and (5) providing tax incentives to independent media.

Golding suggests that third-world nations should explore more alliances to create and support media systems that offer programming and content alternatives to global media. More radically, some scholars, such as Dennis Mazzocco, have argued that private ownership should be abolished and media be placed under ownership of public, nonprofit foundations. Others have taken this even a step farther and argue that capitalism itself needs to be abandoned. Lee points out that the crucial difference between neo-Marxist and non-Marxist critics is the difference between revolution and evolution. "Revolution cannot be limited to the media realm alone; it is a redefinition of the relationship between man and society, media and politics." Mainstream critics reject such ideas, and instead advocate a limited approach, one that involves increasing people's understanding of media through the schools, encouraging companies to focus on nonprofit goals, and creating councils that serve as a clearinghouse for people who have complaints against the media.

Although most critical scholars are extremely guarded and pessimistic about the impact of media globalization, some hold out hope that real change is possible. Herman and McChesney write:

> *For the short and medium term we expect both the global market and global commercial media to strengthen their positions worldwide ... . But beyond that the future is very unclear and remains the subject of human political control. ... The global market system has not ushered in a liberal democratic utopia and history is not at an end; quite the reverse, as economic polarization, ethnic strife, and a market-based paralysis of democracy hold forth possibilities of rapid and substantial social, political and economic upheaval. If it is to change, and in a positive way, it is important that people who are dissatisfied with the status quo should not be overcome and rendered truly powerless by a sense of hopelessness and cynicism. As Noam Chomsky said, "If you act like there is no possibility for change, you guarantee that there will be no change."*

In sum, many scholars believe that global media are destroying the diversity of ideas, good journalism and democratic principles. But are they right?

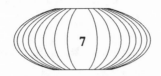

ARE THE
CRITICS RIGHT?

The guest professor was distinguished looking, which added all the more to his credibility.

He had just finished an intellectually challenging lecture on the political economy of the mass media — a neo-Marxist term for describing how corporate or global media are destroying the diversity of ideas, good journalism and democratic principles. Most of the graduate students and faculty in the room were impressed. Except for one.

"Professor, do you think the diversity of ideas in the field of mass communication research has increased or decreased during the last 30 years or so?" Like a cat bumped off a ledge, the seasoned professor landed squarely on his feet. His response drew laughter and admiration from those in the room, but it didn't answer the question.

"But do you think the diversity of ideas in our field has increased or decreased?" Once again the professor dodged the question, drawing more chuckles and admiring glances.

"But you still haven't answered the question, professor," the persistent inquirer said. "All things considered, is the field of mass communication more or less diverse in terms of theories, ideas and perspectives today than it was 30 years ago?"

"I guess in some ways it's more diverse and some ways less," the professor responded, clearly uncomfortable with the question. He went on for another five minutes. But this time the room was silent.

Criticizing the Critics

This professor avoided answering the question because he knew the correct answer would punch a hole in his neo-Marxist theory of mass media. Most neo-Marxist theories assume that corporate media, especially global media, are destroying diversity in the marketplace of ideas. Why? Because, according to the critics, corporate media are more concerned about profits than people or product quality.

But there is little question that the number of ideas and theories about the mass media — especially critical ideas — has grown explosively during the 20th century, particularly in the last 30 years. The professor himself is evidence of this. For more systematic evidence, one only need spend an hour or two at the library or a large bookstore. Thirty years ago only a handful of scholarly journals in the field of communication were devoted solely to critical scholarship. But today there are more than a dozen, and many mainstream journals now welcome such research. Furthermore, neo-Marxist scholars publish thousands of books every year — so many that now there are a dozen or so publishers around the world that specialize in neo-Marxist, cultural studies and postmodern scholarship. In fact, many academics believe that kind of scholarship is becoming the dominant theoretical approach in the field of communication. As Hamid Mowlana, a internationally recognized authority on global communications, put it:

> *The first survey of the state of international communication between 1850 and 1960, which I undertook over two decades ago ... [showed] little work in such areas as cultural analysis, the political economy of communication, discourse analysis, and comparative studies. ... A quarter century later, one is overwhelmed by the amount and extent of research output in international communication with diverse areas of inquiry and highly specialized streams of research.*

The fact that neo-Marxist scholarship flourishes in a capitalist system poses significant problems for global media critics. First, there is the problem of explaining how Western political systems can tolerate such critical scholarship, much of which accuses capitalists of committing great crimes against people and society. Second, there is the problem of explaining how diversity can decrease in the public sector when it is increasing in the academy. The latter problem is particularly difficult for critics because, as I pointed out in the introduction, critical writings and documentaries are increasingly finding their way into mainstream bookstores and libraries.

The failure to recognize and account for the expanding diversity of ideas in our world today is, I believe, the most significant shortcoming in critical models of corporate and global media. But there are other shortcomings, too. The critics have failed to (1) back up many of their claims with sound empirical research; (2) explain social changes that have often benefited groups that challenge tradition or the capitalist system (e.g., women, labor and civil rights organizations); and (3) resolve what economists call the "approved contradiction" — or the illogical notion that professional managers can emphasize profits more than capitalists even though they (the managers) do not benefit as directly from the profits.

The purpose of this chapter is to examine these problems. Before we begin, though, I caution the reader that these shortcomings do not mean all aspects of critical models are wrong. For example, the critics are quite correct when they point out that global media, like all mainstream media, produce content and programming that reinforces dominant institutions and value systems. All media serve a master. Whether you refer to this social control function as "media imperialism," "media hegemony" or simply "maintenance of the status quo," the fact remains that mass media content clearly helps to promote social order. Thousands of studies support this proposition, and I take up the social control function of the mass media in more depth in Chapter 8.

To be sure, critical models have contributed a great deal to our understanding of media and society. But the main problem with those models is that they generally overstated the social control part of the equation and understated the social change component. Let's begin with the diversity issue, and then turn to the other criticisms.

The Expanding World of Ideas

As pointed out in the last chapter, an assumption underlying most theories of democracy is that voters need to have access to a broad range of ideas and opinions on the issues of the day. Therefore, to resolve the diversity debate, it is necessary to ask: Where do ideas come from?

From people, of course. But to be more specific, ideas come from social interaction — that is, from people and organizations communicating with each other, often when they are trying to solve problems.

Think about the last time you tried to solve a problem. It may have been related to work, school, family or even play. It doesn't matter. What does matter is that when you think about the problem, many ideas typically race through your mind. Some simple. Some complex. Some make sense. Some don't. Where did they come from?

Well, some probably came from talking with others. You may have consulted with a spouse, friend, co-worker, boss or even a professor. Or you may have tried to resolve the problem on your own. You may have drawn on your own experiences. Or you may have sought out books, newspaper stories or magazine articles. But even if you relied on yourself, your ideas still had their origins in social interaction, because the experiences you've had and the materials you read are all shaped and produced through social interaction.

Now, if ideas are generated through social interaction, then it stands to reason that if social interaction increases, the number of ideas will increase as well. In other words, if you increase the number of individuals and groups in a society or organization, then isn't it reasonable to argue that the number of ideas will increase? Furthermore, if a social system or group encourages people to come up with different ideas, then the number of ideas could be expected to increase even more. And, if these ideas can be recorded in written or electronic form, they can accumulate over time, building an even larger reservoir of ideas and knowledge.

Diversity in the Academy

Now, can you see in part why the diversity of ideas has increased so much in the field of mass communication? During the last 30 years or so, the number of mass communication scholars and organizations representing them has grown dramatically (from a handful just before World War II to more than 40,000 worldwide). Fifty years ago you could count on one hand the number of theories and hypotheses about mass communication processes and effects. Today there are literally thousands, covering everything from cognitive processes to institutional and global effects. Some have interesting names: Spiral of Silence, Cultivation Theory, Agenda-Setting Hypothesis, Knowledge-Gap Hypothesis, Priming (cognitive and social), Framing, Mass Media Systems Theory, Discourse Theory, Uses and Gratifications, Media Dependency Theory and even Critical Theory.

The growth of these and many other theories in large part stems from an increase in the number of scholars and professional groups representing them, as well as an increase in the number of communications students, who, of course, provide many new ideas. But, as noted above, an increase in the number of social actors is not the only factor. Another is the actual value placed on ideas and diversity themselves. As noted in Chapter 2, historically many religious groups and political rulers discouraged the development of ideas, partly because they were often a threat to their power. Today, however, universities encourage scholars to come up with new ideas and to challenge old ones, and often reward those who do with tenure and pay increases. In fact, professors who don't come up with new ideas will have a difficult time getting published. The academy places a high value on new ideas, debate and criticism, and these values in turn help promote the development of new ideas and theories.

A third factor enhancing the development of ideas is simply the ability to record them. In other words, there are a lot more ideas and theories around today than in the past because we have the ability to record them in writing and electronic form. Technology, especially electronic, is speeding up the process through which ideas are generated and disseminated. Interestingly, one consequence of the ability to transmit knowledge in writing or in electronic form has been a devaluation of "respect for elders." In ancient times and in traditional cultures, older people were respected in part because they were like walking libraries — they had knowledge (memories) about events that affected the local community. Today, we are more likely to turn to experts, books and libraries for such information, and respect is based less on age than on advanced learning and knowledge. That's one of the reasons polls show that professors and physicians have two of the most prestigious jobs in the system.

Although the diversity of ideas has clearly increased substantially in the academy, there are limits even in the academy. As philosopher of science Thomas S. Kuhn pointed out, scholars who propose radical ideas — outside of the mainstream of science — often have difficulty getting published and are marginalized by other scholars. There are numerous examples of this in the history of natural and social sciences, including Albert Einstein's special theory of relativity. But my point is not that diversity in the academy is tolerated in an absolute sense — because it is not. Rather, diversity is increasing in relative terms, and it is increasing faster than at any time in history.

Diversity in the "Real" World

Now let's apply this theory of diversity to the world outside of the academy. First, have the number of people and groups in the world increased? The population has grown exponentially, as you probably already know. But just as important has been growth in the number of groups and organizations. Urban, industrial countries are layered with a myriad number of economic, political and social groups. This includes families, places of work, professional organizations, peer groups, neighborhood groups, community groups, churches, political organizations and social organizations. Most people who live in industrial societies belong to many different formal and informal organizations.

Second, do most societies or nations around the world today encourage ideas? Although many traditional societies and religious groups still discourage ideas — especially those that challenge traditional authorities — it is widely accepted that most urban, industrial societies today are much more tolerant of new ideas, even critical ones, than they were in the past. In fact, most industrial societies are so tolerant that many traditional and nontraditional subcultures often thrive within them. The Amish — a traditional religious group that shuns modern life — is a good example in the United States. Although widely despised, neo-Nazi groups also continue to survive and are not outlawed in most Western countries.

And third, have the number of media and technologies expanded? Incredibly so. Modern technology, such as the phone, computer and mass media, accelerate communication, feeding the "idea fire" even more. In contrast, 500 years ago there were no media. People had limited contact with each other, which limited ideas. The knowledge they needed to get through everyday life was obtained through experience and through contact with others around them. But today modern technology connects people around the world, and the rate of exchange has increased exponentially.

Diversity In Rural and Urban Areas

The notion that the universe of ideas is expanding as societies grow and become more structurally complex can be adroitly illustrated in a comparison of rural and urban areas within a country or between countries.

Rural areas or communities have small populations and a small number of social, economic and political groups. This "social structure" tends to limit social conflict as well as ideas, especially those critical of the system. If you have ever lived in a small town, you know it usually is not very tolerant of a diversity of ideas, especially liberal ideas. Small towns with universities are sometimes the exception because diversity (of ideas) is highly valued in the academy. Nevertheless, small towns generally embrace more traditional ideas and beliefs, which are not great platforms for radicals or those who wish to challenge the status quo.

One consequence of this relative lack of diversity is that the local weekly or community newspaper usually contains very little news that is critical of people or social institutions. Instead, they are usually filled with "booster" news — social and political news that tends to project a view of the community as harmonious and wholesome. Of course, this does not mean there is no conflict in a small towns. There can be and usually is a lot of *interpersonal* conflict in small towns — proportionately, often just as much as in large cities. However, in relative terms there is a lot less *social* conflict in small towns (conflict between groups), because they simply have a fewer number of organized groups than larger communities.

In contrast, urban or metropolitan communities are characterized by a large number of social groups, many of which compete for limited social, political and economic resources. In most large cities around the world, you usually can find political groups representing both the extreme right (fascists) and left (communists), as well as the mainstream political parties (e.g., Democrats and Republicans in the United States). Groups representing the interests of women, minorities, gays, laborers and environmentalists also are in abundant supply.

As a consequence of this structural diversity, the news media in metropolitan communities are filled with stories that reflect the conflict, debate and criticism generated in large part by these groups. Although these stories and editorials are often viewed as threatening to the social order, they often play a significant role in contributing to social order because they introduce alternative

ideas or innovations that enable organizations and institutions to adapt to
changing conditions.

The Critics' Response

In response to these arguments, critics often argue that even if the number of
ideas is increasing, those ideas are narrowly restricted to the needs of political
and economic elites. In other words, the critics see most ideas as serving
capitalist goals and ideals.

I do not dispute the fact that many ideas today are generated for the benefit
of someone's pocketbook. And — let there be no mistake — mainstream
corporate media are highly responsive to political and economic centers of
power and promote values generally consistent with capitalist ideals and elite
interests. In absolute terms, corporate and global media may be faulted for
failing to challenge some of the more repressive features of Western society.

However, the fact that most ideas today generally support existing
institutions, values and ways of thinking does not mean there are fewer ideas
critical of the status quo, or that people have less access today to them than ever
before. If you go into a major bookstore chain, you will find scores of neo-
Marxist, cultural studies and postmodern books and reading materials. In fact,
some of them, especially in sociology, political science and mass
communication, are bestsellers. And talk about diversity — go check out the
lesbian/gay section, the feminist section, or the environmental section. And if
you can't find the time to go to the store, then get online and type in the terms
Marxism or *postmodernism*. Using the search engine Alta Vista, in August 1999 I
generated 37,640 references for *Marxism* and 11,501 for *postmodernism*. Nineteen
months later, in March 2001, I did the search again and produced 158,975
references for Marxism and an astounding 562,266 references for
postmodernism.

Of course, critics will respond that just because there is ample material
about Marxism on the Internet doesn't mean that material has an impact. My
response: Sure, most people aren't interested in reading that stuff, and sure,
Marxists do not have the same access to resources as major corporations. But
the point is that they have a greater choice today than ever before — the
information environment contains 721,241 new sources that didn't exist a
decade ago. Diversity is expanding in relative terms.

Where's the Empirical Beef?

The second major problem with the critical model is that much of the research on media simply fails to support it.

Social scientific research on media systems supports the critics' arguments that the flow of information around the world tends to go from economically and politically powerful countries to poor countries. Western mass media, especially media from the United States, Britain and France, have a disproportionate influence in this regard. Research, including my own, also suggests that corporate media are more profitable. As noted in Chapter 4, larger, more complex organizations benefit from economies of scale and have more human and capital resources.

However, critics have failed to provide convincing evidence that the diversity of ideas is decreasing. They often cite case studies and anecdotes, such as the ones in Chapter 6 about ABC and CBS, to support their arguments. Although these incidents provide support for their argument, the problem with using case studies and anecdotes is that they may not be representative of the entire population of media. As international communications researchers Lars Willnat, Zhou He and Hao Xiaoming point out:

> *[T]he theory of cultural imperialism ... assumes that Western cultural products have deleterious effects on indigenous cultures because of their one-way flow from the West and the undesirable, foreign values embodied in those products. This approach, though rhetorically powerful and political attractive, has gathered only limited empirical support.*

Indeed, Willnat and his colleagues point out that cross-sectional studies, including their own research, show that audiences in developing countries often interpret Western television programs differently from their counterparts in the West and read new meanings into the messages. Consumption of foreign media also does not necessarily lead to a favorable foreign cultural orientation. Moreover, after reviewing the empirical literature on "cultural imperialism," mass communication researcher Michael B. Salwen, concluded that

> *we can readily discard the broad claim that exposure to Western media alone will cause foreign peoples to shed their cultural identities and values and adopt Western values. At the very least, factors inherent within cultures, such as gender roles,*

account for different responses to foreign media messages … . Indeed, some of the
empirical studies suggest active resistance to foreign media messages in some
instances. … Finally, the empirical studies suggest not only negative effects but
positive ones as well, such as the "liberation" of women in male-dominated cultures
… and increased cultural exchange … .

And the most comprehensive survey of the empirical literature to date,
conducted in 1997 by mass communication scholars Michel Elasmar and John
Hunter, concluded:

Based on the concept that foreign TV programs embody a tool of cultural
imperialism, we had expected our meta-analysis to reveal that foreign television
programs have strong effects on the domestic audience members who view them. The
results summarized above reveal that this is not the case. At most, foreign TV
exposure may have a very weak impact upon audience members. This result
contradicts the assertions of Herbert Schiller and his colleagues, who have long
warned against the dangers of cultural imperialism.

Salwen concedes that repeated exposure to Western media messages over
long periods of time may "subtly alter cultural values." Indeed, Elasmar and
Hunter found that exposure to foreign TV leads people in foreign countries to
purchase more foreign products, to hold values similar to those in the country
producing the foreign message, and to acquire beliefs about the country
originating the message. A survey of Filipino high school students by
international mass communication researchers Alex S. Tan, Gerdean K. Tan and
Alma S. Tan also found that American television programs have a small effect
on eroding of traditional Filipino values. Alex Tan argues that Western
entertainment programming offers images of a "better life" to which the poor
in developing countries may aspire. This is a reasonable argument, albeit there
are no longitudinal cohort empirical studies, which are necessary to make a
strong case for the imperialism hypothesis.

Corporate critics also have failed to produce sound empirical evidence to
support their claims that corporate media are greedier or that seeking profits
leads to a lower-quality product. It should come as no surprise to anyone that
profit-making is a concern at corporate and global media organizations — it is
an important goal wherever media are supported by private sources of capital.
The key question is not whether corporate or global media make decisions that
are profit-driven — the question is whether they, as organizational forms, place

more emphasis on profits than noncorporate (or entrepreneurial) media, and what impact this has on content. In other words, to understand the impact that global media are having, one needs to conduct a comparative study, which means studying changes over time or comparing the differences between groups (corporate versus entrepreneurial media).

But critics rarely conduct comparative studies (one exception is Mowlana's study which showed the diversity of research on international communication has exploded in the quarter century). And rarely do they study entrepreneurial media. Consequently, they have a self-generated illusion that profit-making is the only goal at corporate and global media. In addition, critics have never been able to provide convincing evidence that corporatization or globalization of media systems inhibit social change or produce more highly dissatisfied employees. In fact, most critical models are unable to account for social change (see Chapter 9).

In contrast, research strongly suggests that some media (e.g., newspapers) become more critical of the status quo as they acquire the characteristics of the corporate form of organization. For example, of the 18 studies that to date have examined the impact of ownership on editorial vigor, eight show that chain newspapers are more vigorous than independently owned newspapers, seven show no difference or have mixed findings, and three suggest that independent newspapers are more vigorous. As journalism professor Gerald Stone has written,

> *there is no consistent documentation that group ownership of newspapers is inherently bad. The chief changes likely to occur with chain ownership are related to economic considerations, primarily: Chains have a distinct economic advantage derived from their experience and expertise in management, marketing and use of the economies of scale. Evidence is that this financial planning sophistication can make newspapers more profitable businesses without debasing the journalistic product.*

My own research on U.S. daily newspapers over the past decade — which has employed probability survey research methods — also contradicts the critical models. I measure corporate structure as a continuous variable composed of 12 individual items, including structural complexity (number of employees/journalists/news beats; number of promotions a reporter needs to become the publisher); rules and procedures (does newspaper have written code of ethics and employee handbook); ownership structure (chain ownership, public ownership, family ownership, legal incorporation); staff expertise (college degree required to be reporter); and emphasis placed on rationality (efficiency) as an organizational goal. One shortcoming of my research methodology is that it cannot provide a lot of specific information about a particular newspaper, which of course is a strength of the case-study approach. However, I am less interested in explaining the particular than the general, and probability sampling methods enable me to test a theory that is applicable to the entire population of daily newspapers, not just one newspaper.

My research has found that newspapers place less emphasis on profits and more emphasis on product quality as they become corporatized. More important, my data also show that newspapers become more vigorous editorially as they become more corporatized. The greater the "corporatization," the greater the number and proportion of editorials and letters to the editor that are critical of "mainstream" authorities, institutions and values. News sources in communities served by corporate newspapers (i.e., mayors and police chiefs) also perceive those newspapers as being more critical of them, their policies and city hall.

The criticism that corporate and global organizations treat employees unfairly also isn't well documented. Although job satisfaction among print journalists has declined since the 1970s — a trend that may reflect increasing uneasiness about the future of the industry and diminishing opportunities for advancement in news organizations — my surveys show that journalists at corporate newspapers continue to be much more satisfied and that editors at corporate newspapers actually have more, not less, autonomy.

Corporate organizations, because they are larger and more profitable, pay their employees higher salaries and under some circumstances actually give them more autonomy. The increased autonomy is partly a function of the division of labor and role specialization. As the organization grows and managers are managing more people, they have less direct control over any particular employee's daily work. At corporate newspapers, the owners and publishers actually play a smaller and smaller role in day-to-day decisions regarding news content, and editorial editors play a greater role. Also, role specialization enables some journalists to become "experts" in various areas, which in turn reduces even further the ability of their manager to control their work. Research also shows that corporate organizations promote women and minorities more quickly than entrepreneurial organizations. Disney, for example, pays benefits to same-sex partners, which has irked some conservative religious organizations.

And even though corporate newspapers may be staffed with editors who have fewer ties to the local community, there is no evidence to support claims that it leads to a breakdown in social order in the community. In fact, corporate newspapers, which appear to place more emphasis on nonlocal news, may help integrate local communities into larger, more complex or global social systems. This, in turn, can help these communities adapt to political, economic and social change.

Technically, my research cannot be applied to other media systems or to other countries. There are many difficulties in studying communication processes across media industries and at a global level. However, my research does call into question some key aspects of critical models. For example, remember from Chapter 6 the story of Frank A. Munsey, the U.S. newspaper owner who built a chain of newspapers during the early 1900s? Although Munsey profited substantially from his newspaper transactions, he also published *Munsey's Magazine*, a mass-circulation muckraking publication that crusaded against corruption and social injustice. Mass communication historians Jean Folkerts and Dwight Teeter also point out that when Munsey merged newspapers, he often strengthened them. Most of his $20 million fortune, by the way, was willed to New York's Metropolitan Museum of Art.

Unfortunately, critics of corporate and global media systems routinely ignore and rarely cite research that contradicts their ideas. Also, it should be noted that some cultural critics dismiss the empirical research literature on philosophical (i.e., epistemological) grounds because they believe reason and logic are much more important criteria for assessing the validity of ideas. Although reason and logic are extremely crucial in any form of knowledge, most scholars, even critical ones, believe research helps sort good from bad ideas.

What About Social Change?

One of the hallmarks of modern society — if not *the* identifying feature — is social change. If we conceptually define social change as the difference between current and antecedent conditions in the social structure (which I define as including not only the enduring patterns of social relationships but also values, norms, laws and social goals, which serve to establish and maintain such relationships), then most scholars would agree that many social changes have taken place in the United States during the last century.

But none of the critical models adequately accounts for social change and the role of mass media. As noted in Chapter 6, the critics assume that as media become more corporatized, the more they promote the interests of their owners and other corporate and business elites. Corporate or global media are expected to have less capacity to publish information that challenges or questions dominant ideas and institutions.

Of course, many acknowledge that news content may, on some occasions, promote the goals or interests of social movements; or that audiences may interpret media messages in a manner that is contrary to the "preferred reading" (which is defined as content that supports the interests of political and economic elites); or that people may use that information to protest against the dominant culture or elite groups. However, the overwhelming focus of critical scholarship has been on how media ignore or criticize the goals of social movements (especially liberal movements), and how the media serve (unwittingly or not) as "social control agents" for powerful elites and the institutions they control.

Corporate and global media are almost always portrayed as organizations that work to the disadvantage of all except a small group of political and economic elites. Even when a series of investigative news reporting uncovers wrongdoing and the political system makes statutory changes that benefit the disadvantaged, critics typically see this as an anomaly that has virtually no impact on changing the power structure, even in the long run. Moreover, mass media can do little to help the cause of social movements.

The problem with this antichange position is that it is inconsistent with history and a large body of empirical research. During the last century in particular, newspapers have played an important role in legitimating and sometimes promoting (though rarely initiating) the goals of many social movements, which in turn have led to a number of social changes. The most notable example of this occurred at the turn of the century, with the rise of the so-called "muckrakers" (see Chapter 9). Their investigations into monopolies, slum housing, the meat-packing industry, and political corruption led to a number of reforms. Media in Western nations also have played a role in legitimating decisions from the courts and government that expanded rights and opportunities for women, minorities, the working class, environmentalists, homosexuals, and the poor. Such changes certainly have not eliminated inequalities, discrimination or injustices, but they have significantly altered the power structure in most Western countries during the 20th century.

As media studies scholar James Lull puts it:

Social change, the defining characteristic of world history, unmistakably demonstrates that ideology is negotiated and contested, not imposed and assumed. Individual persons, social groups, nations, and cultures should not be considered victims of dominant social forces. We must conclude that the media/cultural imperialism thesis ... therefore, is not wrong but incomplete. Furthermore, the more complex theory of ideological and cultural hegemony — wherein institutional forces are said to converge on behalf of the vested interests of society's political-economic elite — is also ultimately unsatisfying. ...

The other side of the coin is popular resistance to dominant ideology and culture. But, just as social institutions including mass media cannot completely control their audiences, the autonomy and power of individuals and subjugated groups is also limited. For this reason I do not want to argue completely against the essential line of reasoning that underlies theories of imperialism or hegemony.

What About the "Approved Contradiction?"

Another shortcoming of the critical perspective is that it has failed to resolve what economist John Kenneth Galbraith calls the "approved contradiction." Basically, the question is this: How can organizations managed and controlled on a daily basis by professional managers rather than the owners (i.e., corporate organizations) be expected to maximize rewards for others (owners) but not themselves?

The notion that professional managers seek to maximize profits for the owners contradicts some basic economic assumptions about human behavior. If one assumes that humans usually seek to maximize their benefits and minimize their costs (as critics assume of corporate media owners), then managers cannot be expected to maximize profits for the owners, because most of their rewards come through a fixed salary and not profits. Although a minimum level of profitability is necessary to prevent the board of directors from removing top management, managers are likely to pursue some of their own interests, which are not always related to the bottom line. They include organization growth and increased emphasis on quality.

More formally, the "managerial revolution" holds that as organizations become more corporatized, power and control over day-to-day operations shifts from the owners to the professional managers. The shift occurs in large part because increasing complexity in organizational structure forces the owners to rely more and more heavily on highly skilled experts and technocrats for key decisions. A recent study that I conducted supports this "power shift." U.S. daily newspaper owners and publishers play less and less of a role in day-to-day decisions about editorial matters as the newspaper exhibits the characteristics of the corporate form of organization, which gives editors a more prominent role.

This shift in power does not mean that the owners or their representatives (board of directors) have no say in the operation. However, their authority over day-to-day decision-making is greatly weakened. Increasingly, the experts — the journalists and other managers — make the decisions, and the owners become increasingly dependent upon their knowledge and advice. At the entrepreneurial media organization, on the other hand, the owner is usually involved in daily editorial decisions and maintains direct control over managers in all areas.

This shift in power also does not mean that managers or editors at corporate media are not concerned with profits. They are, because profit-making is crucial for the survival of any business. However, corporate organizations place less importance on profit-making because most managers do not benefit directly or as directly from profits, as most of their income is derived from a fixed salary. Instead, managers place much more importance on maximizing growth of the organization, which, research shows, does contribute directly to higher salaries and greater power. Also, managers place greater importance on product quality and other nonprofit goals because, as professionals, they place a higher value on intrinsic rewards (e.g., peer recognition) as opposed to just extrinsic rewards (salary). "Doing a good job," in fact, is canonized in many codes of ethics that serve journalists and other professional managers.

Some critics charge that managers at corporate media have an MBA mentality. Undoubtedly this is true, as MBAs have the requisite knowledge and training to operate a complex business organization. But the increased concern with profits is more apparent than real. Profit-making is much more likely to be a topic of conversation at a corporate medium because that organization is more likely to be publicly owned. In addition, the corporate medium is more likely to be absentee-managed, which means the local publisher or general manager often seeks the assistance of other managers in making the organization profitable. In contrast, profit-making is less likely to be a topic of discussion at entrepreneurial media, because those organizations are family owned or privately owned, and the owners rarely want to reveal their income to the community or their employees.

Some critics also argue that corporate media organizations which pay professional managers higher salaries or stock bonuses pursue profits more vigorously. However, I recently re-analyzed compensation data collected by *Business Week* and found that corporate pay for top media executives has no relation to either shareholder return or profitability. Rather, it's total sales that counts: The bigger the company, the more it pays, regardless of profitability or shareholder return. In fact, for every one percent increase in sales, the pay of top media executives increases by one-half percent. These findings, I concluded,

fail to support executives' arguments that job performance drives their paycheck. They also fail to support the position of corporate media critics, who argue that corporations which pay more are greedier and place more emphasis on profits than on nonprofit goals (e.g., producing a higher quality news and entertainment product).

But the findings will come as no surprise to many postindustrial theorists, who have argued for some time that managers seek not only to serve the owners but also themselves. The managerial revolution has not eliminated the profit motive, to be sure. All businesses seek profits. But the managerial revolution has decreased the power of the owners (i.e., non-management stockholders) relative to the managers. The golden parachute is a visible example of this power shift. And short-term profit maximization is not always in the best interests of the top managers. ...

[P]rofessional managers often place more importance on maximizing growth of the organization. To be sure, growth may benefit owners in the long-run. But managers often stand to gain a great deal in the short run. Growth helps fend off hostile takeovers, explain low profits, increase managerial power, make stockholders more dependent upon management, and, of course, increase managerial pay. Indeed, this study shows that growth is the surest way to increase top executive pay.

An in-depth analysis of the managerial revolution hypothesis, including a review of the empirical literature, is contained in Chapter 10.

What About the Zero-Sum Problem?

Another major problem with the critics' perspective is the zero-sum assumption. If a medium maximizes profits, then critics assume that it has less to spend on collecting news, improving the product or serving the public. Admittedly, this zero-sum argument has a certain amount of intuitive appeal. However, the paradox is that media which make more money theoretically have more money to spend on improving the operation.

Although the evidence is still scanty, research by media economist William Blankenburg suggests that one large (i.e., corporate) newspaper spends more money in absolute and relative terms on the editorial content than two smaller newspapers of equal size. Blankenburg's research does show that publicly owned corporate newspapers are more profitable than privately owned family newspapers — a finding that is consistent with the notion that corporate media, because they are larger and benefit from economies of scale, are structurally organized to maximize profits.

Whose Interests Do Global Media Serve?

In sum, theory and evidence support the critics' arguments that media organizations are growing and becoming more profitable, partly because they benefit from economies of scale and better resources. There also is little question that corporate and global media produce content that supports the status quo. However, the evidence does not support the critics' charges that as media become more corporatized, the diversity of ideas shrinks, or that media content becomes less critical of those in power, or that media content contains fewer ideas.

But if corporate and global media are not simply lap dogs for the rich and powerful, then whose interests are they serving?

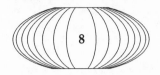

GLOBAL MEDIA
AND SOCIAL CONTROL

Sometimes — no matter what you do — you can't please anyone.

Just ask CNN correspondent Peter Arnett, who was one of the few Western journalists allowed to cover the 1991 Gulf War from inside Iraq. Iraqi officials didn't trust him, so they censored parts of the news reports he filed from Baghdad. But his reports didn't please U.S. officials either — especially the reports about civilian casualties, the bombing of an alleged baby formula factory, and his interview with Saddam Hussein. For example:

- Gen. H. Norman Schwarzkopf told Barbara Walters that Arnett's reports of the civilian deaths made the United States look like it was "lying to the American people when we (American military) told them we were deliberately trying not to target civilian targets."
- American military officials argued that the baby formula factory was actually a biological-weapons facility, but Arnett's reports strongly implied this was not the case.
- Arnett's interview with Saddam, *The New York Times* reported, "gave the Iraqi ruler an opportunity to restate his certainty of victory, to suggest that he might use unconventional weapons if forced and to

express gratitude to 'noble souls' in the West who have been
demonstrating against the war."
- Sen. Alan Simpson called Arnett an Iraqi "sympathizer."
- A coalition of right-wing groups called him a "traitor" and "an
  unpaid propagandist" for Saddam Hussein.

Ironically, though, after the war, left-wing mass communication scholars
around the world charged CNN and other global news media of reporting the
conflict with a pro-Western bias — not an Iraqi one! They argued that global
media coverage helped legitimate and justify the West's attacks on Iraq. In fact,
polls showed that the U.S. public opinion became much more supportive of
President George Bush and his policies after the shooting started. So, in the
end, the only organization apparently pleased with Arnett's coverage was CNN,
whose audience ratings soared during the war and helped boost the network
into one of the world's top television news networks.

In response to his critics, Arnett says he was just doing his job. "Why
shouldn't we show what bombs do when they hit a country?" he asked an
audience at the University of California in San Diego. Many journalists agreed.
Arnett was simply reporting events as objectively as possible, they argued.

But if his reports were objective, then why did they generate so much
criticism? Can news really be objective? Can news from global media
corporations be objective? Is there really any difference between the way global
media and nation-based media cover events like the Gulf War? And whose
interests are global media serving?

The Ethic of Objectivity

The ethic of objectivity is one of the most important principles guiding Western
journalists today. Although definitions vary, three major ideas or tenets underlie
most conceptions of objectivity: (1) Journalists should keep their personal
opinions and the opinions of their newspapers out of their news stories; (2) All
sides to a story should be covered and reported; and (3) All sides to a story
should be given an equal amount of coverage.

The origins of objectivity are often traced to the 1830s and the so-called
Penny Press in the United States, which sold newspapers for a penny apiece and
became the first "mass" medium. But it took nearly a century for the concept
to gain widespread acceptance. And despite another century of practice, the

notion that the news media are objective is under greater assault today than at any time in history.

On one side are the conservatives, who vociferously argue that mainstream media, including global media, have a liberal bias. In their book, *And That's The Way It Is(n't): A Reference Guide to Media Bias*, L. Brent Bozell III and Brent H. Baker argue that

> *America's most influential media outlets report the news through a liberal prism. With reprints, excerpts and summaries of more than 40 studies conducted over the past decade, (this book) provides the most thorough analysis ever compiled proving the liberal political slant in the national press.*

On another side are the liberals, who — you guessed it — accuse the media of having a conservative bias. As media critics Jeff Cohen and Norman Solomon put it:

> *One of the most enduring myths about the mainstream news media is that they are "liberal." The myth flourishes to the extent that people don't ask pointed questions: If the new media are liberal, why have national dailies and news weeklies regularly lauded those aspects of President Clinton's program that they view as "centrist" or "moderate," while questioning those viewed as liberal?*

Of course, the third perspective comes from the journalists themselves, who argue that the news is neither liberal nor conservative. "We don't take sides," they often tell me. "We are neutral, objective, and nonideological. Indeed, our professional ethic of objectivity holds that we must be unbiased observers of the world. We are supposed to keep our personal opinions to ourselves, cover all sides of the story, and give roughly equal weight to all sides. Opinions are properly expressed only on the editorial and op-ed pages, or in news analyses."

Although journalists readily concede that "pure" objectivity is impossible to achieve, they nonetheless are committed to following a number of news-gathering rules — such as attributing information to sources and quoting different sides to a controversy — that allegedly produce "objective," unbiased news accounts. As former ABC News President James Hagerty put it:

We're trying to be objective ... we are reporters! We get interpretations from other people and present them. If anyone on this network is expressing his own opinion — well, if I catch him [sic] I won't permit it.

So who's right? The conservatives, the liberals or the journalists? None of them, I will argue in this chapter.

The news does contain a bias, to be sure. But when viewed from afar, it is neither extremely liberal nor conservative. It is *mainstream*, centrist, or middle of the road. And global media, because they rely heavily upon mainstream Western elites for news, also have a mainstream Western bias.

The Mainstream Bias

The mainstream bias means that Western news media rarely give positive news coverage to extremist groups on either the left or right. For example, communists and others on the "far left" rarely get sympathetic press coverage in daily newspapers or on national television. But the same holds for neo-Fascists and others on the "far right." Virtually all of the coverage given to these groups — in commentaries as well as straight "hard news" stories — is negative or critical. The only notable exception is when one of the extremist groups is denied freedom of speech, in which case the news coverage focuses on the free-speech issue rather than on the ideological goals of the groups. This has happened on several occasions to the neo-Nazi groups in the United States. However, let there be no mistake, the goals of those groups are strongly condemned and criticized by the mainstream news sources cited in the news stories.

So what is the mainstream ideology? In the United States, it is embodied in the Democratic and Republican parties. In England, it is the Conservative and Labor parties. And throughout much of Europe, it is the Social Democrats. These are the groups that get preferential coverage in the news and generally get the most positive coverage. To be sure, there is a lot of critical news directed at mainstream parties — especially when they criticize each other. When that occurs, the mainstream news media usually cover both mainstream sides of a dispute.

However, news media rarely seek the opinions of groups that are considered to be outside of the mainstream. In fact, the more extreme the group, the less the coverage it will receive and the less favorable the coverage will be. Conversely, as a rule, the more the group's goals fall within mainstream values and norms, the more coverage it tends to get and the more favorable that coverage.

Bias in a U.S. Presidential Election

A good way to illustrate the mainstream bias is to examine a U.S. presidential election. All presidential races include more candidates than just those in the Democratic and Republican parties. In 1996, for example, 21 people ran for president (albeit not all names were on all 50 state ballots).

To be purely objective, a reporter ideally should give each candidate in a presidential election equal coverage — that is, each should receive the same amount of space, the same placement and the same balance of views. This ideal is sometimes possible when there is only one Democratic and one Republican candidate, because both are from the political mainstream. However, because presidential elections also include candidates from nonmainstream parties, the coverage has never come close to the ideal of objectivity. Some candidates receive more coverage than others.

For example, in 1996 the media gave much less coverage to Green Party candidate Ralph Nader, Libertarian candidate Harry Browne, and Socialist Workers Party candidate James Harris. The vast bulk of the coverage went to Bill Clinton and Robert Dole. Ross Perot received less coverage than Clinton or Dole but more coverage than the other nonmainstream candidates. Why? Because (1) his views were closer to the mainstream than most of the other candidates, (2) he had a relatively large following (more political power than the other nonmainstream candidates), and (3) he was a curious anomaly (a billionaire running for office).

Now, you may ask, why do the "alternative" candidates get so little coverage? Through the years, I've asked many journalists this question. And the answer is almost always the same. Because the alternative candidates have no chance of winning and because the public wants to hear about the mainstream candidates. The public does not want to hear the views of socialist or Green Party candidates, they argue.

There is, no doubt, some truth to this. Most of the alternative candidates have no chance of winning, and the public generally is less interested in their views. But this doesn't change the fact that — and most journalists will concede this — the election coverage is not objective. The alternative candidates are "marginalized," meaning that they are assumed not to be viable candidates.

Mainstream Bias in Other News Stories

The mainstream bias is more difficult to see in other stories, especially in those that are not controversial. But it is there.

For example, the very day I am writing the copy you are now reading, *The* (Spokane, Washington) *Spokesman-Review* published a story titled, "White separatists to be featured at survivalist expo." The story outlined how leaders of neo-Nazi, right-wing Christian separatist, antiblack and anti-Semitic groups would be speaking at the Spokane Convention Center. But the focus of the story was not on what the speakers would say — as it might have been for Republican and Democratic speakers. Rather, the focus was on how the views of these groups were contrary to the dominant values of the community. None of the extremist leaders was interviewed, but there was a generous sampling of critics' views.

"From a legal standpoint, there's nothing we can do to block this kind of event," one city official is quoted as saying. "Do we condone it? Do we want it to be there? The answer is, 'Hell no!'" Says another city official: "Like civil libertarians, I am concerned with ... (respecting) ... First Amendment freedoms. But as the human rights specialist, I will continue to speak against supremacy and hatred, and I encourage citizens who want to live in a respectful community to do the same."

With this example I am not trying to defend the position of these right-wing groups — in my opinion, their views are repugnant and based on ignorance. However, in terms of analyzing the media coverage, this example illustrates quite clearly how the media marginalize extremist groups and, in the process, provide support for dominant groups and community values.

Another front-page story in the same *Spokesman-Review* edition extolled the virtues of a Russian human rights champion who was tormented in prison during the Soviet days of "totalitarian repression." The moral lesson: Communism is bad.

Another story details one of the possible motives why a deputy sheriff charged with murder may have shot his wife. Adultery, which violates virtually all mainstream religious groups' codes of morality, can lead people astray. Still another story in the newspaper noted that a new diabetic drug could reduce the need for insulin. This story reinforced social norms and values about the importance of scientific research and helped the U.S. Food and Drug Administration get the word out to the public.

I must emphasize again that I am not passing personal judgment on these stories or the values promoted in them. In fact, I believe many of them are noble and worthy of coverage. However, my point is that the news is not objective in any absolute sense, despite what journalists may claim. At the same time, the news is not nearly so conservative as the liberals would have us believe or as liberal as the conservatives would have us believe. Rather, in all cultures, news in the mass media generally promotes the dominant values of that culture and the powerful social institutions. And, at election time, the mainstream bias helps to guarantee that changes in national leadership do not come quickly or radically.

By the way, if you want to understand why some people believe the news media are too liberal or too conservative, simply ask them for their political orientation. As a rule of thumb, the more conservative the orientation, the more likely they are to see the media as liberal. The more liberal the orientation, the more likely they are to see the media as conservative.

So much for objectivity.

Is the Mainstream Bias Good or Bad?

Of course, the answer to this question depends on whether you're a member of a mainstream party or not. During the 1992 presidential election, Dr. Lenora B. Fulani, the only black female candidate in the race, asked reporters why they were not covering her campaign. "Because you didn't raise much money and because you don't have a chance of winning," they told her. Her response: "How can I raise money and win if you don't give coverage to my campaign?" Classic Catch-22.

Needless to say, news coverage that focuses primarily on the mainstream candidates has the consequence of legitimizing those candidates and helping them maintain their advantage in the election. Once again, I must point out that I am not passing judgment on this fact — I am simply pointing it out. Many journalists and elites would defend the current practice of giving less coverage to alternative candidates. They would argue that the country might fall into the hands of some radical element if all alternative candidates were given as much coverage and as favorable coverage as mainstream candidates. Perhaps. But the point remains that the coverage is not objective — it supports a mainstream view of the world, and that has consequences for the distribution of power in societies. Specifically, the mainstream bias helps to maintain the status quo.

Values in the News

The news coverage of presidential elections highlights one of the major values promoted in the news — *moderatism*. In other words, excess or extremism in politics should be avoided.

Sociologist Herbert J. Gans also has identified seven other enduring values in the news: ethnocentrism, altruistic democracy, responsible capitalism, small-town pastoralism, individualism, (social) order and national leadership. Although he was writing about U.S. media, these values actually can be applied to news media in most Western and many other nations around the world (including global news media corporations), and to most forms of entertainment programming on television, at the movies and on radio (more on this below).

By *ethnocentrism*, Gans means that the news media value their own nation above all others. This ethnocentrism is most explicit, he says, in foreign news, "which judges other countries by the extent to which they live up to or imitate American practices and values ... ." War news and humanitarian efforts provide the clearest expression of this principle. Recent examples include coverage of the ethnic conflict in Yugoslavia and the 1991 Gulf War. Western media coverage helped legitimate intervention by NATO and Western countries.

The value of *altruistic democracy* is highlighted in stories about corruption, conflict, protest and bureaucratic malfunctioning. The news implies that politics should be based on the public interest.

The value of *responsible capitalism* means that the news has an optimistic faith in capitalism, the good life and competition, and that unreasonable profits and gross exploitation of workers is wrong. Stories about corporate investors who violate federal laws reinforce this value.

Small-town pastoralism refers to the love-affair that most Americans and Westerners have with the idea of small-town life, and to the problems posed by industrialization: urban crime, increasing social conflict and urban decay. British author Peter Mayle's books about rural French life, such as *A Year in Provence*, strongly support this value.

Individualism promotes the idea of freedom of the individual both within and against the system. People are expected to participate in society and act in the public interest but on their own terms.

Although it is often argued that the United States places much more value on individualism than other countries — and there may be some truth to this — the idea of individuality itself was not born in the United States. Individualism is largely a product of modernization, or more specifically, social differentiation and the division of labor. Traditional societies and groups do not give individuals much freedom or autonomy. The "collective" takes precedence over the individual. There is very little tolerance for alternative lifestyles. However, as cities grew and industrialism spread, the number and variety of groups (occupational, social, political) also increased. This means that people in urban areas or modern societies have more options and opportunities. Of course, one of the adverse consequences of greater freedom and autonomy (i.e., individuality) is that many people feel estranged from the community. Sociologists argue that this is one reason for higher crime and suicide rates.

Gans also argues that *strong leadership* also is highly valued, because it is the way through which order and moral values are maintained. In all countries around the world, news media provide substantial coverage of their leaders.

As noted in Chapter 5, the news also reinforces the value of *order and social cohesion*. Whenever a major disorder occurs, such as a riot or protest, the first thing the media call for is calm. Violence is never the way to solve problems. One must always work peaceably for change, even if the system is highly repressive. Well, almost always. There are some interesting historical exceptions to this rule.

For example, in the United States, accounts of the American Revolution are almost always written in a way to justify the use of force and violence against England. Of course, history books would be quite different today if the British had won. But it is fairly safe to say that today virtually no group in America — except the police and armed forces — could use violence and obtain positive news coverage, no matter how overwhelming the repression they face.

Mainstream Bias in Entertainment Programming

We have spent most of this chapter talking about the mainstream bias in Western news media reports. And for good reason. News media play a major role in shaping or influencing public policy. Politicians, bureaucrats, corporate executives and special interest groups depend heavily on news to achieve their goals.

But the mainstream bias also exists in Western entertainment programming, and the impact of entertainment programming should not be underestimated, as people spend much more time with it than with the news.

Finding examples of entertainment programming that support the mainstream values and institutions is not difficult. Take, for instance, law and order. As noted in Chapter 5, one of the most significant themes of Western television and movie programs is that "crime doesn't pay." Despite all of the gratuitous violence in such programming, most television and movie programming clearly does not encourage people to engage in criminal activity. Lawbreakers are almost always caught, killed or punished. And those that get away usually have noble motives or are up against a corrupt system.

Mass communication scholar George Gerbner argues, quite correctly I believe, that these tales of morality define the boundaries of acceptable behavior, reinforce laws that punish lawbreakers, and provide support for authoritarian police practices and laws. Although Gerbner's social control model makes a lot of sense, some critics believe television violence produces antisocial behavior, including criminal behavior. Indeed, social science research has shown for more than three decades that violent programming produces aggressive behavior in small children. However, no study has ever been able to show a direct link between violent programming and adult law-breaking activity. Nor is it likely to. The reason is that television programs and movies are only one possible influence on human behavior, and they usually are not the most important.

There are many other influences, including schools, families, churches, the legal system, and the work place. The vast majority of our experiences with these institutions tell us that under most circumstances it is wrong to use violence to solve our problems. Consequently, even though most of us have seen thousands of acts of violence on television and in the movies, we do not become violent offenders, because we have internalized the value that violence is wrong. But even for those of us who commit violent acts, television cannot be blamed as the most significant factor. Violent behavior is a complex phenomena — the product of many social, economic and political factors.

Entertainment programming also reinforces many other values that contribute to social order and mainstream views. For example, television programming and movies frequently extol the virtues of a good education and a successful career , but the self-absorbed "filthy" rich and those who turn their backs on materialism (the ascetics) both tend to be marginalized or are portrayed as kooks. Education is also highly revered, because it is seen as the ticket to success in the capitalist job market.

Most Western mass media do not support a particular religious institution, because their societies and communities have a variety of religious groups. But they all place a great deal of importance on the idea that religion is important for social cohesion and stability. Generally, it's also good to be religious, but both fanatics (members of cult groups) and religion-hating atheists are usually portrayed as bad.

Although many television comedies, particularly in the United States, portray characters in nontraditional family situations, the emphasis is almost always on love, friendship, honesty, sincerity and treating others well. And then there is love, perhaps the most commonly found theme in media next to violence. Western media idealize the notion of romance and love, and who could conceive of a more powerful aphrodisiac for social control?

Of course, social control is not the only function performed by mass media. In the next chapter, we'll talk about how such news and entertainment programming may also promote social change.

Empirical Research and Social Control

A great deal of research provides support for the notion that Western media and global media in particular promote dominant Western values and institutions. There are so many, in fact, that we don't have the time or space to review them all. But let me outlines some general findings of that literature.

First of all, many studies show that mass media rely heavily on bureaucratic, especially governmental, institutions for the news, and they eschew alternative, unorthodox points of view and promote values generally consistent with capitalist ideas and elite interests. One consequence of this is that social problems are usually framed from the perspective of those in power. Agenda-setting studies show that media play an important role in transmitting the political and economic priorities of elites to the masses.

Challenging groups also seek to use the media to influence public and elite opinion, but they are often marginalized by elites and, thus, are perceived by the media to be less credible and newsworthy. A number of studies have shown that labor unions receive less favorable news coverage than big business when labor disputes break out. Similarly, Vietnam War protestors were almost always portrayed as spoiled brats who needed old-fashioned discipline. Groups that are perceived as being outside of the mainstream also tend to get less favorable coverage in the news. Contrary to the watchdog metaphor, studies show that most journalists identify very strongly with the governmental news sources they cover. And international news tends to have a strong pro-Western bias.

Studies of television programs indicate that institutionalized groups, such as the police, are usually portrayed humanely and sympathetically, whereas other characters are portrayed in negative ways. Media avoid discussing class conflict issues, and media owners clearly have strong business ties to other powerful governmental agencies and corporations. In short, as a general rule of thumb, the greater the power of a group or organization, the greater its ability to get favorable coverage in the mainstream media.

Origins of the Mainstream Bias

The mainstream bias is not the product of some sort of conspiracy on the part of journalists, film producers or elites in Western countries. Media in all social systems reflect the general concerns and interests of those in positions of power. If they didn't, they would have a difficult time surviving.

Imagine, for instance, what would happen if the media were to take a position that was sympathetic to extremists views, such as those of the neo-Nazis. Community and mainstream political groups would strongly criticize the media. Many advertisers would pull their ads, and many readers would drop their subscriptions. In other words, the dependence that media have on profits to survive is also a mechanism for keeping the media "in line" — and it helps protect the status quo.

The mainstream bias is the product of a number of complex legal, cultural, social and economic constraints that media face to survive in the marketplace. These forces did not just emerge yesterday. They go back to the origins of mass media themselves.

The first newspapers in England and the United States faced major legal constraints. If they published content that was critical of the authorities, the newspaper could be shut down and the publisher prosecuted. In fact, the first newspaper in the United States was shut down after the publication of its first issue in 1690, because it published stories about an attempt to bribe Native Americans to turn them against the colonists and about a scandal involving the French king and his daughter-in-law.

Legal constraints, which include libel law (content that harms a person's reputation), continue to play an important role in regulating what people can say. However, they are only a small part of the picture. Cultural and social factors also play a key role.

When John Campbell began publishing a newspaper in the American colonies in 1704, he was well aware that he had to stay within certain moral and ethical boundaries — not just to please the British authorities but to please community leaders as well. At that time, a story about women's rights or sexual relations, for example, would have offended many clergymen and sparked much criticism of the newspaper. Most mainstream media, in fact, did not support women's right to vote until after 1916, when President Woodrow Wilson declared his support for the 19th Amendment. And Wilson's change of heart no doubt was influenced at least in part by the fact that Australia and New Zealand had already given women the right to vote.

Although times have changed and stories about women's rights and sex are much more common today, media are still bound by cultural values and by the interests of those in power. Women and minorities in most Western countries still struggle to find legitimacy in mainstream media, and they have yet to achieve equality in the workplace. And the media rely heavily on political and economic elites — not the general public — for news, which means the news tends to legitimize the institutions these elites run.

The dependence that media have on elites for news can be traced to the development of news beats. Prior to the 1830s, the content of most newspapers was composed of national or international affairs. The accounts were usually lifted from newspapers in other countries or from official government documents. Local news stories, when they appeared, were often gleaned from other local newspapers, private letters, correspondence and, occasionally, personal contacts with governmental officials. Newspapers were directed largely to elite audiences, which included government officials, politicians and business people. Most newspapers were highly partisan in character, and many were supported by political parties. Although colorful, such papers had limited appeal — generally to members of their political party.

This changed dramatically with the emergence of the Penny Press in the 1830s. As the title implies, some newspapers in New York and other major cities cost only one cent, which meant the average citizen could afford one. The Penny Papers also focused not just on economic and governmental news but on social news, which included reporting the affairs of the local police, courts and community groups. These papers were very popular. Circulation and advertising revenues grew rapidly. To maintain a continuous flow of news copy, newspapers created "beats." These beats were anchored in the centers of power in a community, which included governmental sources (police, courts, city hall), businesses (Wall Street), community groups (religious, social) and, eventually, lifestyle beats (sports, food, women's pages).

It was through the Penny Press that the ethic of objectivity in reporting began to emerge. Gradually throughout the 19th century newspapers began to shed their partisanship in favor of a more neutral stance. This appealed to more readers, which in turn boosted advertising sales and revenues. Whereas the ethic of objectivity did mean that newspapers were now printing more than one opinion when covering a controversial issue, it did not mean that newspapers were objective in some absolute sense. They still obtained news and information from the powerful elites, and those outside the mainstream power groups were still marginalized. According to media historian Dan Schiller:

> *Objectivity developed in tandem with the commercial newspapers' appropriation of a crucial political function — the surveillance of the public good. By means of periodic exposures to violations and infringements of public good — most notably in crime news, a blossoming genre — the newspaper at this juncture presumed to speak as "the public voice." In one jump the newspaper moved from the self-interested concerns of partisan political warfare to the apparently omniscient status of protecting the people as a whole.*

Media historian Michael Schudson also argues that the penny papers contributed to the development of a market economy in two ways. First, through advertising, the penny papers enlarged the potential market for manufactured goods. Second, the penny papers transformed the newspaper from something that was read at the club or library to a product consumed in the home. The penny press became the first mass medium for delivering consumers to producers.

In short, the mainstreaming effects of the news media are not a product of a conspiracy; rather, they are the product of organizational constraints on the news operation. Through a unique set of historical circumstances media linked themselves to the centers of power, and the outcome was also beneficial for the media. By cooperating with the media, elites helped to legitimate the role of the media in covering news. And the profit motive ensures that media will not stray too far beyond the interests of elites. It is inconceivable, for example, to imagine stories that would attack representative democracy as a political system or capitalism as an economic system. Any Western or global medium taking such a stand quickly would find themselves without readers and advertisers.

Relative Objectivity

Having pointed out that news is not objective in any absolute sense, I now face the problem of *relativism* — if there is no objectivity, then is every news account of an event equivalent and is there no truth? No, and I will pull myself out of the quagmire of relativism by building a case for what I call *relative objectivity*. Basically, what I'm going to argue here is that contemporary Western-style journalism incorporates more points of the view than ever before, even if it still promotes the dominant values and institutions in a society to the detriment of other groups. And Western-style journalism incorporates more points of view than one can get in communist or totalitarian media.

Let me begin with a little history. During the 19th century, most newspapers in Europe and the Americas were highly partisan, usually siding with and sometimes being financially supported by political parties. Many contemporary critics of journalism wish for that kind of press again — one that allegedly contained a robust debate. But, as might be expected from a partisan press, the stories and columns in those publications were often vitriolic, inaccurate and self-serving. Not only that, they also excluded the other point of view. You only got one side of the story. Moreover, most people didn't get more than one side to a story because they just read their own political party's paper. They didn't read the other party's paper, and this, of course, had the effect of limiting the debate.

But the ethic of objectivity changed all that. Increasingly newspapers became less partisan and restricted opinion and commentary to special pages. News stories now contained not just one point of view, but two or more views. Of course, to a certain extent, this took some of the bite out of the partisanship. But, at the same time, it improved the accuracy of the news accounts and, more importantly, brought the story to a broader range of people. Now people who were members of different parties could read the same publication and get the views of not only the leaders of their parties but also the opposition. Paradoxically, then, the ethic of objectivity actually broadened the debate on public issues.

At the same time, the mass media became more open and more responsive to alternative groups and ideas (in relative terms). For example, at the turn of the century in the United States, a form of investigative reporting called "muckraking" began exposing graft and corruption in government, unhealthy conditions at meat-packing plants, monopolistic practices in the oil and other industries, slum landlord practices, police corruption and the underworld. To be sure, these exposés did not radically change the power structure in society. However, they led to reforms that helped cool down the radical factions, especially the socialist movements, which had millions of followers back then.

In the next chapter, I shall argue that relative to most other social institutions in society — including the church, government, the legal system and schools — the news media are more responsive to alternative groups and ideas. And this helps social systems adapt and change. These topics will be taken up in more depth in the next chapter. But let me just add here that, from a broad perspective, news media in Western societies and global media in particular may be likened from time to time to a tempered social reformer, drawing attention to various problems in society or the world (e.g., sexism in the military, discrimination in the workforce, police brutality and corruption).

Global Media Mainstreaming

So what does the mainstream bias mean in terms of understanding the role and function of global media in a world system?

Because global media are creations of Western culture, are profit-seeking organizations and are dependent upon powerful governmental and corporate sources for news, the content of global media will continue to generate strong support for Western values and institutions, such as responsible capitalism and representative democracy. Alternative economic and political systems or ideas still will be marginalized. This helps to explain in part why global media coverage of the Gulf War as well as the NATO bombing of Yugoslavia contained a pro-Western bias.

However, because global media audiences transcend national boundaries, the content of global media also will be less nation-centric. When an international dispute emerges, global media cannot afford to alienate audiences in different countries. This could severely impact advertising or subscriptions. Media coverage of the NATO bombing of Yugoslavia — although generally favorable to NATO — often portrayed NATO in a negative light, especially when innocent civilians were killed.

So, in relative terms, the tone of the global media coverage is likely to be less biased in favor of a particular county, even though the most powerful countries, such as the United States and England, will still have the edge. This helps to explain why U.S. officials were so upset about Arnett's coverage from inside Iraq.

So what are the long-term consequences of a world dominated by global news media? One can expect mainstreaming toward a Western view — that is, toward a world dominated by a free-market economic system and a representative democracy political system. At the same time, the ability of political and economic elites within a country to dominate their media systems will diminish. In some cases, this will produce social conflict. The probability of this happening will be greatest in nations that reject Western values, especially the Middle East, where many Western values are despised (see more on this in Chapter 11).

Yet, the emergence of global media also increases the probability for social change that lessens discrimination and injustice, as I shall argue in the next chapter.

GLOBAL MEDIA
AND SOCIAL CHANGE

Washington, D.C. — June 17, 1972.

Five men are arrested while breaking into Democratic Party national headquarters at the Watergate complex in Washington, D.C. For two years investigative reporters from *The Washington Post, The New York Times* and other media dig out a story that implicates President Richard Nixon and, in addition, discovers that his administration has been spying illegally on U.S. citizens, harassing political opponents and attempting to obstruct justice through a cover-up. Under pressure of impeachment and conviction, Nixon resigns on August 8, 1974.

No story in the history of journalism has generated more praise for U.S. mass media. *Washington Post* reporters Bob Woodward and Carl Bernstein took the lion's share of credit, helping their newspaper win a Pulitzer Prize. The media coverage seemed to support H. L. Mencken's claim that the primary function of a "free press" is "to comfort the afflicted and to afflict the comfortable." According to press theory, the news media are supposed to be *watchdogs* for the people, especially the powerless and those who have no organized voice in the system. The media are supposed to be an adversary, not an advocate, of the government and the powerful, and they are supposed to challenge authority and promote democratic ideals.

Without question, news media coverage of Watergate played the key role in forcing the resignation of the most powerful person in the world. But do media really comfort the afflicted and afflict the comfortable? Do they really fight for democratic ideals and institutions? And do they really challenge the dominant power groups, as suggested by the watchdog notion?

Professional journalists have no difficulty answering "yes" to all of these questions. But many scholars who study mass media and their relationship to society argue that media act more like *lap dogs* for the rich and powerful than watchdogs for the poor and weak. Media are agents of social control.

The truth, as I shall argue in this chapter, lies somewhere in-between these two extremes — or what we might call the *guard dog* role. The news media, as well as entertainment media, clearly generate content and programming that supports the status quo. But they also provide content that, at times, helps promote social change. Watergate is a good example of this. The Watergate stories, as I shall elaborate in detail subsequently, reinforced dominant values and norms in the system, but they also stimulated legislative action that changed the election funding rules. And these changes, in turn, may have led to a strengthening of the social order.

In this chapter, I shall also offer a more general theory of social change that links changes in society to changes in media organization. Specifically, I shall argue that the more media exhibit the characteristics of the corporate (or global) form of organization, the greater is their capacity to promote social change that eliminates economic and political inequality. This theory stands in sharp contrast to many of the neo-Marxist models of corporate and global media.

Watergate and Social Control

On the surface, it may seem strange to argue that Watergate is a good example of the social control function of the media. After all, didn't the news media bring down the most powerful individual in the world? Yes, they did, but this doesn't mean the coverage didn't contribute to social order. To the contrary, Watergate is a prime example of how media support the system. And to understand why this is the case, we first need to make a distinction between the individual and social structure.

Almost from the beginning, the problem of Watergate was defined primarily as an individual problem, not as a problem of the social structure. In other words, the media spotlight was focused on the illegal actions of various individuals connected with the Nixon administration, who were defined as "bad actors." The media did not focus on the social structure as the problem — that is, that there was something wrong with the laws or structure of the American system of democracy. This distinction is important. When problems are defined in individual terms, problems are resolved by punishing or controlling the individuals. This generally does not lead to much social change. But when the problem is defined as *systemic*, then the social system must be changed to correct the problem, and this can have a much greater impact on people's lives now and in the future.

A *social system* may be defined as two or more people or organizations who depend upon each other to achieve their goals. As I use the concept here, system also refers to the values, rules (or norms) and laws that govern those relationships and enable *social actors* (individuals or organizations) to achieve their goals. Most societies, like the United States, have rules and laws that punish people who burglarize offices, tap telephones, engage in political espionage or lie. The system also is composed of institutions, organizations and special interest groups — such as Congress, the FBI and the Supreme Court — that have the power to create and enforce those values and laws. By drawing attention to the "abuses of power" that occurred during Watergate, the media played an important role in preserving the basic values and rules of the system.

Mass communication researchers Phillip J. Tichenor, George A. Donohue and Clarice N. Olien call this the *guard dog* function of the media. They argue that media act more like a guard dog for the system than a watchdog for the powerless or a lapdog for the powerful. Watergate is a good example. If the media were like a watchdog, they would have directed a lot of criticism at the system (its structure) that gives power to some groups and individuals and not to others. But that was not their main focus. They were focused on individuals. Conversely, to be a lapdog, the media coverage would have supported Nixon and his administration. But this clearly was not the case.

The notion that media coverage of the Watergate scandal generated support for the system was confirmed by Gerald Ford the day after Nixon resigned and Ford became president. "Our long national nightmare is over," Ford said, adding that Watergate demonstrates that "our system (of governance) works." He praised the press, and then urged the country to turn to other issues. In short, the problem of Watergate did not stem from the system itself — it stemmed from a handful of individuals who violated the rules. The media played a crucial role in defining which rules were broken, and to that extent reinforced the status quo.

From a broad perspective, all investigative reporting can be seen as helping to support the social system. That's because all investigative stories have a moral lesson embedded within them. They either draw attention to the violation of some law or norm or they suggest that the system needs a law or norm to correct a wrong. As mass communication researchers James S. Ettema and Theodore L. Glasser put it: "Investigative journalism defends traditional virtue by telling stories of terrible vice ... investigative journalism maintains and sometimes updates consensual interpretations of right and wrong, innocence and guilt ... ." In Watergate, the moral lesson was that politicians should not engage in dirty tricks, violate the trust of the people, lie or steal.

Ironically, though, investigative journalists appear to be unaware of the morality tales in their stories, according to Ettema and Glasser. "These reporters do acknowledge that their stories do not 'speak themselves,' but they maintain that their narrative skills are employed strictly in the service of cognition. ... the selection and sequence of facts is determined by a 'logical progression,' not, of course, by any moral order." In other words, reporters see themselves as fact gatherers, not as preachers of right and wrong.

Nevertheless, all investigative reporting has a moral lesson. And to the extent that it does, investigative reporting can help contribute to social order. But it doesn't end there.

Watergate and Social Change

Admittedly, press exposure of the Watergate scandal did not change the system a whole lot. The institution of the Presidency continues to be very powerful — in fact, probably more powerful today than at any time in history. And many politicians still engage in dirty tricks (e.g., the latest fashion in the United States is negative political advertising).

But it is unfair to say that the Watergate story had no effect on the system. In the months and years after Watergate, Congress (and many states) passed a series of "good government" bills or rules designed to restore faith in the political process. Among other things, these actions

- limited individual contributions to candidates for federal office to $1,000 for each primary, election and runoff, and to $5,000 for political action committees;
- required candidates running for federal office to identify people and organizations that contribute $100 or more to a campaign;
- eliminated office "slush" funds, limited spending on direct mail to constituents, and eventually banned honoraria;
- required elected officials to file annual reports detailing some aspects of their income and investments; and
- resulted in the enactment of an independent prosecutor law.

To be sure, none of these changes has radically altered the distribution of power in American society. As a consequence, some scholars, like Ettema and Glasser, argue that investigative journalism is politically conservative. They point out that the stories rarely address questions of what has gone wrong in the system, who should be accountable, and how things should be changed. In many cases, journalists consider such matters as going beyond the bounds of "objectivity" in reporting (see Chapter 8).

Many other examples in which investigative reporting has had little or no impact on the system could be cited. However, there also are many examples that have contributed to significant social change — change that has benefited the disadvantaged and disenfranchised.

For example, during the early part of the 20th century, capitalism was clearly "out of control." Factory workers in Europe and the United States worked up to 16 hours a day, were paid poor wages and worked in unsafe and unsanitary conditions. Few laws regulated industry. But the abuses drew the attention of small group of journalists, dubbed "*muckrakers*" by Teddy Roosevelt, who gave them that derogatory title because they had exposed corruption in the U.S. Senate. Turning Teddy on his head, so to speak, the journalists appropriated the muckraker title as a badge of honor. Their stories led the federal and many state governments to enact a number of laws or regulations that broke up monopolies in the oil industry, placed greater sanitary regulations on the meat-packing industry, improved working conditions for factory workers, recognized the right of laborers to unionize, limited working hours for children, improved housing conditions and increased penalties for government abuse of power. From a systemwide perspective, these reforms no doubt helped to "cool down" radical groups and reduced the potential for violent or revolutionary change.

Although investigative reporting often promotes social change, it is important to point out that everyday journalism often has the same impact. For example, mass media historian Dolores Flamiano found that during the early part of the 20ᵗʰ century mainstream newspapers and magazines "helped to bring the concerns of the birth control movement to a larger, more heterogeneous audience."

Articles in The New York Times *and several well-circulated magazines also reflected the fact that birth control was increasingly recognized as a public issue, not a private matter. Scientific discourses made contraception socially acceptable and no longer obscene, leading to the eventual legalization of contraceptives (under a doctor's supervision) in the 1930s.*

During the 1950s and 1960s, routine news coverage of the U.S. Supreme Court and Congress helped legitimate a number of decisions or laws that expanded or protected civil rights for minorities and women. At the same time these decisions were being made, newspapers like *The New York Times*, *The Nashville Tennessean* and *The Atlanta Constitution* were publishing news reports about acts of discrimination and racism against African Americans. In the early 1960s, *The News York Times* gave prominent coverage to the civil rights movement and Martin Luther King's "I Have a Dream" speech.

In 1968, journalists in Vietnam rebuffed U.S. military propaganda about the Tet Offensive, and their reports helped turn public opinion against the war — so much so that after those reports a majority of citizens opposed the war. "The media's negative assessment proved more convincing than Washington's statements of victory because it confirmed the sense of frustration that most Americans shared over the conflict," according to Vietnam historian Sandra C. Taylor.

During the 1960s and 1970s, mainstream media increasingly began covering social movements seeking greater rights and opportunities for women and protection of the environment. Beginning in the 1970s, journalists at many large, corporate newspapers across the United States investigated reports of police brutality, and their stories helped contribute to the formation of many civilian review boards. *Philadelphia Inquirer* reporters Donald L. Barlett and James B. Steele also made a name for themselves with a number of investigative reports on the criminal justice system and Washington's relationship with special interest groups. In 1990, the Pulitzer Prize for investigative reporting went to the (Minneapolis) *Star Tribune* and its investigation of a former fire chief, who allegedly was involved in fire insurance fraud schemes. The city of St. Paul and the state legislature in Minnesota responded by passing laws regulating firefighters' consulting activities.

So what does all this have to do with global media?

My point is that investigative reporting is primarily the product of large, corporate media organizations, and global media are at the top of the corporate "food chain." They are the ones that have the resources — both human and capital — to undertake such projects. Indeed, research by mass media scholars Thimios Zaharopoulos and Ronald E. McIntosh shows that large corporate newspapers are the ones that typically win the Pulitzer Prize and other rewards for best reporting. In addition, media scholars Philip Meyer and David Arant found that newspapers that win a lot of Pulitzer Prizes also make fewer spelling and editing errors. In short, corporate media organizations are the only ones with enough power to challenge big business and massive governmental bureaucracies. And global media systems, with their vast resources, are in the best position to undertake in-depth reporting projects.

Empirical Research and Social Change

But don't take my word for it. Let me summarize some of the empirical research.

Although journalists tend to have personal beliefs that support Western value systems, research shows that they generally are much more liberal than elites as well as the general public on a wide variety of social and political issues. Polls and historical research also show that conservatives are more critical than liberals of investigative reporting. Journalists also are often sensitive to the concerns of minorities and consumer groups, are often critical of corporations and believe that private business is profiting at the expense of Third World countries.

Media reports also have helped to legitimize rural grassroot protest groups in Minnesota, who sought to block construction of a power line that would serve a large, metropolitan area. One study found that, contrary to hegemonic theory, media gave much more favorable than unfavorable coverage to gay and pro-choice protest marches in Washington, D.C. And, as noted in Chapter 7, although ownership of newspapers in the United States and most Western countries has become more centralized (i.e., reduction in the number of owners), to date there is little evidence showing that this has led to a reduction in message diversity. In fact, studies show that media in larger, more pluralistic communities cover a broader range of topics and contain more news.

Other research has found that veteran reporters at mainstream newspapers often write stories that challenge elements of the so-called dominant ideology. A Canadian study found that commentaries, columns and op-ed pieces often challenged the official government position. A study in India suggests that news stories can contribute to public awareness of problems with the status quo, which in turn can promote discontent and support for social change. Researchers in the United States found that investigative stories on police brutality produced swift changes in regulations regarding police misconduct.

Research also shows that alternative (nonmainstream) media, which are tolerated in most capitalist systems, often challenge dominant ideologies and contribute to mobilizing and promoting social movements or causes. One participant observation study concluded that reporters at an alternative radio station created oppositional news using conventional reportorial techniques. A historical review reported that alternative media have helped promote the American Revolution, abolitionism and equality for women, minorities and gay rights groups. In April 1999, U.S. President Bill Clinton criticized Afghanistan's ruling Taliban (a religious militia group), because it was preventing girls from attending school, forcing women from the workforce, preventing women from traveling alone without a male relative, and publicly beating women who defied the Taliban's edicts. Global news media organizations gave prominent coverage to the story.

A study I conducted in the late 1980s also found that television may actually promote beliefs that oppose economic inequalities. The data came from a national probability survey of U.S. adults, which found that people who benefit most from the system — men, whites, conservatives and those who have high incomes, education and occupational prestige — are most likely to favor economic inequalities. However, television viewing reduces support for beliefs that promote economic inequality, even when controlling for all of the other factors. I contend that entertainment programming generally portrays capitalists and economic disparities in a negative light. This bias stems partly from the liberal orientation of television and movie writers. Another recent study that supports my study found that people who watch a lot of situation comedy programming are less critical of alternative family lifestyles. The argument is that these programs, which often portray characters in nontraditional family situations, are creating more tolerance for alternative lifestyles.

Finally, mainstream corporate media may also help promote the causes of social movements. I devote the next section to this topic.

Media and Social Movements

Although investigative journalism is often cited as a source of social change, it is not the most significant source in modern society. Social movements, many sociologists would argue, are much more important. Without social movements, today's world would be much different.

Consider, for instance, what it was like to be a woman before the late 20th century. Nowhere in the world did you have the right to vote. You had limited access to a college education — many schools would not accept women. But even if you had a college education, you didn't have access to the best jobs in the public or private (corporate) world. Teaching school was your best bet.

Or consider what is was like to be an African American living in pre-Vietnam War America. You could not eat in many restaurants. You had to sit at the back of the bus. You could not drink out of water fountains reserved for whites. Your children could not attend the best schools. You were denied access to good jobs. And, in some areas of the Deep South, you lived in fear for your life.

Today, there is little question that opportunities and social conditions for women, African Americans and many other historically oppressed groups have improved in the United States and most Western countries. Women are guaranteed the right to vote. Minorities and women have better access to jobs and education. Factory laborers are no longer required to work 16 hours a day. Pollutants and emissions from factories and motor vehicles are much more highly regulated. People now have access to contraceptives. The elderly have social security and health care. The stigma associated with being homosexual has lessened considerably, and some corporations (such as Disney) and governments have extended employment benefits to same-sex partners.

To be sure, these changes and the passage of time have not eradicated discrimination, inequality, income disparities, disregard for the environment, unwanted births, lack of access to opportunity, poor health care and poverty. Sociocultural patterns are deeply embedded, and elites and the institutions they control nearly always resist change, because it usually means a loss of political, social and economic power. But elite resistance to challenges from less advantaged groups is not always effective in preventing social change that benefits those groups. As the preceding examples show, social movements often have played a pivotal role in altering, however subtly, the balance of power between traditional elite groups and the masses. That's one reason why U.S. civil rights leader Jesse Jackson says he remains upbeat and optimistic — despite past and current problems, the civil rights movement, in his view, has won significant battles since the 1960s.

To be sure, social science research clearly demonstrates that all social systems have ideological and coercive means of social control, and that the content of mainstream mass media generally supports those ideologies and those in power (see Chapter 8). We know that all modern social movements need the mass media to achieve their goals in a representative democracy. Media play an important role in legitimating (or delegitimating) the goals of social movements and accelerating (or decelerating) public attention to the social problems movements identify.

We also know, thanks to media researcher David L. Protess and his colleagues at Northwestern University, that investigative reporting is most likely to promote change when journalists and policy makers actively collaborate to set policy-making agendas prior to story publication. However, we don't know a whole lot more about the conditions when mass media may help promote or hinder social change, partly because, I contend, this topic generally has been ignored by critics of corporate and global media.

Nevertheless, despite the shortage of research, several statements can be made. One is that, historically, mass media have tended to ignore social movements until they gain power. Although the civil rights and women's movements were founded in the 19th century, they did not garner significant favorable media coverage until the 1950s and 1960s. This coincides with a substantial growth in the size and power of those movements. The same thing happened to the environmental movement. Not until 1962, with the publication of Rachael Carson's *Silent Spring*, which drew attention to the problems of pollution, did mainstream media begin giving substantial coverage to environmental issues.

However, since then, mainstream media — especially media in large, pluralistic cities — have published or aired many stories that have lent support to the goals of these movements, and news coverage has been much more favorable. Television entertainment programming in the United States also has become more favorable to women and those with alternative lifestyles. Today, even same-sex relationships are getting some positive portrayals (e.g., the former ABC comedy *Ellen*).

Overall, then, it is clear that mainstream mass media, which include global media, are no agents of radical change. But throughout the 20th century, corporate media have published many stories that have helped promote or legitimize social reforms. As Herbert Gans sums it up:

> *News is not so much conservative or liberal as it is reformist; indeed, the enduring values are very much like the values of the Progressive movement of the early twentieth century. The resemblance is often uncanny, as in the common advocacy of honest, meritocratic, and anti-bureaucratic government, and in the shared antipathy to political machines and demagogues, particularly the populist bent.*

And comparing the media to legal systems, sociologist Jeffrey Alexander observes:

> *In distinguishing the news media from the law, the significant point is the media's flexibility. By daily exposing and reformulating itself vis-à-vis changing values, group formations, and objective economic and political conditions, the media allows "public opinion" to be organized responsively on a mass basis. By performing this function of information-conduit and normative-organizer, the news media provides the normative dimension of society with the greatest flexibility in dealing with social strains.*

A Theory of Corporate Structure and Social Change

How did corporate media gets their reformist bent? Why do corporate media have a greater capacity to promote social change? And why do global media have the greatest capacity to promote social change?

In this section, I attempt to answer these questions through a formal theory of corporate structure and social change. But to appreciate how this theory works, we need to look at the history of the corporate form of organization. Many critical analyses imply that capitalists consciously created the corporate form of organization to maximize profits. This is not true. The corporate form emerged in large part to solve the problem of organizational continuity (i.e., continuation of an organization after the death of a principal). Later, it was granted special legal privileges.

A Brief History of the Corporation

Although corporate groups existed during the Roman empire, organizational theorists usually trace the origins of the modern corporation to the late Middle Ages and the rise of major trading centers. Before then, work and other social activities revolved almost exclusively around the family and the local community. The economic and social division of labor was very limited. The vast majority of people worked the land or tended herds, and the availability of work outside of agriculture was limited in part because there was little surplus in food production. People shared a common value system and work environment.

But advances and improvements in agriculture gradually increased food production, freeing more and more people from the land. These surpluses, in turn, promoted the growth of specialized economic, political and social groups, each of which developed unique interests, needs and goals.

Artisan guilds, local boroughs and ecclesiastical bodies were some of the earliest corporate groups. Two key factors distinguished them from other social formations. The first was that they were consciously created instruments of self-governance designed to promote the interests of their members. They decided who could join their groups and reproved members who violated group norms and goals. Many justified their existence in part through claims that they served in the public interest and would protect the public from charlatans and quacks. But this didn't mean they always served the public interest. They often monopolized markets and controlled prices. Nevertheless, French sociologist Emile Durkheim argues that the primary functions of these groups were to curb individual egoism, foster solidarity among workers, and act as a check on the abuses of employers, industrial organizations and the state.

The second factor distinguishing the corporate groups from other groups was that they survived beyond the lifetime of any single member. This permanency enhanced the power of the corporate group relative to individuals and other, more transitory social formations (i.e., kinship, friendship structures).

Contemporary professional groups, such as doctors and lawyers, and modern business corporations can trace their roots to these early corporate groups. One of the earliest forms of the business corporation was the joint-stock company, which was created in the 16th and 17th centuries to fund large-scale public works projects, such as canals or sewers, or overseas trading expeditions. Through the sale of stock, these organizations could accumulate large sums of capital in a short period of time. Shares of these companies could be easily transferred from one person to another. However, unlike the modern legal corporation, the owners of joint-stock companies were personally liable for the company's debts, and many lost money because of unscrupulous promoters and risky ventures.

In response to these events, many Western nations passed laws during the late 1700s and early 1800s limiting the liability of a stockholder to the actual amount of money invested. If the corporation went bankrupt, the personal assets of the investor were protected. The laws also were changed to give the corporation a legal personality so that it could enter into contracts, sue or be sued, and enjoy other privileges of legal citizenship.

These changes promoted capital investment, which, in turn, had a profound effect on the development of the business organization. In the early 1800s, most businesses were very small relative to other competitors in the market, but by the late 1800s, many had grown to powerful proportions, wielding substantial market power. At the turn of the century, for example, Standard Oil Company controlled 90 percent of the refined petroleum sold in the United States. (Note: This didn't last long, however. Ida Tarbell, one of the original muckrakers, wrote a series of stories about the company's ruthless business practices, and Congress eventually passed antitrust laws that broke the company up into smaller companies.)

Today, of course, the modern business corporation is the dominant form of organization around the world. In 1996, the 500 largest manufacturing corporations in the United States held more than 70 percent of the manufacturing assets. Although the corporate organization is often praised for its efficiency and increased productive capacity, as noted in Chapter 6, it is also strongly criticized for having too much power. The major fear, of course, is that the corporate organizations will act only in their own self-interest, not in the interest of the community or their customers.

The Rise of Corporate Media

The first mass medium to earn the title "corporate" was the newspaper. Its origins are usually traced to the late 19th century; however, the transition should be seen as a gradual process rather than as a sudden event. Prior to that time, the typical newspaper, even in the largest cities, was owned and operated by an individual or family who employed only a handful of people. The publisher usually performed many roles, including that of editor, printer and advertising salesperson. But by the 1870s, the leading metropolitan dailies in Europe and America were becoming complex organizations. On the editorial side, they had a chief editor, a managing editor or night editor, a city editor, two dozen reporters, a telegraph editor, a financial editor, a drama critic, a literary editor and editorial writers; and on the production side, there were printers, pressmen, typographers and photo-engravers, each of whom was represented by a different union.

The number and size of newspapers grew dramatically in the late 1800s. Between 1870 and 1900, for example, the number of general-circulation daily newspapers in the United States quadrupled (from 574 to 2,226). Daily circulation increased five-fold (three million copies to 15 million) and household daily circulation nearly tripled (.34 to .94 copies per household). The modern chain newspaper also emerged in the late 19th century. Although chains existed before the U.S. Civil War, what distinguished the groups after the war is that they survived long beyond the death of the original owners.

At the turn of the century the typical newspaper was still owned and managed by individuals or families, as opposed to joint-stock companies. But in large newspapers around the world, such individuals increasingly had less and less say about day-to-day operations. Specialized roles had developed more fully, and functional areas such as advertising, circulation and news at large newspapers were increasingly being managed by individuals who possessed specialized skills and knowledge in those areas. Publishers and owners increasingly had less and less to say about day-to-day operations — these decisions were left to editors and professional managers.

The trend toward specialization in reporting also has continued. Most large newspapers now have beats that cover the environment, science and technology, and the Internet. Most reporters also have some specialty. Corporatization of the industry also continued. In 1900, the typical U.S. daily had a circulation of 7,500; only 27 of the 1,967 dailies, or 1.4 percent, were owned by a chain or group. But by 1990, the typical daily had a circulation of 38,000 and was owned by a chain or group headquartered in another city or state. Nearly 80 percent of the 1,626 dailies, or 1,217, were part of a chain or group.

In sum, the corporate form of organization offered two great advantages over other forms of organization. First, it survived the death of its member/owner(s), which gave the organization continuity and permanence. This enabled groups to exercise greater control over the production of a particular product or service. The second advantage is that it offered the investor limited liability. If the business venture failed, the investor only lost the amount invested, not his or her entire assets.

Why the Corporate Form?

At the societal level of analysis, the emergence of the corporate form can be attributed in large part to two other more general trends: urbanization and industrialization. As sociologist Robert Park remarked in 1923: "The growth of great cities has enormously increased the size of the reading public. Reading which was a luxury in the country has become a necessity in the city. In the urban environment literacy is almost as much a necessity as speech itself."

The reason is interdependency. Unlike the relatively self-sufficient pioneer farmer, who was able to live off the land and produce other goods (e.g., clothes) necessary for survival, the city dweller depends more heavily on others to survive and achieve goals (e.g., to eat, find employment, dispose of garbage, etc.). This increased dependency means the urbanite has a greater need for news and information. To find the lowest prices for food, to find a job and to learn about changes in garbage collection services, the urbanite turned to the newspaper. Industrialization also contributed toward the growth of the newspaper, as manufacturers needed ways to reach buyers. Newspaper advertising helped deliver consumers to producers.

At the industry level of analysis, the emergence of large, complex news corporations can be explained largely as a byproduct of increasing competition. As Karl Marx pointed out, competition encourages capitalists to innovate, which in turn lowers production costs and prices and eliminates weaker competitors (see Chapter 4 for more details). Barriers to entry (i.e., expensive start-up costs) keep newcomers out of the field. Larger, "corporate" firms have an advantage because they generally benefit most from economies of scale. In Marx's view, concentration and centralization of ownership would continue until an industry would become dominated by one or a handful of companies (oligopoly) over time. Although antitrust laws and advancing technology have reduced the centralizing tendencies in many industries, Marx's general principle still holds true: Capitalism contains the seeds of its own destruction.

Consequences of Corporate Structure

If the corporate form of organization, then, is in large part the product of increasing economic, social and political complexity in a social system, or what some sociologists call *structural pluralism or structural differentiation* (i.e., an increase in the number and variety of groups in a social system), then what might we expect the consequences of that social form to be in terms of coverage of the status quo? More criticism, for two major reasons.

First, because corporate media are themselves the product of increasing structural pluralism, they are more likely to be located in communities that contain more social conflict and criticism of dominant groups and value systems. A well-documented research finding is that newspapers in small, homogenous communities contain less conflict news and criticism of established institutions and elites. The amount of social conflict and criticism is low partly because the community contains a limited number of alternative or challenging groups and organizations.

In contrast, social conflict is a much more common feature of large, pluralistic communities. The conflict is greater in pluralistic communities in part because they contain a greater number and variety of special interest groups competing for limited social, political and economic resources. Decision-making in such communities is expected to take into account diverse perspectives and views. Although stories and editorials that contain conflict or criticism are often viewed as threatening to the social order, such stories often play a significant role in contributing to system stability because they introduce alternative ideas or innovations that enable organizations and institutions to adapt to changing conditions. Moreover, coverage of social movements and their events may have the effect of "cooling down" those groups, inasmuch as they see that coverage as promoting their goals or giving them a say in public discourse.

In short, global media contain more social conflict and criticism of established authorities and ways of doing things because they are themselves a product of the most pluralistic countries in the world.

The second reason corporate and global media would be expected to be more critical of the status quo is that their publishers and editorial staffs are more insulated from special interests and parochial political pressures. Owners and top managers of corporate media are much less likely to grow up in the community their medium serves. They also work for a medium for a shorter period of time, are oriented more to the corporation than to the local community, and are more strongly committed to professional norms and values, which place a higher premium on truth and criticism at the expense of local or national boosterism. Strong ties to a local or national community, in other words, inhibit criticism of local and national elites and power groups. Former international television news reporter Jim Upshaw, now a journalism professor, also argues that the

> *crushing, deadening routines of corporate media, instituted for efficiency, help to deter either owner or managerial interference in content. Process transcends personality in some organizations ... .*

Thus, in contrast to the conventional wisdom, the argument here is that increasing structural pluralism and corporatization of the media industries produces greater, not lesser, criticism of the status quo. The key strength of this macrosocial model is that it helps to account for social change and the role that mass media often play in promoting such change. As social systems become more pluralistic, news content is expected to become more critical of traditional ways and established institutions. Media reflect to some degree the diversity of the communities they serve, and increasing role specialization and professionalization, which are byproducts of community growth, help to insulate journalists from parochial political pressures.

A key assumption underlying this model is that the increased level of criticism that allegedly emerges from these structural forces contributes to discourse that places increasing pressure on existing institutions to change. Admittedly, social change does not always emerge from media criticism of the system; in fact, increased criticism may lead those in power to become even more repressive (e.g., martial law). But this is not a deterministic model. The argument here is that in representative democracies, the probability of change is generally enhanced, not thwarted, by media criticism.

Research on Corporate Structure

Although few studies have examined the relationship between media structure and critical content, what has been done lends support to the hypothesis.

Several years ago I conducted a comprehensive review of studies that examined the relationship between corporate structure and editorial-page practices and content. Of the 18 studies identified, eight found that corporate newspapers were more vigorous editorially than independent newspapers, seven had mixed findings or no differences, and three found corporate newspapers were less vigorous. On balance, the literature suggests that corporate media engage in practices or produce content that is more critical of the status quo.

My own national probability surveys of newspapers and sources also supports these findings. The more a newspaper exhibits the characteristics of the corporate form of organization, the greater the number and proportion of editorials and letters to the editor that are critical of mainstream organizations and institutions. Other studies also support the argument that chain newspapers are more critical of the status quo. One found that Gannett newspapers were far more likely than a sample of non-Gannett newspapers to oppose positions taken by the White House and Supreme Court on three major issues.

Journalists from corporate newspapers also appear to be more likely to emphasize an active, interpretive, investigative and critical role for the news media. Mass communication researcher George Gladney reported that editors at large circulation newspapers — which is a good proxy measure of corporate structure — were more likely than those at small newspapers to rate "editorial courage" and "editorial independence" as primary indicators of newspaper excellence. Media scholar Roya Akhavan-Majid and her colleagues concluded that editors of chain-owned newspapers are more likely than their independent counterparts to emphasize an active, interpretive, investigative and critical role for the press, and support for these values increased as the size of the chain increased. Newspaper researcher Randall Beam found that newspapers which employ a strong market-oriented management style (a characteristic of corporate structure) are more likely than those that employ a weak market-oriented style to endorse an adversarial role for journalists and to profess a commitment to publishing an excellent journalistic product and public affairs content.

A study I conducted recently of news sources also supports the argument that corporate media are more critical of dominant institutions and value systems. I hypothesized that mainstream news sources in communities served by highly corporatized newspapers would perceive news coverage in those papers to be more critical of them and their policies than sources in communities served by less corporatized newspapers. A national probability survey of mayors and police chiefs in 200 U.S. communities supported the hypothesis. The more corporatized the newspaper, the more the mainstream sources perceived that newspaper to be critical of them and their policies and the more biased and less fair they perceived that newspaper's coverage.

A third factor that helps corporate/global media provide fuel for the engine of social change is the managerial revolution. This topic is so important that I've devoted the entire next chapter to it.

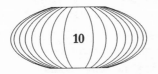

THE GLOBAL
MANAGERIAL REVOLUTION

Let's say you're the chief executive officer of a major media corporation. Profits from your publishing divisions have been relatively stable for some time, so you've made an offer to merge with a major film and cable television company. This is a long-term strategy that will complement your existing holdings and give you a major global presence. Two weeks before the deal is expected to go through, another media company makes an offer to buy your media corporation. The offer is sweet — the buyer will pay $200 per share, or nearly twice the value of your stock six months earlier. Stockholders clearly will support the sale. And the deal will make you extremely rich.

What should you do?

Snub the buyer, withdraw the merger offer, and spend $15 billion to buy the film and cable television company outright. What? Yup, that's exactly what Time Inc.'s CEO J. Richard Munro and board of directors did in the summer of 1989. Time Inc. spent so much money to purchase Warner Brothers that Paramount Communications could no longer afford to purchase Time Inc. Too much debt. As it turned out, Munro and the executives at Time Inc. still made a pile of money, as did the executives and stockholders at Warner Brothers. But Time Inc. stockholders didn't fair too well. The value of their stock fell to $70 a share. And since then Time Warner has generated mostly small profits. (However, the share value of the stock has risen substantially since 1997.)

On the surface, it doesn't seem to make sense. Why would the top executives of a major corporation turn down an offer that would have had everyone at that corporation, including themselves, laughing all the way to the bank? The answer, according to Munro, is that they wanted to preserve the journalistic history that Henry Luce, founder of *Time*, had created.

"This is my legacy," Munro, 58, told a *Fortune* magazine reporter. "I did not work here 33 years to bust the company up." He and other Time Inc. executives owned a lot of company stock and could have gotten extremely rich on the Paramount offer. And had Time stockholders been given a chance to vote on the Paramount buy-out, there is no question that they would have approved it.

But Munro and others in top management did not give the stockholders a chance to vote on the measure. The acquisition was imposed upon the stockholders.

The Managerial Revolution Hypothesis

Since the turn of the century, a number of scholars have argued that control of corporate organizations in modern societies has been shifting from the owners, or capitalists, to professional managers and highly skilled technocrats. This proposition, also known as the *managerial revolution hypothesis,* occupies a prominent place in postindustrial theories of society, which contend that knowledge, rather than capital, is becoming the key source of power in society.

The notion that power may be shifting in corporate organizations has significant consequences for media managers, scholars and public policy makers. Corporate and global news media organizations are often accused of placing more emphasis on profits than on quality journalism, restricting journalists' autonomy, alienating employees, destroying community solidarity, supporting the interests of big business over those of the public, and, perhaps most serious of all, failing to provide a diversity of ideas crucial for creating or maintaining a political democracy. But if power in the modern corporate news organization is shifting from the owners to the managers and the technocrats (e.g., editors), and if managers pursue not just profits but others goals, such as maximizing growth of the organization or producing a high-quality product, then these criticisms may be off target.

Research generally supports the idea that most stockholders play a relatively limited or no role in day-to-day operations at most large corporations. However, social scientists still disagree on the question of whether power is really shifting in the system. Some argue that top-level managers are still under the thumb of big investors. Although this is no doubt true in many companies, the key question is whether managers have more autonomy from owners and big investors, and whether they pursue goals other than profits. Research on nonmedia organizations produces mixed results on this question. But my own research on U.S. daily newspapers clearly shows that power has shifted, that owners and publishers play less of a role in controlling news content, and that newspapers place less emphasis on profits as an organizational goal and more on product quality as they become more corporatized. My research also shows that media companies which pay their executives more are not more profitable and do not have higher stock values.

A Brief History of the Managerial Revolution Thesis

The origins of the managerial revolution hypothesis are not fully known. Ironically, though, some of the seeds appear to have been planted by Adam Smith and Karl Marx, neither of whom likely would have viewed it with much favor.

Smith originated the idea that manager-controlled firms place less emphasis on maximizing profits than owner-controlled firms — a proposition that still occupies a prominent position in contemporary research programs. Owner-managers could be expected to keep an eye on the bottom line because their pocketbook was directly affected. But this same diligence could not be expected for joint-stock companies that were controlled by non-owning managers, because

> The directors of such companies ... being the managers ... of other people's money than of their own ... cannot ... be expected ... (to) watch over it with the same anxious vigilance with which the partners in a private copartnery frequently watch over their own. ... Negligence and profusion, therefore, must always prevail, more or less, in the management of the affairs of such a company.

As noted in Chapter 4, Marx is partly responsible for the idea that, as businesses grow and capital becomes more concentrated, ownership becomes more, not less, dispersed. Concentration of capital leads to an increase, not decrease, in the number of owners, because, over time, capital is divided among family members, often through inheritance, and earmarked for new ventures. Although ownership tends to become diffused and decentralized as a firm grows, Marx countered that this process is slow and is more than offset by centralization of capital, which he defined as the combining of capitals already formed — that is, a reduction in the number of competitive firms in a particular sector of industry through merger, bankruptcy or acquisition.

Although Smith underestimated the staying power of the corporate form of organization and Marx overestimated the revolutionary potential of the workers, their ideas nonetheless stimulated other thinkers. In the late 1800s, social democratic theoretician Eduard Bernstein argued that the corporate form of organization led to the splitting up of property into "armies of shareholders" who represented a new "power." The shareholder, he argued, expropriates the capitalist class, transforming it "from a proprietor to a simple administrator."

The writings of the sociologist Max Weber at the turn of the century also may be interpreted as anticipating more formal arguments of later writers, even though he personally disagreed with the idea that managers were gaining power over capitalists. The appropriation of managerial functions from the owners, he argued, does not mean the separation of control from ownership. Rather, it means the separation of the managerial function from ownership. Nevertheless, Weber's writings are somewhat ambiguous. Elsewhere, he observed that bureaucrats, or the technical experts of government, often attempt to control the flow of information to both policy makers and the public.

> The question is always who controls the existing bureaucratic machinery. And such control is possible only in a very limited degree to persons who are not technical specialists. Generally speaking, the trained permanent official is more likely to get his way in the long run than his nominal superior, the Cabinet minister, who is not a specialist.

The first comprehensive analysis of the notion that the proprietors or owners of the means of production were ceding power did not appear until the early 1930s. In *The Modern Corporation and Private Property*, Adolf A. Berle and Gardiner C. Means, an economist and a lawyer, argued that "ownership of wealth without appreciable control and control of wealth without appreciable ownership appear to be the logical outcome of corporate development." The trend toward separation of ownership from management, they argued, occurs because the capital required to operate and own large corporations is often beyond the resources of any single individual or company. As companies grow, they need to draw upon more and more sources of capital, which over time diminishes the percentage of shares owned by any single individual or entity. Berle and Means believed managers, unlike the owners, would be guided by a broader social conscience and professional values, rather than a selfish profit motive.

In the early 1940s, sociologist James Burnham argued that the trend toward separation of management from ownership was leading to the rise of a new class that would replace the capitalists. Growth of business means more than just increasing scale; it also means increasing technical complexity, and this in turn means that the owners must depend more and more on experts and highly skilled managers to run the new means of production. Organizational skills and technical knowledge are the bases of managerial power. However, in contrast to Berle and Means, Burnham believed managers would act in their own self-interest, not necessarily in the public interest.

During the 1940s, economist Joseph Schumpeter made similar arguments. He contended that highly skilled managers and technical specialists, not the capitalists, were the creative force behind the innovative process in modern capitalism. In early capitalism, the capitalist was the entrepreneur, the innovator. Capitalists are driven by profits. But as organizations grow, this role becomes more specialized and routinized and is delegated to highly educated and trained specialists. Because entrepreneurs in modern organizations are not usually the direct beneficiaries of profit, according to Schumpeter, they are driven not by profits but by social status.

By the 1950s many theorists treated the managerial revolution as an empirical fact rather than a hypothesis or theory. Sociologists Talcott Parsons and Ralph Dahrendorf both believed that class relations were being replaced by an occupational system based on individual achievement, in which status was determined by functional importance. In fact, public opinion polls showed then and now that physicians and professors are two of the most prestigious positions in society.

During the 1960s and 1970s, Galbraith and Bell continued this line of thinking, incorporating the managerial revolution hypothesis into larger, more comprehensive theories of social change. Galbraith argues that the "decisive power in modern industrial society is exercised not by capital but by organization, not by the capitalist but by the industrial bureaucrat." One consequence of the shift in power, he says, is less emphasis on profit maximization as an organizational goal. Hence, it would be irrational to argue that those in control (i.e., managers) will maximize profits for others (i.e., stockholders).

As noted briefly in Chapter 7, Galbraith calls the belief that managers are more profit-maximizing the "approved contradiction." In other words, how can corporate media organizations be more profit-oriented when they are more likely to be controlled by professional managers and technocrats, who do not benefit directly or as directly from the profits as the owners? As Galbraith puts it:

> [I]t is now agreed that the modern large corporation is, quite typically, controlled by its management. The managerial revolution — the assumption of power by top management — is conceded. So long as earnings are above a certain minimum, it would also be widely agreed that such management has little to fear from the stockholders. Yet it is for these stockholders, remote, powerless and unknown, that management seeks to maximize profits. Management does not go out ruthlessly to reward itself — a sound management is expected to exercise restraint. Already at this stage, in the accepted view of the corporation, profit maximization involves a substantial contradiction. Those in charge forgo personal reward to enhance it for others.

More important to managers than maximizing profits, Galbraith argues, is prevention of loss, because low earnings or losses make a company vulnerable to outside influence or control. All businesses must earn a minimum level of profit, Galbraith argues, but professional managers place greater emphasis on organizational growth, planning, knowledge, autonomy and expertise, because these factors are recognized as the basis of power in the organization and are essential for long-term survival of the organization (and their jobs).

Applying this logic to the Time Warner incident, one might postulate that Munro and other executives were attempting to secure their jobs for the long term, as well as build an even bigger media empire. After all, that's where all the fun is. Top-level managers like money, to be sure. But most professionals also like their work. They derive a sense of power from it and a sense of identity. In addition, the decision to buy Warner did not entail a great deal of risk to the top-level executives, because they didn't have to spend their own money. So, even if the managers received most of their income from profits through stock options or other incentives, one would still argue that they, in contrast to nonmanagerial owners, would place more emphasis on nonprofit goals. For professional managers, work is a calling, not just a job.

Bell's *The Coming of the Post-Industrial Society* contends that theoretical (or scientific) knowledge, rather than capital or practical knowledge, is the primary source of innovation and social organization in a postindustrial society. In the economy, this change is reflected in the decline of manufacturing and goods and the rise of service industries, especially health, education, social welfare services and professional/technical services (research, evaluation, computers, systems analysis). A postmodern society is an information society. Education rather than heritage or social position is the key means of advancement, and rewards are based less on inheritance or property than on education and skill (i.e., a meritocracy). Bell contends that these structural changes foster a new class structure — one based on the supremacy of professional, managerial, scientific and technical occupations (the knowledge or intellectual class) — that gradually replaces the bourgeoisie as the ruling class.

In sum, the managerial revolution is being fueled by at least three factors or trends: (1) *the death of major entrepreneurial capitalists or stockholders,* whose concentrated economic power is dispersed over time as it is divided among heirs; (2) *organizational growth,* which forces companies to draw capital from more and more sources, diluting the proportion of ownership of any single owner; and (3) *increasing complexity in the division of labor and market competition,* which forces owners to rely more and more on the expertise of highly skilled professional managers and technical experts to manage day-to-day operations of the organization. A fourth trend may also be added to the list: (4) *the growth of pension, insurance, mutual and trust funds,* which invest heavily in corporate stocks and are managed by professional investors, not the owners. Over time, these factors and others are expected to promote the growth of a professional-technical class that will replace existing capitalists as the new ruling class.

But does the research support the managerial revolution hypothesis?

Empirical Research on the Managerial Revolution Thesis

The empirical research can be divided into two major categories or approaches. One attempts to answer the question: Is ownership becoming more diversified as organizations and the economic system have grown? The research here is primarily descriptive and focuses on how much stock is controlled by families or individuals and the extent to which they are involved in top management.

The second line of research attempts to answer the question: Even if ownership is becoming more diversified as organizations grow and become more structurally complex, are those organizations still serving the interests of the owners above managers or other groups? Research on this question involves explanatory analysis and examines the relationship between organizational structure and organizational outcomes (i.e., profit maximization, job loss, product quality).

All of the research that has specifically tested the managerial revolution hypothesis except one have been conducted on nonmedia corporations. The media study involved a national probability survey of daily newspapers and is addressed in depth following this review.

Is Ownership Becoming More Diversified?

Research on this question strongly suggests that owners play less and less a role in the day-to-day operations as organizations grow, that the proportion of manager-controlled firms has increased, and that most large companies are manager- rather than owner-controlled. These findings are generally applicable to mass media industries as well.

Using data compiled from Standard's *Corporation Records, Moody's* manuals, *The New York Times* and *The Wall Street Journal,* Berle and Means concluded that families or groups of business associates owned more than half of the outstanding voting stock in only 11 percent of the top 200 largest nonfinancial corporations. Using 10 percent stock ownership as the minimum criterion for family control, they classified 44 percent of the top 200 largest nonfinancial corporations as management controlled.

In 1937, the Securities and Exchange Commission, using more reliable and comprehensive data, reported that minority ownership control existed in the vast majority of the nation's largest corporations. However, Robert Aaron Gordon challenged the government study, pointing to a number of shortcomings and concluding that probably fewer than a third of the companies were controlled by families or small groups of individuals. A study by *Fortune* magazine in the 1960s also concluded that 71 percent of the 500 largest industrial corporations were controlled by management.

Using a methodology similar to Berle and Means, Robert J. Larner concluded that only three percent of the largest 200 nonfinancial corporations were controlled by families in 1963. At the same time, 84 percent of the companies were controlled by managers, nearly double what Berle and Means had found. The remaining 13 percent were partially controlled.

However, a year later Philip H. Burch challenged Larner's and Berle and Means' findings, arguing that they had used a too restrictive definition of control. Burch argues that control should include not only some measure of stock ownership but also membership in top management or on the board of directors. Using this broader definition, he found that about 36 percent of the top 300 public and private industrial corporations were probably family controlled in 1965. However, Burch also found that the proportion of family-controlled firms had declined about three to five percent a year since 1938, when they controlled about 50 percent of all large companies. These data support Larner's and Berle and Means' argument that family or individual control declines as a company grows.

Do Managers Serve Themselves or Owners?

The second line of research has focused to a large extent on Smith's 200-year-old hypothesis, which posited that managers are less likely to serve the interests of the owners than themselves. Often this has involved examining whether managerial-controlled firms or large corporations are less profitable or place less emphasis on profits. Noneconomic researchers have also examined the impact on organizational goals and practices, with the expectation that managers will place greater value on organizational growth, product quality and innovation. Findings are mixed.

Several studies are interpreted as supporting the managerial revolution thesis. Joseph Monsen and his colleagues examined the impact of ownership structure on the level of profitability for the 500 largest industrial firms. They found that over a 12-year period the net income to net worth ratio (return on owner's equity) for owner-controlled firms was 12.8 percent, compared with 7.3 percent for manager-controlled firms.

John Palmer also found that manager-controlled firms operating in markets with a high degree of monopoly power report significantly lower profit rates than owner-controlled firms, but no major differences emerged between firms in moderate or low monopoly markets. The reasoning here is that managers can pursue goals other than maximum profits only in the absence of competition, which acts as a constraint on all types of organizational structure. Larner found that manager-controlled firms have slightly lower profit rates.

In contrast, other studies have found no differences or that manager-controlled firms are more profitable. Neil Fligstein and Peter Brantley, for example, found that manager-controlled firms actually outperformed family- or bank-controlled firms in terms of profits. However, they argue that ownership overall has little effect on the economic actions undertaken by large firms; rather, the key determinants are existing power relations within the firm, the concept of control that dominates the firm's actions and the action of competitors.

Several other studies also have found that management control exerts no important influence on profit rates. David R. James and Michael Soref studied the relationship between dismissal of corporate chiefs and five measures of managerial/owner control and found that corporate heads are retained or fired on the basis of profit performance, not ownership structure.

One major problem with these studies, however, is that they tend to focus on the largest 100 to 500 corporations. These corporations are not representative of all businesses, and the restricted variance reduces the ability to detect differences between more-or-less corporatized organizations. In contrast, newspapers are the ideal mass medium for testing the managerial hypothesis, because they range greatly in size and complexity.

Research on Newspapers

Breaking with previous theorists, I have argued that a positive correlation between managerial-control and high profit rates is compatible with the managerial revolution thesis. This would be expected, because the corporate form of organization is structurally organized to maximize profits. However, the corporate organization places less emphasis on profits as an organizational goal because professional managers pursue goals other than profits.

These hypotheses are supported by my national probability samples of daily newspapers in the United States. In several studies, I have found that corporate newspapers are more profitable than smaller, less "corporatized" ones. I argue that corporate newspapers are more profitable because they benefit from economies of scale and superior management and human resources. However, corporate newspapers also very clearly place less emphasis on profits as an organizational goal and more emphasis on other, nonprofit goals — such as product quality, maximizing growth of the organization, using the latest technology, worker autonomy and being innovative — because they are controlled by professional managers and technocrats, not the owners.

As mentioned earlier, my research also shows that journalists at corporate newspapers are more satisfied with their jobs because they have more autonomy, status and prestige than journalists at noncorporate or entrepreneurial newspapers. And, more importantly, I found that as organizations become more corporatized, editorials and letters to the editor published in them become more, not less, critical of mainstream groups and ideas. In addition, established news sources (mayors and police chiefs) in communities served by corporate newspapers also believe that those newspapers are more critical of their policies and city hall. I trace the growth and development of the corporate newspaper to the economic and social division of labor in society (i.e., structural pluralism or social differentiation), and I argue that the corporate form of organization helps to explain many of the social changes that have taken place, especially in the last century (see Chapter 9).

Despite these findings, a fundamental question remains: Can these changes be generalized to other industries as well? The newspaper industry is widely believed to operate in markets where there is little direct competition, which is not characteristic of most markets. Thus, these findings may not be representative of businesses as a whole. At the same time, however, the empirical research by economists and sociologists also cannot be generalized to the entire population of businesses, because virtually all of it is based on national data for only the largest corporations — populations of firms have rarely been studied.

In another study, I attempted to circumvent these problems by examining changes in source attributions in news stories over time. The assumption underlying this approach is that media content reflects in a crude way the power structure of a society. If this power-reflection proposition is correct, then one could postulate that changes in the power structure should be reflected in the sources that journalists use to report on the news. More specifically, I hypothesized that *during the 20th century attributions of capitalists declined, while attributions of scientists, technicians, researchers and others whose roles involve the production of theoretical knowledge increased.* A content analysis of source attributions on the front page of the *New York Times* over a 90-year period during the 20th century supported this hypothesis. Attributions of capitalists declined from 8.8 percent in 1903 to 4.0 percent in 1993. In contrast, attributions of technocrats increased, going from 2.7 percent to 10.5 percent. Although illustrative, the findings from this study should be interpreted cautiously, as they assume that attributions are a measure of the power structure in a society.

Finally — and perhaps most importantly — in 1996 I conducted a national survey of U.S. daily newspapers and asked publishers, owners and editors what role they play in making decisions about editorial and news content. Because this is the only study to directly test the managerial revolution hypothesis in the media industry, I devote the rest of the chapter to it.

A Theory of Corporate Management Control

The logic behind my theory of corporate management control is not complex. Basically, it posits that owners and publishers lose control over the editorial content because of increasing role specialization.

More specifically, as the scale and size of an organization increases, roles generally become more specialized and the division of labor expands. These structural forces increase the productive capacity of the organization and reduce costs; however, they also increase the complexity of the decision-making process. A highly complex organization depends heavily on a highly educated and skilled workforce to achieve its goals. At newspapers, this means that editors and other newsroom experts, not the owners and publishers, have the requisite knowledge and skills to make such decisions. Owners (whether proprietors or absentee stockholders) and other top-level managers (publishers) depend heavily on experts and highly skilled managers to run the organization. And the owners' and publishers' roles also become more specialized; that is, they tend to focus more on budgetary matters and long-term planning rather than on day-to-day matters.

In sum, I hypothesized that *the more a newspaper exhibits the characteristics of the corporate form of organization:*

(H1) the less role owners (proprietors and stockholders) and publishers will play in making decisions that affect editorial content (i.e., what to cover, what to publish on the front page, whether to publish a controversial story, and what positions to take in editorials); and

(H2) the greater the role editors and reporters will play in making decisions that affect editorial content.

Method and Measures

The data were collected through a national probability mail survey of top-ranking managers at daily newspapers in the United States. A two-page questionnaire was mailed in October 1996 to the top-ranking editorial manager (usually the editor or editor-in-chief) and the top-ranking noneditorial manager (usually the publisher) at 314 dailies randomly selected from the *1996 Editor & Publisher International Yearbook*. No sample frame for owners of newspapers exists to the knowledge of this researcher. However, respondents were asked to indicate whether they owned any interest in their newspaper and, if so, how much (in proportions). Of the 628 respondents included in the sample pool, valid responses were obtained from 412, for a response rate of about 66 percent. The respondents represented 269 of the 314 dailies (86 percent).

Although individuals responded to the questionnaires, it is important to point out that the newspaper — not the individual — is the unit of analysis study. To conduct such an analysis, the findings were aggregated for each newspaper that had two respondents. For continuous measures (i.e., ordinal, interval and ratio level measures) and dichotomous nominal measures, the final value used in the analysis represented the mean of the ratings given. In cases where the values for one of the respondents were missing (e.g., failure to answer a question), the values of the other respondent(s) were substituted.

As in my previous studies, the independent variable (corporate newspaper structure) was composed of five dimensions and 12 individual measures, including: (1) *Structural Complexity* — number of full-time employees; number of full-time reporters and editors; number of beats or departments; number of promotions needed for reporter to become top editor; (2) *Ownership Structure* — whether the newspaper was owned by chain or group (no=0; yes=1); whether public ownership was possible (no=0; yes=1); whether the newspaper was a legally incorporated business (no=0; yes=1); whether the newspaper was controlled by one family or individual (no=1; yes=0); (3) *Rules and Regulations* — whether the newspaper has "its own formal, written code of ethics"; whether the newspaper has "its own employee handbook of rules and procedures"; (4) *Rationality in Decision-Making* — amount of perceived importance top management places on "finding the most efficient way to solve problems"; and (5) *Staff Expertise* — whether "reporters normally need a bachelor's degree to be considered for employment at your newspaper" (no=0; yes=1)."

To measure control over editorial content, respondents were asked to rate how much role the owners (and/or stockholders), local publisher (or top manager), top editor, managing editor (or equivalent), editorial editors and reporters have when it comes to making one or more of four editorial-content decisions. The four decisions and the exact wording of the questions were as follows: "When it comes to making decisions about ... (1) what stories to publish, (2) what stories to publish on the front page, (3) whether to publish a controversial story, and (4) what positions to take in editorials, ... how much of a role do each of the following individuals play?" Responses were recorded on a seven-point scale ranging from "plays no role" (value of 1) to "makes all decisions" (value of 7).

Respondents rated owners, publishers and editors on all four decision conditions. Managing editors were rated on only the first three, because at many newspapers they have little role in influencing editorial-page content. Reporters were rated only on the first measure, because they usually have little involvement in the other decisions, and editorial editors were rated only on the last measure. For the owner, publisher, top editor and managing editor roles, the individual decision conditions were summed to create indices, and those indices were then divided by the total number of decision conditions, which standardized the ratings to the original seven-point scale.

Findings

Interestingly, the mean ratings indicated that, regardless of corporate structure, most owners in general play a relatively limited role in making decisions about editorial content. Averaging across all four content measures, the mean rating for owners was 1.9 (on a 7-point scale, where 7 means a high degree of control), compared with 4.3 for publishers, 5.8 for top editors and 6.0 for managing editors. In terms of making decisions about what stories to cover, reporters received a mean rating of 5.0, and editorial editors garnered a mean of 5.7 when it came to making decisions about what positions to take in editorials. Although the mean for owners was low, the variance was greater for that measure than for any of the other variables (1.36 versus .59 to 1.35 for the other measures). In other words, some owners play a much more active role in decision-making than other owners.

Hypothesis 1. The data support the first hypothesis, which expected that owners and publishers would play less of a role in making decisions about editorial content as a newspaper becomes more corporatized. The table below shows that less than one percent of the owners at highly corporatized newspapers (0.9 percent) say they play a major role in editorial decision-making (i.e., major is defined as values five, six or seven on the seven-point scale), compared with 11.3 percent of the owners at newspapers scoring low on the corporate index measure. Similarly, only 17.5 percent of the publishers at highly corporatized newspapers say they play a major role in editorial decision-making, versus 38.4 percent of publishers at the least corporatized newspapers. The odds of these findings occurring by chance alone are less than one in 1,000. In short, the higher a newspaper scores on the corporate index, the less role owners and publishers play in controlling news content.

TABLE 1. EFFECT OF CORPORATE STRUCTURE
ON CONTROL OF EDITORIAL CONTENT

Percent of respondents in the following groups that play a major role in controlling editorial content	Corporate Newspaper Index		
	Low (n=105)	Moderate (n=125)	High (n=119)
Owners	11.3%	4.3%	0.9%
Publishers	38.4%	38.1%	17.5%
Top Editors	80.5%	88.5%	81.7%
Managing Editors	84.0%	89.7%	94.6%
Reporters	28.8%	33.6%	47.0%
Editorial Page Editors	67.1%	80.6%	86.6%

How to read the table: As the value for corporate structure increases, owners and publishers play less of a role in controlling editorial content, whereas managing editors, reporters and editorial page editors play a greater role. There are no significant differences for top editors — at all newspapers, most of them play a major role in controlling editorial content. *SOURCE:* National probability survey of U.S. daily newspapers in 1996.

Hypothesis 2. The data also generally support the second hypothesis, which expected that editors and reporters would play a larger role in controlling news content as corporate structure increases. This finding applies to managing editors, editorial editors and reporters. The only exception was top editors, for whom corporate structure does not make a difference, because most top editors at all newspapers play a major role in controlling editorial content.

More specifically, Table 1 shows that more than 81.7 percent of the top editors at highly corporatized newspapers say they play a major role in controlling content, versus 80.5 percent of editors at the least corporatized newspapers and 88.5 percent of those at moderately corporatized newspapers. None of these differences is significant.

However, managing editors at highly corporatized newspapers are much more likely than their counterparts at the other papers to say they play a role in controlling content (94.6 percent versus 84.0 percent and 89.7 percent, respectively). Even more dramatic, nearly half of the reporters at highly corporatized newspapers (47 percent) say they play a major role in deciding what stories to cover, compared with only about a fourth (28.8 percent) of those at the least corporatized newspapers. Finally, nearly nine of 10 editorial editors at highly corporatized newspapers say they play a major role in deciding what positions to take in editorials. Additional analysis showed that the relationship between the role variables and corporate structure remained about the same when controlling for respondent's job function (i.e., editor, publisher, owner, reporter, managing editor) and for demographic characteristics (education, age, gender, income).

Summary

This probability survey of U.S. daily newspapers provides strong support for the managerial revolution hypothesis. Owners and publishers of newspapers exert less control over news content as the organization acquires the characteristics of the corporate form of organization. Such decisions are left primarily to high-ranking editors, who, it was argued, have the requisite knowledge and skills to make decisions about content. And, contrary to some studies of autonomy, editorial editors and reporters play a larger, not lesser, role in making decisions about the content they produce as the newspaper becomes more corporatized.

These findings bolster and reinforce the findings from previous studies, which show that corporate newspapers place less emphasis on profits and more emphasis on product quality and other nonprofit goals. The findings also support studies which show that corporate newspapers publish more editorials and letters to the editor that are critical of mainstream groups and values.

At a minimum then, this study and the social scientific literature in general suggests that arguments that dismiss outright the notion that managerial and technocratic occupations are gaining power relative to capitalists are premature. At a maximum, the literature suggests that a major transition of power is taking place in society. I believe the latter is true and, if it is, this transfer of power has at least two major implications for media managers, scholars and policy makers.

First, the managerial revolution casts doubt on arguments that the growth of the corporate form of organization in mass media industries is leading to greater emphasis on profits at the expense of product quality or a diversity of ideas. Instead, the managerial revolution hypothesis suggests that professional managers and editors are placing greater emphasis on information diversity, product quality and other nonprofit goals.

Second, if a transition of power is taking place, then corporate media would be expected to have a greater capacity to promote social change. This does not mean that hegemonic models are wrong; rather, they just overstate the social control consequences of the mass media and understate the media's capacity to promote social change. The growth of corporate media, in fact, may help to explain many of the social changes during the last century or so that have benefited disadvantaged groups (e.g., increasing rights for consumers, women, environmentalists and minorities).

To the extent that media managers and technocrats control the news production process, one might also expect that these groups will have a disproportionate impact on public policy. Future research should focus more closely on the impact that media management structure has on organizational goals and behaviors, as well as the impact dependence on technocrats has on audiences and policy makers.

Finally, I would like to point out that the managerial revolution is the most underappreciated trend in the media industry today. In my opinion, one of the main reasons for this is the overwhelming bias among mass communication scholars toward any perspective that may even hint that corporations have the potential to pursue goals other than profits. Scholars who take the road less traveled are quickly branded "apologists for corporations." Although not all of the research evidence supports the managerial revolution, the failure to study changes in the structure of corporate management has seriously compromised many analyses of business and media systems.

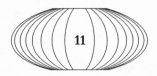

11

GLOBAL MEDIA
IN THE 21ST CENTURY

In the second edition of his book *The Media Monopoly,* former journalist and retired professor Ben H. Bagdikian predicted in 1987 that "if mergers and acquisitions by large corporations continue at the present rate, one massive firm will be in virtual control of all major media by the 1990s." He added that, "Given the complexities of social and economic trends, that is not inevitable." In the fifth edition of the book, published in 1997, Bagdikian qualified that observation a bit more, changing the last clause from "... that is not inevitable" to "... it is unlikely to result in one owner." Good thing, because the century is almost over and the U.S. media industry is still a long way off from one single owner.

Although ownership in many media segments has become more concentrated, Bagdikian's prediction underscores how risky the crystal ball business can be — and he only had to project a decade into the future. By training, most scholars are cautious and avoid making predictions because they are afraid a mistake will haunt them. Certainly it would be foolhardy to try to predict what will happen in the years to come to any of the major global media corporations. Although most organizations and people resist change, no one can say for certain what will happen to specific media organizations.

However, the inability to make sound predictions about specific organizations doesn't mean that social science research cannot provide some insights into trends that will affect mass media industries and mass communication processes in general. I believe it can, and in this chapter I share with you my vision of media in the 21st century. Of course, those trends assume that nuclear war, environmental degradation or a natural disaster won't destroy our world. They also assume that the world will continue to become more structurally (or socially) differentiated — a topic I have touched on before (Chapter 7) but one which now needs further elaboration.

Trend #1 — Structural Differentiation

One of the most visible and important changes taking place in most societies today — and this trend is likely to continue in the 21st century — is increasing structural (or social) differentiation. In other words, the number and variety of groups and organizations in societies around the world are increasing, and many organizations are themselves becoming more structurally complex (i.e., the number of departments, units and/or specialized roles are increasing).

Another term often used interchangeably with differentiation is the division of labor. It is important to point out, however, that structural differentiation involves growth not only in the economic sector (businesses) but also in most aspects of social (nonbusiness) life. Thus, the number of service, recreational, philanthropic and nonprofit groups also is increasing and diversifying.

Structural differentiation has important consequences for media systems. As social systems become more differentiated, needs for information and knowledge also increase. This, in turn, helps promote growth in the number and variety of media. In fact, historically, the emergence and growth of all forms of mass media, including global media, are directly related to the growing demands for information brought on by urbanization and industrialization, which are two visible indicators of structural differentiation (see Chapter 2).

Urbanization increases the need for information because it requires collective cooperation to deal with a broad number of social needs and problems, including food distribution, shelter, crime, poverty, waste disposal, public health, pollution and land control. Political elites — who have most of the power for dealing with such problems — depend heavily upon the mass media for information to help them make policy decisions. They also depend upon news reports to help generate support from other elites and the public for the decisions they make. Media coverage helps legitimize such actions, while at the same time conveying the notion that the citizenry in general plays a major role in the decision-making process (even if it doesn't). Urban residents also rely more heavily on newspapers and other mass media than residents of rural or undifferentiated societies, because they depend more heavily upon other individuals and organizations for everyday needs (food, clothing, shelter and public services, such as water and police protection).

Industrialization under capitalism also requires that people work together, but now the purpose is to produce products and services for sale in a market that ultimately earns a profit for the business firms. Manufacturers need access to large, heterogeneous markets, and one efficient method for reaching such markets is through advertising. The dramatic growth of the newspaper in the 19th century is directly related to the growth of advertising in the private sector, with the penny press emerging in the 1830s as the first mass media to offer access to mass markets (see Chapters 2 and 8). News about markets, politics and natural disasters also is crucial for business. Business managers must constantly monitor their economic and political environments to adapt to changing conditions and to lobby for change when necessary.

Increasing urbanization and industrialization, growth in population and the world economy, and expansion of technology also will promote increasing specialization in the business world. Many businesses will become more structurally complex, offering more differentiated products and services. This means creating and marketing goods and services that target specialized markets, consumers and audiences. Market segmentation, target marketing and niche marketing will continue to be the buzzwords of the business world. Professional organizations also will continue to grow and specialize in response to an increasingly differentiated and segmented workforce. It means the "professionalization of everyone," as one sociologist once remarked.

But the economy isn't the only area that is becoming more structurally differentiated. Most aspects of social life are differentiating as well. This includes governmental agencies and institutions around the world, which will be offering more and more services to more and more people. School systems, especially colleges and universities, will be offering more and more programs in specialized areas. Distance learning via the Internet will become much more common. But even public schools for precollege youth and children will offer an increasing diversity of courses and curricula. People also will have a greater choice of recreational and leisure activities or services (e.g., sports, hobbies, travel, clubs). And, despite a continuing trend toward secularism around the world, many new religious groups will emerge. Scientific rationality will not bring an end to beliefs in the supernatural. In fact, religious, mystic or cult groups will flourish. And many of these religious groups will be highly critical of materialism, capitalism and science.

As alluded to in Chapters 6 and 7, professors in the social sciences and the humanities and journalists also will become more and more critical of capitalism, Western ideas and the notion of scientific progress. Many will continue to argue that differentiation is creating a fragmented society, one in which social order is breaking down. Although most societies are clearly more differentiated and the social sciences are unable to solve many social problems, such as crime and drug abuse, there is little evidence to suggest that most societies are breaking apart or that most people's faith in science is waning. Advances in the natural sciences and technology will continue to make daily life easier and advances in the medical sciences will continue to extend the lifespans of most people around the world. In fact, most societies or nations will be more stable than at any time in history, even though there will be a greater number of groups pursuing fewer resources than ever before.

But an important question remains: If many societies are differentiating and the diversity of ideas is increasing, then what is holding them together? Part of the "glue" comes from the division of labor, which generates needs for information and knowledge and increases interdependence between people.

Division of Labor and Needs for Information

To see how the division of labor contributes to social order, let's compare life in small organizations or in small, relatively undifferentiated societies or groups to that in large organizations or societies. In small organizations or societies, nearly all of the activities crucial for the existence of these groups can be accomplished through interpersonal communication. The social and economic division of labor is limited. Group solidarity and homogeneity in shared sentiments and values tend to be high. Social conflict is minimal, and competition between social actors for scarce resources is limited.

However, as a group or social system grows, competition for scarce resources and social conflict typically increase. This often threatens the stability and existence of these groups. Historically, for example, when a society grew beyond the resources in its environment, its leaders often sought more territory or the society broke up into smaller groups that moved into new territories.

Civil war or colonization (exploitation of another society) also solved the problem, even though many people suffered. However, the division of labor is another solution to the problem of scarce resources, because it usually leads to increased efficiency and productivity. As Adam Smith pointed out, when tasks are divided into discrete steps, an organization can produce a lot more goods and services at a fraction of the time and cost (see Chapter 4).

The historical trend toward the division of labor is certainly not automatic or unilinear. Many cultures, even today, resist such trends. The division of labor also requires greater cooperation among the specialized units and roles to accomplish a goal. As groups and organizations grow and become more structurally differentiated, interpersonal communication as the sole basis for social organization becomes inadequate. The primary reason is that it is inefficient. In large organizations, for instance, it is impossible for even one individual to communicate personally with all others on a regular basis.

More generally, as the number of social actors in a group or organization increases, the amount of interpersonal contact between any single social actor and all others declines. But even if interpersonal communication on a grand scale were possible, it could not, by itself, deal with the problems of coordination and control that accompany increases in the division of the labor and role specialization. For the division of labor to expand, various tasks and functions and jobs generally must be routinized, formalized and standardized. As a rule of thumb, these three elements become more crucial as the organization grows in size. But, in any case, to accomplish these tasks efficiently, organizations and social systems usually need to develop formalized sources and media of communication.

The types of sources and media employed will vary depending upon the level of analysis. For example, within organizations, such sources and media include, but are not limited to, the development of formalized goals and policy statements, written rules and procedures, job descriptions, interdepartmental memos and letters, bulletin boards, newsletters and e-mail. Within industry segments, specialized media, such as magazines and newsletters, emerge to help organizations cope with management problems and changes in the industry. And within communities or social systems as a whole (e.g., nations), mass media, including newspapers, television and radio, provide information about system-wide problems and issues that cut across organizational boundaries and groups. Such media are also important for connecting consumers to producers via advertising.

Today, the growth of large-scale global media and the Internet is driven primarily in response to the growth of world-wide markets and the need for information that integrates the structurally diverse businesses and organizations. Although the types of media and content may vary considerably within and between the three levels mentioned above, in all cases they perform at least one similar function: They link social actors to one another, reducing social distance and enabling them to accomplish their goals more effectively and efficiently.

Thus, in complex societies, people and groups increasingly depend upon each other and the media to achieve their goals. Specialization breeds dependence. And dependence generally leads to social order and integration. This principle is captured in the popular phrase, "You scratch my back, and I'll scratch yours." The city dweller depends on the farmer for food; the farmer depends on city dwellers to purchase his/her products. The university depends on students for tuition income; the student depends on the university for learning; the business community depends on universities to train future workers; and so on. This interdependence does not guarantee harmony and cooperation, but it can create structural conditions that generally promote social integration.

Paradoxically, although differentiation often produces a much greater diversity of perspectives and ideas, there is also much greater tolerance of others. Large, complex cities, for example, are often safe havens for alternative lifestyles and perspectives. Sit on a street corner in any major city in the world and you'll see what I mean. Large complex systems also can tolerate more social conflict because they have more structural mechanisms for dealing with such conflict (e.g., court systems, moderators, labor boards, administrative judges, public hearings).

Because there is a greater diversity of perspectives in pluralistic systems, shared values also tend to become more general. But agreement on all values is not necessary for people to accomplish their individual goals. And people around the world will continue to share some common values, such as the sanctity of human life, human rights, love, friendship and honesty.

Global Capitalism and the Nation-State

As we travel through the 21st century, you also notice that more and more countries follow a capitalist or a free-market model. Planned economies, such as those under communist states, are virtually gone. The problem was that they could not efficiently produce and distribute goods and services. The market is much more efficient, even if it continues to be highly inequitable. Huge income inequities between nations and groups continue, but market-driven economics continue to raise the absolute standard of living for most people around the world. This helps to cool down dissidents.

Although capitalism appears to have triumphed at a global level, this doesn't mean the economy operates on truly free-market principles or that there is no criticism of capitalism. More appropriately, the world economy has elements of socialism and capitalism. Capitalism cannot solve many of the world's problems, such as poverty, crime and poor health care. So the state (governments) must fill in. Social welfare will continue to consume larger portions of the economic pie.

As postindustrial theorists have predicted, the trend toward a service and information-based economy will continue. But Karl Marx's ghost will continue to haunt Wall Street via the transnational corporation. Although neo-Marxists interpret this as a tightening of the capitalist noose, John Kenneth Galbraith points out that oligopolies reduce risk and enable large companies to pour more resources into research and development. Also, because companies are controlled by managers rather than the stockholders, they place more emphasis on nonprofit goals, such as organizational growth and product or service quality (see Chapter 10). They can do this partly because they have market power and don't have to worry as much about making a profit. From time to time, governments will step in and enforce antitrust laws.

The nation-state as a geopolitical unit will not disappear any time soon, despite the recent trends in the European Union and many predictions to the contrary. Government bureaucrats and political elites resist change, and increasing concern for multiculturalism and cultural sovereignty will temper moves to do away with the state. However, there is little question that over time economic globalization will siphon off some of the power of the nation-state. The United Nations or some entity like it will increase in power and influence. This is especially true as the world consumes its resources and pollutes the environment. In fact, a threat to the world's environment may very well prove to be more instrumental in global integration than economic interdependence.

In sum, the most significant trend that will affect global media and mass communication in general is structural differentiation. Given this general outline, let's now turn specifically to trends in media.

Trend #2 — Global Media Growth and Differentiation

Over the next couple of decades and probably longer, there is little question that the number and size of global media organizations will continue to increase. This growth is partly a function of increasing globalization of other nonmedia companies, which are looking for efficient ways to advertise their products around the world. Global media will deliver consumers to them.

Some scholars have argued that the amount of dollars spent on advertising will decrease as ownership in many industries becomes more concentrated. However, there is no evidence to suggest that advertising revenues in general are declining — in fact, they are increasing — and there is no evidence to suggest that the number of new businesses or the number of units within existing businesses will decline. In fact, most corporations, including global media, will tend to become more structurally differentiated over time. Global media companies, in particular, will offer a multitude of news, information and entertainment services to billions of people around the world. China and Asia will offer the biggest growth potential.

But this growth will not be limited to the big players. The Internet and Internet II (which enables much faster transmission of data and information) also will create new business opportunities in information services and other areas, and this will increase pressures for decentralization of economic power in many industries. With the Internet, small companies and sole proprietors can offer highly specialized information services that larger companies will shun.

Although no one can predict what will happen to global media corporations like AOL Time Warner and Disney, it is a safe bet that many more mergers and acquisitions will take place in the years to come. Economies of scale will be a driving force. New markets and growth in the world's population also will stimulate growth in the size of media organizations. And to reduce risk, global media increasingly will engage in more joint ventures. In some cases, this will diminish competition, but competition overall will continue to increase.

Although media critics and social scientists will continue to raise concerns about concentration and centralization of power in the media industry, few efforts to regulate media industries will be successful. That's because media proponents can easily fight off such efforts by raising concerns about governmental control over media systems. But even more important, proponents of global media will point out that the marketplace now has many new media organizations and alternative sources of information, news and entertainment programming that enhance competition. Indeed, they will be right.

As global media organizations grow and expand, the number and variety of information and entertainment services, especially teleservices (television or online video), they offer will continue to grow and become more specialized. There will be channels for every professional and recreational interest imaginable. Not all of these services will be successful. And, despite fears of increasing social fragmentation, some media services and programs will appeal to large segments of the world population (e.g., business and political news). But the trend definitely will be toward identifying groups and markets with specialized needs for information and entertainment programming. As noted above, market segmentation and target marketing will be key to the success of most media organizations.

Trend #3 — Bigger Media But Proportionately Less Powerful

Although global media corporations will grow and reach more people, paradoxically their ability to control the information and entertainment marketplaces will decline. In metaphorical terms, the pie and its slices are getting larger, but each slice is proportionately smaller than the slice in the previous pie. In comparative terms, no single company or program will be able to dominate the global market to the degree that the state-run or private television networks did in Western countries during the 1950s and 1960s. There will be too many choices. Consumers and audiences will have access to thousands of information and entertainment services.

To be sure, news media organizations like CNN (an AOL Time Warner company) will continue to reach hundreds of millions and probably billions of people, and their audiences will expand. But needs for information will continue to become more specialized, and many alternative news channels and outlets will emerge to serve those specialized needs. In fact, the trend toward specialized information and entertainment services will continue to grow exponentially, thanks to the Internet and new technologies. Anyone with a computer terminal can create a news, information or entertainment service — and not necessarily for profit; it may just be for fun or entertainment.

Contrary to the predictions of the neo-Marxists, the Internet and the World Wide Web (or whatever we call those technologies in the future) will continue to help decentralize control over information. One example of this comes from the music world, where artists are bypassing the recording companies and are now marketing their music directly to consumers, who can directly download digitally recorded songs. This trend toward less centralized control over information is not new. It goes back to the printing press, which challenged the authority of the church and state (see Chapter 2). But in the future most people will be able to reach many others around the world through the Internet.

Of course, large-scale media companies will continue to have a competitive advantage, even in many specialized areas, because they have the capital and resources to produce the kinds of products and services that meet the needs of an increasingly globalized and market-driven world economy. Global media corporations will continue to rake in the lion's share of revenues. However, specialized media services will continue to grow and expand because they will provide services that cannot be easily or profitably offered by global media organizations. Larger companies prefer large, undifferentiated audiences that offer the highest level of profit. But convergence of technologies will make it more difficult for them to control the market.

Trend #4 — Convergence of Technologies

For the near future, global media will continue to deliver their services directly to consumers in a variety of ways — through cables, satellites, over the air and telephone lines. However, as technology advances, the trend will be toward convergence on the Internet, which offers video, audio and print media services all in one package.

This tendency toward convergence will blur the boundaries between traditional print and electronic media, especially news media, even further. Although traditional forms of media, such as the printed newspapers and magazines, will continue to exist, the online versions will be less expensive to produce and distribute and will offer multimedia formats (e.g., film clips, live reports) — something the printed copy cannot do. News media companies that currently own both print and electronic news services are best positioned to adapt to changes in technology in the 21st century.

Convergence on the Internet also will increase competition. Conventional forms of delivery (cable TV, over the air television, radio, print news media) won't die out immediately. But the media delivery market will become much more diversified, and growth in the traditional forms of delivery eventually will slow or decline, especially in those cases where an electronic version saves the consumer money. The newspaper is particularly vulnerable over the long run, because printing and delivering a hard copy can consume more than 35 percent of the total expenditures. Convergence also will decentralize control even more over information and ideas.

Although convergence of technology on the Internet will blur the lines between print and electronic media, it is important to point out that increasing access to information on the Internet will not kill off the news-gathering business. News media organizations will continue to have a privileged status in Western countries because of the ethic of (relative) objectivity (see Chapter 8). In other words, traditional news media organizations offer a more objective account of the world relative to the news sources they cover. Moreover, despite all of the criticism of news media, polls show that more than two-thirds of the public trusts the reports they get in the news media, and the public will continue to depend very heavily on news media for news and information.

Trend #5 — Increasing Diversity of Ideas

Critics of corporate and global media organizations have made many predictions and claims that growth in size of media organizations is leading to less diversity and greater homogeneity in the news, information and entertainment programming people consume. Although case studies of certain media organizations and media industries (e.g., newspaper industry) may support such claims, when national or global media systems are examined, their predictions do not hold up very well. The trend clearly has been toward an increase in the number and variety of media outlets, as well as an increase in the diversity of content and programming they produce.

The case for increasing diversity is presented in Chapter 7. Let me just add here that the causes of this increase are largely a function of structural differentiation. Interestingly, as global media grow, so will the criticism of them. In fact, the number of critical books, articles, documentaries and web sites will explode over the next couple of decades. Much of this criticism will be based on isolated events or anecdotes, which are true. Global media are no messiah. They are profit-seeking corporations that sometimes make decisions that are self-serving and harmful to disadvantaged groups and alternative ideas.

However, as Chapters 7-10 tried to show, much of this anecdotal evidence is not representative of the bigger picture. Probability surveys show that corporate media do publish content that is more critical of traditional value systems and dominant institutions, and news sources perceive those media as being more critical of them. Ironically, though, probability research is unlikely to have much impact on scholars. As philosopher of science Thomas S. Kuhn pointed out, scientific paradigms are difficult to change. This is especially true in the social sciences, where there is continued disagreement even about basic issues of logic and research. Nevertheless, the beauty of increasing structural differentiation is that people have greater access to more perspectives, ideas and theories than ever before. This diversity can only promote better debate and research.

Trend #6 — Spread of Western Values

Because global media are creations of Western political and economic systems and need profits to survive, global media will continue to produce news content and entertainment programming that generally promote Western values, such as responsible capitalism, racial and gender equality, representative democracy, a diversity of ideas, religious tolerance and — yes — materialism and consumerism. This doesn't mean these values are automatically or uniformly adopted by non-Western peoples. As noted in Chapter 7, local cultures often interpret Western media messages in ways different from the culture that produced them.

However, despite exceptions to the rule and variances within cultures, there is little question that Western values are spreading and will continue to threaten traditional cultures and ways of doing things. Even highly isolated tribal cultures (e.g., Amazon basin) will find it increasingly difficult to insulate themselves from Western materialism and popular culture. And the comforts and conveniences of modern capitalism, once tasted, are rarely given up — just ask the neo-Marxist scholars, who themselves draw down comfortable salaries at major universities around the world.

But traditional media effects models have not done a good job explaining how Western values are transmitted and adopted. Those models hypothesize that foreigners who consume greater amounts of Western media content are more likely to adopt the values embedded in those messages. To be sure, empirical research provides some support for this proposition (see Chapter 7), and it would be illogical to argue that repeated exposure to such messages over long periods never has any effects. But it is erroneous to assume that cognitive changes of this sort play the key role in spreading Western values, or that most indigenous citizens need to adopt such values as a prerequisite for social change. In most social systems at most times in history, most people (ordinary citizens) have little power to change things. This is true even in today's so-called "representative democracies." Most power resides with political and economic elites, who make most of the decisions that affect most people. So, although changing the opinions of the typical citizen may help promote change, it is not a necessary condition. Changing the values of elites is much more important.

Historically, perhaps the best example of this is Peter the Great — the Russian Czar who associated with Westerners at an early age and later borrowed many Western technologies and practices to modernize the Russian government and military. Similarly, today the role of Peter is played by young foreign students who are educated at Western universities. Partly through personal experience and partly through exposure to mass media in the host countries, many acquire a "Western view," or at least an understanding of it. It is important to point out again that these experiences and exposure to Western mass media do not lead to wholesale adoption of Western values. Like Peter the Great, foreign visitors like some of the things they see in the West and dislike others. They do not accept everything at face value, but when they return to their own countries, they share many of these Western ideas and practices with others and sometimes they adopt them (if there are no structural barriers to doing this, such as a communist economic system). But, taken as a whole, a Western education tends to promote better understanding and appreciation for the Western view — an observation also supported by the fact that many foreigners educated in the West often stay and get jobs in Western countries.

This "elite cognitive model" does a much better job at explaining how Western values are disseminated around the world. However, the impact of this social psychological theory should not be overestimated. Historically, in fact, one might argue that coercion has spread Western values much more thoroughly than indigenous acceptance. In modern times, colonialism was the economic tool for doing this. Great Britain, France, Spain and the United States, among other countries, colonized many indigenous peoples around the world. Yet, despite much resistence to the colonizers, when the colonizers pulled out their influence did not end there. Rather, many elements of Western culture and values were embedded in those countries' legal, social and economic systems. Most of the empires are now gone. But the structural ties and influence of the Western countries are still there, and the content of global media continues to help maintain and support those structures.

For example, remember the 1997 Asian economic crisis discussed in Chapter 5? Western economists placed the blame for the crisis squarely on those countries, and their allegedly anti-free-market practices (i.e., high protective tariffs, vertical integration of industries, nepotistic business practices, bribery, lack of competition). But as a condition for helping to bail out those Asian countries, the International Monetary Fund and Western countries did not ask elites or ordinary citizens to change their personal values about capitalism. Rather, the IMF and Western countries simply required those countries to change some aspects of the structure of their economic and political systems. In essence, the West was saying: "Implement our market reforms, or we won't give you economic aid."

Thus, the imposition of Western culture came not through changes in psychology but through changes in the social structure, and global media like CNN helped play a supporting role. Their news reports relied heavily on Western economic and political elite sources. Acting as a guard dog for Western values, the news reports helped reinforce and legitimate the Western diagnosis of the illness as well as the prescription for a cure. Although many of the Asian countries continue to resist taking the medicine (i.e., they have been slow to implement reforms), the long-term prognosis for such resistance is not good in a global competitive world. In short, the spread of Western values, especially capitalism, may be structurally imposed, and countries that fail to adopt such practices may find themselves alienated politically and economically (e.g., North Korea).

The argument that Western values are structurally imposed rather than culturally adopted can be seen as an extension of the work of three British sociologists who analyzed the Marxian claim that a capitalist ideology explains the stability and permanence of capitalism. Nicholas Abercrombie, Stephen Hill and Bryan S. Turner studied the subordinate and dominant classes in feudalism, early capitalism and late capitalism and concluded that in all three periods those classes had very different belief systems. The ruling classes subscribed to the ideas that supported the prevailing economic and political institutions, but, contrary to the Marxian model, the subordinate classes did not. Abercrombie, Hill and Turner argue that capitalism persists not because subordinate classes tacitly accept the dominant ideology, but because they are controlled by the "dull compulsion" of economic relationships, the integrative effects of the division of labor and the coercive nature of law and politics. Although Abercrombie, Hill and Turner reject the idea that ideology incorporates the lower classes, they argue that ideology does have significant effects on the dominant class. "What has been important for the stability of capitalism is the coherence of the dominant class itself, and ideology has played a major role in securing this," Hill writes.

But the impact of structural constraints and the extent to which global media influence traditional cultures also should not be overstated. Western culture and ideas are never fully incorporated. Traditional cultures do not easily pass into history. More accurately, they become overlaid with another sheet of structural and value complexity. The paradox of Western culture also is that many alternative groups and unorthodox cultures are able to survive and thrive in structurally differentiated societies. As mentioned earlier, part of the reason is increased tolerance for such groups. Representative democracies also place a high value on the diversity of ideas, which itself will help protect certain aspects of traditional culture and life.

Of course, the spread of Western ideas, however slow and incomplete, will not necessarily be perceived as a bad thing even by ordinary citizens in Western or indigenous cultures. In fact, for those who believe in the values of responsible capitalism, racial and gender equality, representative democracy, a diversity of ideas and religious tolerance, the new global media order will be more liberating than disabling. In contrast, for those who dislike commercialism, materialism, consumerism and commodification, the new global media order will be despised. But in either case, there is little doubt that over the long term Western values and ways of doing things will threaten traditional cultures.

Although the content of global media may help liberate some people and integrate many areas of the world, this doesn't mean global media content will automatically lead to less social conflict. In fact, global media have the potential to increase conflict, I believe, between some Western and Muslim cultures. Predictions are difficult here, to be sure. It is safe to say that most Muslim countries will continue to limit imports of Western media products and services. But clearly time is not on their side. Muslim media systems are, at this point, unable to compete on a global level, and some forms of technology (satellite transmission, cellular phones, fax machines) are making it more difficult for governments to control information within their borders. Perhaps even more important is the economic dependence (i.e., oil revenues) that many Muslim countries have on the Western world. That dependence is likely to keep the conflict between cultures low key for the time being. But should oil supplies dry up or Western demand for Middle East oil drop substantially, then Western control over global information may do little to ease the conflict. At this point, the safest prediction is that the ideas and values promoted in global media, as they permeate other cultures, will be changed and adopted to fit the needs of the host culture. Again, this should not be interpreted as a case of full-fledged hegemony, but rather as another level of complexity.

In short, the spread of Western values is facilitated by both ideology and social structure. In this respect, I am turning both the critical/cultural theorists and the traditional media effects scholars "on their heads."

Trend #7 — Increasing Knowledge Gaps

One likely consequence of the growth of global media systems will be increasing gaps in knowledge between nations and between individuals within nations. For critics and others who seek to reduce disparities in knowledge between peoples, this trend can be interpreted as having adverse consequences for developing countries.

The knowledge gap hypothesis was proposed in 1970 by University of Minnesota media sociologists Phillip J. Tichenor, George A. Donohue and Clarice N. Olien, who argued that

> *As the infusion of mass media information into a social system increases, segments of the population with higher socioeconomic status tend to acquire this information at a faster rate than the lower status segments, so that the gap in knowledge between these segments tends to increase rather than decrease.*

This hypothesis can be applied to individuals, groups or to nations. From a worldwide perspective, the argument is that the "information rich" countries (e.g., France, Great Britain, Japan, United States) are gaining more power and influence over the "information poor" countries (e.g., African and Latin American countries). The logic is straightforward: High-status people are better educated and have more resources to obtain and understand information.

The "Minnesota Team" tested their theory using longitudinal public opinion data on sending an astronaut to the moon and cigarette smoking. Prior to World War II, for example, most people, regardless of status, didn't believe it was possible to send a spaceship to the moon. However, as technology advanced and media began publishing reports that space travel was possible, the gaps in knowledge between high-status and low-status individuals widened. That's because high-status people were reading more and were talking about science more than low-status people. Similarly, as media began publishing more information linking cigarette smoking to cancer, high-status individuals acquired this information at a faster rate than low-status individuals.

Mass communication scholars Cecilie Gaziano, Kasisomayajula Viswanath and John R. Finnegan Jr., who have reviewed the literature on the knowledge gap hypothesis, generally find support for it. But aside from making information more readily available, there is little agreement on what can be done to reduce gaps. Even then, the problem isn't solved.

Take, for instance, the popular children's television show *Sesame Street*, which originated in the United States and is broadcast in many countries around the world. When first proposed in the 1960s, the goal was to help disadvantaged children living in inner-city areas catch up intellectually to their peers from the more affluent suburbs (e.g., to correct a knowledge gap). By the way, that's one of the reasons the show is filmed on a television set modeled after an urban neighborhood. Studies showed that the program boosted the verbal and math test scores of children from disadvantaged backgrounds. However, the program also boosted scores for children from advantaged backgrounds — even more. In fact, the knowledge gaps got even bigger. Why? Because parents of high-status children were giving their children more encouragement to watch the program, and were spending more time with them during the programming.

Because *Sesame Street* produces greater gaps in knowledge, should the program be discontinued? Similarly, should global news and information programming be halted because it produces knowledge gaps? Many people see this as throwing the baby out with bath water. Limiting information or access to it is clearly not the answer. And developing countries are caught in a bind, as mass communication Professor Chin-Chuan Lee points out:

For how long can the Third World reject modern communication technologies and their potential benefits? It is undesirable for them, on the one hand, not to enjoy the benefits of technology; continued resistance may widen the gap between them and the richer countries. It is more undesirable, on the other hand, that they have to tolerate a continued or heightened Western media hegemony and the concomitant cultural dependence. How to resolve this paradox while formulating a sound communication policy will undoubtedly be a blend of art and science.

Although there is no easy solution to the knowledge-gap problem, a good starting point, I would argue, is the "new communication strategy" adopted in 1989 by United Nations Educational, Scientific and Cultural Organization. That strategy, adopted by a consensus of its member states, has three major objectives: (1) to encourage the free flow of information at both national and international levels; (2) to promote a wider and more balanced dissemination of information, without any obstacle to freedom of expression; and (3) to strengthen the communication capacities of the developing countries, in particular through the International Programme for the Development of Communication. UNESCO Director-General Federico Mayor adds that

> *There can be no doubt that the future of the new democracies will depend in part on the development and strengthening of free, independent and pluralist media in both the public and private sectors, since the spread of knowledge and values is impossible without freedom of communication. The importance of this principle in democratic societies is undeniable: free communication enables ordinary citizens to express themselves and make their voices heard and, as a result, to influence the events that shape their daily lives.*

Conclusion

So, are global media a menace or a messiah? The primary goal of this book was to answer that question. And the answer, if it is not already clear, is that neither of these extreme typifications accurately captures the social consequences of global media and their content.

Global media, like all corporate media organizations, produce news and entertainment programming that in general supports the dominant values and social institutions in the societies they serve. This support occurs partly because corporate media depend heavily upon political and economic elites for news and upon advertisers for economic support. Global media also are constrained by Western values, laws and norms. They rarely promote radical ideas or radical change. Like the government, church and schools, global media play an important social control function — they provide information and entertainment programming that help social actors achieve their goals within the constraints of a neocapitalist economic system. This social control function is not a conspiracy, nor is it necessarily a nefarious thing. However, to the extent that people are unhappy with the dominant values or disagree with the decisions of social institutions, global media may themselves be seen as a menace.

At the same time, however, this book also argued and presented empirical data to show that, comparatively speaking, corporate and global media organizations have a greater capacity than previous forms of media organizations, such as entrepreneurial or owner-managed media, to criticize dominant values and institutions. This increased criticism is partly a function of the environment — corporate and global media are themselves a product of complex social systems, which contain more social groups and more social conflict. The increased criticism also is a function of the fact that corporate global news media organizations are more insulated from parochial national political pressures. They are controlled on a day-to-day basis by professional managers, who pursue not only profit goals but also nonprofit goals, including product quality.

One consequence of these changing structural conditions is an explosion in the diversity of ideas — especially ideas critical of corporate business, capitalism, and Western political elites and ideas. As noted in Chapters 7 and 9, this diversity helps explain many of the social changes that have taken place during the 20th century — changes that have, from time to time, benefited the poor and disadvantaged. At various times in history, these changes may have cooled down groups that might have sought revolutionary change. In short, corporate and global media can promote from time to time social change.

Finally, what do I think about all these trends? Quite frankly, I am not as worried about the future as most scholars. Many seem to be infected with what I call the "Chicken Little Syndrome" — the sky is always falling. They get a lot of attention, by the way, for trying to find the worst in media systems. And, admittedly, there is a lot to be found. Most journalists are sadly unaware of the extent to which their reports help justify and support political and economic systems that are often unjust and unfair. The same applies to producers of entertainment programming. I wish journalists and media producers could see how the content they produce socially constructs problems and reality. That awareness still wouldn't guarantee change in the system, because media are structurally dependent upon on advertisers, sources and consumers. However, I cannot buy into the argument so often expressed in the academy that "we're all going to hell in a handbasket." I think mainstream media systems are more responsive to the needs and problems of the disadvantaged and alternative groups today than ever before. And I think a more constructive approach is to increase the search for ways to make media systems more responsive. I hope this book has made a small contribution toward that goal.

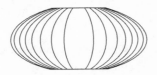

APPENDIX

WHAT IS THE CORPORATE FORM OF ORGANIZATION?

The notion that global media are advanced forms of what has been called the *corporate form of organization* can be traced to the famous German sociologist Max Weber.

Writing in the early part of the 20th century, Weber defined a corporate organization as a group controlled by an administrative staff engaged in a continuous purposive activity. Corporate organizations may or may not pursue economic profits, but they all establish and maintain boundaries for admission and continued membership. In other words, one must be hired or be allowed to join the group to become a member, and one is expected to abide by its rules. The rules are enforced either by a head or by an administrative staff.

Weber also distinguished between bureaucratic and nonbureaucratic corporate forms (a distinction that is no longer commonly recognized today because the broader term *corporate* has become synonymous or interchangeable with Weber's more restrictive concept of *bureaucracy*). A bureaucracy is a corporate organization in which behavior is goal-directed and decision-making is *rational*. By rational, he means that bureaucratic organizations try to reduce the production and distribution of goods or services into routines so as to find the most efficient and effective way to reach a goal. The reader can see that this use of the term *rational* is clearly different from the common sense meaning of "reasoning" or "reasonableness." The focus is on how to find the most efficient way to produce a product or service.

In addition to rationality, Weber argues that bureaucracies are characterized by a hierarchy of authority, employment and promotion based on technical qualifications, a set of rules and procedures that define job responsibilities and show how tasks are accomplished, formalistic impersonality and a highly developed division of labor and role specialization.

Weber pointed out that authority in a bureaucracy is vested in the position rather than in the individual. This minimizes the disruption that occurs when an individual leaves the organization. Selection for employment or promotion is based on technical competence or expertise rather than patronage or social position, and loyalties are given to the organization and its set of rules and procedures, not to individuals. In exchange, employees are given monetary compensation, promotions or other rewards. Interpersonal relations in bureaucracies are more impersonal than those in nonbureaucratic organizations, but Weber argued that such impersonality was necessary to efficiently accomplish the goals of the organization. In other words, when people are too close to or friendly with each other, this can interfere with job performance (e.g., too much socializing). Tasks in a bureaucracy are highly specialized and delegated to individuals who ultimately are accountable for their performance. Rules and regulations control and standardize behavior, enabling managers to control the actions of a large number of workers. And the division of labor and role specialization generate economies of scale and increase the productive capacity of the organization.

Although Weber believed bureaucratic organizations are very efficient, he did not see them as a panacea. He believed they tend to monopolize information, resist change and threaten individual freedom and democratic principles. Many critics of global media strongly agree. A number of empirical studies also have questioned the extent to which bureaucracies are rational or efficient. Others even argue that bureaucracies are self-destructive.

All these criticisms have some merit. Who among us hasn't experienced the coldness of bureaucratic red tape? Time, however, has demonstrated that despite these problems corporate organizations often are capable of adapting to changes in the environment, and they still remain the most effective and efficient way to coordinate the work of large numbers of people. In fact, no other organizational form has displaced the corporate form, and nearly all aspects of modern life are interpenetrated by it.

Employing a Weberian model, then, *a global medium may be defined as a transnational corporate organization that is characterized by (1) a highly complex hierarchy of authority, (2) a highly developed division of labor and role specialization, (3) a formalized set of rules and procedures, (4) employment and promotion based on performance and technical qualifications (e.g., professional managers make most of the decisions), (5) greater rationality (efficiency) in decision-making, and (6) more formal relations between workers or employees.* For comparison purposes, the opposite of the global or corporate form of media organization is the *entrepreneurial media organization,* which scores low on the six characteristics listed above and has operations in only one country. Although professionals and scholars often talk in terms of these dichotomies (corporate versus entrepreneurial, global versus nonglobal), in the real world these ideal types are better conceptualized on a continuum, in which all media organizations may be ranked as higher or lower than each other. Global media represent one extreme end of the continuum — they are the largest, most complex corporations in the mass communication industry. The smallest locally owned and managed country weekly newspapers anchor the other end of the continuum.

Corporate structure can be measured using many different indicators. This includes popular items like (a) whether a medium is owned by a chain or group; (b) whether a medium is publicly owned; (c) the number of media owned by a group; and (d) whether the medium is a legally incorporated business. All of these ownership items are seen as indicators of corporate structure, because they tend to correlate with organizational complexity. However, it is important to point out that these four items are not always good indicators, because they are very crude (all except item "c" are dichotomous) and do not do a good job of discriminating between highly complex organizations. For example, none of those measures, or even all four taken together, could discriminate between many small daily newspapers (which are often owned by a public chain that is legally incorporated) and a global media giant like Disney, but quite clearly their organizational forms are different.

Total sales can also be used as a measure of corporate structure, because it tends to be correlated with structural complexity. However, total sales is also a measure of demand, and as such is better if supplemented with other measures (the numbers correspond to the six items above) such as (1) number of promotions needed for reporter to become top editor; (2) number of full-time employees; number of full-time reporters and editors; number of beats or departments; (3) number of rules and procedures; (4) the amount of education or work experience required for various jobs; (5) amount of perceived importance top management places on "finding the most efficient way to solve problems"; (6) and the self-reported closeness that employees have to each other and their employer.

Although not all researchers accept this conceptual or operational framework, to date none has offered any alternative conceptualizations, and Weber's corporate structure approach continues to be the most sophisticated and advanced method for studying the impact of organizational structure in mass communication.

NOTES

Introduction

For data on media use, see pp. 6-7 in *Hoover's Guide to Media Companies* (Austin, TX: Hoover's Business Press, 1996).

The most widely recognized critic of corporate and global media is Noam Chomsky, a linguist at MIT who has spent much of the last quarter century criticizing U.S. media. Chomsky has almost developed a cult following. Even a film has been made about his ideas and theory of propaganda. See, e.g., Edward S. Herman and Noam Chomsky, *Manufacturing Consent: The Political Economy of the Mass Media* (New York: Pantheon Books, 1988).

My theory of corporate structure is formally laid out in David Pearce Demers, *The Menace of the Corporate Newspaper: Fact or Fiction?* (Ames: Iowa State University Press, 1996). A brief summary can be found in David Demers, "Corporate Newspaper Bashing: Is It Justified?" *Newspaper Research Journal* (in press). Also see David Demers, "Corporate News Structure, Social Control and Social Change," pp. 375-398 in David Demers and K. Viswanath (eds.), *Mass Media, Social Control and Social Change: A Macrosocial Perspective* (Ames: Iowa State University Press, 1999).

180 NOTES

Chapter 1 — The Good, the Bad and the Global

Brief economic histories of The Walt Disney Company can be found in Richard A. Gershon, *The Transnational Media Corporation* (Mahwah, NJ: Lawrence Erlbaum Associates, 1997); Edward S. Herman and Robert W. McChesney, *The Global Media: The New Missionaries of Corporate Capitalism* (London: Cassell, 1997); and *Hoover's Guide to Media Companies* (Austin, TX: Hoover's Business Press, 1996). For a biography of Walt Disney, see Leonard Losley, *Disney's World: A Biography* (Chelsea, MI: Scarborough House, 1990). Also of interest: Alan Bryman, *Disney and His Worlds* (London: Routledge, 1995) and Ron Grover, *The Disney Touch: How a Daring Management Team Revived an Entertainment Empire* (Homewood, IL: Business One Irwin, 1991).

The *Newsweek* quote is taken from "Of Mice and Men," *Newsweek* (September 5, 1994), p. 41.

The McChesney quote is from Robert W. McChesney, "The Global Media Giants: The Nine Firms that Dominate the World," *Extra, 10*(6), (November/December 1997), p. 11.

The most vocal critics of corporate structure include C. Edwin Baker, *Ownership of Newspapers: The View from Positivist Social Science,* (Cambridge, MA: The Joan Shorenstein Center, Harvard University, September 1994); Jean Baudrillard, "The Masses: The Implosion of the Social in the Media," *New Literary History, 16*:577-589 (1995); Edward S. Herman, "Media in the U.S. Political Economy, pp. 75-87 in J. Downing, A. Mohammadi, and A. Sreberny-Mohammadi (eds.), *Questioning the Media: A Critical Introduction* (Newbury Park, CA: Sage, 1990); Edward S. Herman, "Diversity of News: Marginalizing the Opposition,"*Journal of Communication, 35*(3):135-146 (1985); Edward S. Herman and Noam Chomsky,*Manufacturing Consent: The Political Economy of the Mass Media* (New York: Pantheon Books, 1988); Edward S. Herman and Robert W. McChesney, *The Global Media: The New Missionaries of Corporate Capitalism* (London: Cassell, 1997); Douglas Kellner, *Television and the Crisis of Democracy* (Boulder: Westview Press, 1990); Herbert Marcuse, *One-Dimensional Man* (Boston: Beacon Press, 1964); Robert W. McChesney, *Corporate Media and the Threat to Democracy* (New York: Seven Stories Press, 1997); John H. McManus, *Market-Driven Journalism: Let the Citizen Beware* (Thousand Oaks, CA: Sage, 1994); Graham Murdock and Peter Golding, "Capitalism, Communication and Class Relations, pp. 12-43 in J. Curran, M. Gurevitch and J. Woollacott (eds.), *Mass Communication and Society* (London: Edward Arnold, 1977); Graham Murdock and Peter Golding, "For a Political Economy of Mass Communication, *The Socialist Register,* 205-234 (1973); and Herbert I. Schiller, *Culture, Inc.* (New York: Oxford University Press, 1989).

The Gershon quote is from Richard A. Gershon, *The Transnational Media Corporation* (Mahwah, NJ: Lawrence Erlbaum Associates, 1997), pp. 215-216.

The quote from Time Warner CEO Gerald M. Levin is taken from a corporate statement posted on the company's World Wide Web page <www.timewarner.com>.

Chapter 2 — The World Is Shrinking

This historical review was synthesized from a number of sources, including Warren K. Agee, Phillip H. Ault and Edwin Emery, *Introduction to Mass Communications*, 9th ed. (New York: Harper and Row, 1988); Shirley Biagi, *Media/Impact: An Introduction to Mass Media*, 2nd ed. (Belmont, CA: Wadsworth, 1994); James Burke, "Communication in the Middle Ages," pp. 80-89 in David Crowley and Paul Heyer (eds.), *Communication in History: Technology, Culture, Society*, 2nd. ed. (White Plains, NY: Longman, 1995); T. F. Carter, "Paper and Block Printing — From China to Europe," pp. 94-105 in David Crowley and Paul Heyer (eds.), *Communication in History: Technology, Culture, Society*, 2nd. ed. (White Plains, NY: Longman, 1995); Warren Chappell, *A Short History of the Printed Word* (Boston: Nonpareil Books, 1970); Melvin DeFleur and Sandra Ball-Rokeach, *Theories of Mass Communication*, 5th ed. (New York: Longman, 1989); Melvin L. DeFleur and Everette E. Dennis, *Understanding Mass Communication: A Liberal Arts Perspective* (Boston: Houghton Mifflin, 1996); Joseph R. Dominick, *The Dynamics of Mass Communication*, 5th ed. (New York: McGraw-Hill, 1996); Michael Emery and Edwin Emery, *The Press in America*, 6th ed. (Englewood Cliffs, NJ: Prentice-Hall, 1988); Robert S. Fortner, *International Communication: History, Conflict, and Control of the Global Metropolis* (Belmont, CA: Wadsworth, 1993); Richard A. Gershon, *The Transnational Media Corporation* (Mahwah, NJ: Lawrence Erlbaum Associates, 1997); Harvey J. Graff, "Early Modern Literacies," pp. 125-135 in David Crowley and Paul Heyer (eds.), *Communication in History: Technology, Culture, Society*, 2nd. ed. (White Plains, NY: Longman, 1995); Edward S. Herman and Robert W. McChesney, *The Global Media: The New Missionaries of Corporate Capitalism* (London: Cassell, 1997); Ray Eldon Hiebert, Donald F. Ungurait and Thomas W. Bohn, *Mass Media II: An Introduction to Modern Communication* (New York: Longman, 1979); Alexander Marshack, "The Art and Symbols of Ice Age Man," pp. 10-20 in David Crowley and Paul Heyer (eds.), *Communication in History: Technology, Culture, Society*, 2nd. ed. (White Plains, NY: Longman, 1995); John C. Merrill, *Global Journalism: A Survey of the World's Mass Media* (New York: Longman, 1983); Wilbur Schramm, *Mass Media and National Development: The Role of Information in the Developing Countries* (Stanford, CA, and Paris: Stanford University Press and UNESCO, 1964); Anthony Smith, *The Newspaper: An International History* (London: Thames and Hudson, 1979); James Watson and Anne Hill, *A Dictionary of Communication and Media Studies* (London: Edward Arnold, 1993); Stan Le Roy Wilson, *Mass Media/Mass Culture: An Introduction* (New York: Random House, 1989); and John Vivian, *The Media of Mass Communication*, 3rd ed. (Boston: Allyn and Bacon, 1995).

Also see the history of the corporate form of organization in the U.S. newspaper industry in Chapter 2 of David Pearce Demers, *The Menace of the Corporate Newspaper: Fact or Fiction?* (Ames: Iowa State University Press, 1996).

Robert McChesney, "The Political Economy of Global Communication," pp. 1-26 in Robert W. McChesney, Ellen Meiksins Wood and John Bellamy Foster (eds.),

Capitalism and the Information Age: The Political Economy of the Global Communication Revolution (New York: Monthly Review Press, 1998), p. 12.

The material from Weber is summarized from two sources: Max Weber, *The Theory of Social and Economic Organization*, trans. A. M. Henderson and Talcott Parsons (New York: The Free Press, 1964 [1947]), pp. 329-339, and H. H. Gerth and C. Wright Mills (eds.), *From Max Weber* (New York: Oxford University Press, 1946), pp. 196-198 and pp. 204-209.

The direct quote from Weber is from Gerth and Mills, *From Max Weber*, p. 215.

Chapter 3 — The Global Media Playing Field

Much of the data on the global media corporations was obtained from their web sites. Recent histories of global media also can be found in Richard A. Gershon, *The Transnational Media Corporation* (Mahwah, NJ: Lawrence Erlbaum Associates, 1997); Edward S. Herman and Robert W. McChesney, *The Global Media: The New Missionaries of Corporate Capitalism* (London: Cassell, 1997); Emma Duncan, "The Technology and Entertainment Survey," *The Economist* (November 21, 1998), pp. 3-18; *Hoover's Guide to Media Companies* (Austin, TX: Hoover's Business Press, 1996).

Also see Annabelle Sreberny-Mohammadi, Dwayne Winseck, Jim McKenna and Oliver Boyd-Barrett (eds.), *Media in Global Context: A Reader* (London: Arnold, 1997); Elizabeth Bell, Lynda Haas, and Laura Sells (eds.), *From Mouse to Mermaid: The Politics of Film, Gender, and Culture* (Bloomington, IN: Indiana University Press, 1995); James Lull, *Media, Communication, Culture* (New York: Columbia University Press, 1995); Nicholas Garnham, *Capitalism and Communication: Global Culture and the Economics of Information* (London: Sage, 1990); Philip M. Taylor, *Global Communications, International Affairs and the Media Since 1945* (London: Routledge, 1997); George Gerbner, Hamid Mowlana and Kaarle Nordenstreng (eds.), *The Global Media Debate: Its Rise, Fall, and Renewal* (Norwood, NJ: Ablex, 1993); William A. Hachten, *The World News Prism*, 4th ed. (Ames: Iowa State University Press, 1996); Hamid Mowlana, *Global Communication in Transition: The End of Diversity?* (Thousand Oaks, CA: Sage, 1996); and Ali Mohammadi (ed.), *International Communication and Globalization: A Critical Reader* (London: Sage, 1997).

Chapter 4 — The Paradox of Capitalism

For data on competition, mergers, consolidations and acquisitions, see Alan B. Albarran and Sylvia M. Chan-Olmsted, *Global Media Economics: Commercialization, Concentration and Integration of World Media Markets* (Ames: Iowa State University Press, 1998); Alison Alexander, James Owers and Rod Carveth (eds.), *Media Economics: Theory and Practices* (Hillsdale, NJ: Lawrence Erlbaum Associates, 1993); Richard A. Gershon, *The Transnational Media Corporation* (Mahwah, NJ: Lawrence Erlbaum Associates, 1997); Edward S. Herman and Robert W. McChesney, *The Global Media: The New Missionaries of*

Corporate Capitalism (London: Cassell, 1997); *Hoover's Guide to Media Companies* (Austin, Texas: Hoover's Business Press, 1996); Gary W. Ozanich and Michael O. Wirth, "Mergers and Acquisitions: A Communications Industry Overview," pp. 95-107 in Alison Alexander, James Owers and Rod Carveth (eds.), *Media Economics: Theory and Practices* (Hillsdale, NJ: Lawrence Erlbaum Associates, 1993); and Nancy J. Woodhull and Robert W. Snyder (eds.), *Media Mergers* (New Brunswick, NJ: Transaction Publishers, 1998).

Smith's ideas are contained in Adam Smith, *An Inquiry Into the Nature and Causes of the Wealth of Nations* (Buffalo, NY: Prometheus Books, 1991[1776]). The quote from Smith is taken from page 10. Also see W. A. Eltis, "Adam Smith's Theory of Economic Growth," in Andrew S. Skinner and Thomas Wilson (eds.), *Essays on Adam Smith* (Oxford: Clarendon Press, 1975).

Marx's theory is in Karl Marx, *Capital: A Critique of Political Economy*, Vols. 1-3, trans. by Samuel Moore and Edward Aveling (New York: International Publishers, 1987). The quote from Marx is taken from page 586. Also see Karl Marx, "Economic and Philosophic Manuscripts of 1844," pp. 66-125 in Robert C. Tucker (ed.), *The Marx-Engels Reader*, 2nd ed. (New York: W. W. Norton & Company, 1978).

The McChesney quote is from Robert McChesney, "The Political Economy of Global Communication," pp. 1-26 in Robert W. McChesney, Ellen Meiksins Wood and John Bellamy Foster (eds.), *Capitalism and the Information Age: The Political Economy of the Global Communication Revolution* (New York: Monthly Review Press, 1998), p. 14.

Chapter 5 — The Global Media Village

The War of 1812 illustration was inspired by Ben Bagdikian, *The Information Machines: Their Impact on Men and Media* (New York: Harper Colophon, 1971), pp. 28-45.

Steven Livingston, "Beyond the 'CNN Effect': The Media-Foreign Policy Dynamic," pp. 291-318 in Pippa Norris (ed.), *Politics and the Press: The News Media and Their Influences* (Boulder: Lynne Rienner, 1997).

Much of the material in this chapter is drawn from my personal conversations with media economists and from masked reviews of my work submitted to *Journal of Media Economics* (e.g., David Demers, "Revisiting Corporate Newspaper Structure and Profit-Making," *Journal of Media Economics*, 11(2):19-35 [1998]; David Pearce Demers, "Corporate Newspaper Structure, Profits and Organizational Goals," *The Journal of Media Economics*, 9(2):1-23 [1996]). Free-market media economists are baffled with the neo-Marxist argument that higher profits means lower quality or less diversity. To them (the economists), higher profits mean more resources to improve the media product. A good summary of the free-market position can be found in Richard A. Gershon, *The Transnational Media Corporation* (Mahwah, NJ: Lawrence Erlbaum Associates, 1997).

Marshall McLuhan's arguments are outlined in *Understanding Media: The Extensions of Man* (New York: McGraw-Hill, 1964) and *The Gutenberg Galaxy: The Making of Typographic Man* (Toronto: University of Toronto Press, 1967). McLuhan's writing is often turgid. A rather interesting introduction is provided by W. Terrence Gordon, *McLuhan for Beginners* (London: Writers and Readers, 1997).

The quote from James Grunig comes from "Turning McLuhan on His Head," pp. 3-20 in James Grunig (ed.), *Decline of the Global Village: How Specialization Is Changing the Mass Media* (New York: General Hall, 1976), p. 17.

Herbert J. Gans, *Deciding What's News* (New York: Vintage, 1979).

Gerald M. Levin's quote is taken from a corporate statement posed on the Time Warner's World Wide Web page <www.timewarner.com>.

The Murdoch quote is from Cherian George, "Do Not Fear Me, Says Murdoch," *The* (Singapore) *Straits Times* (January 13, 1999), p. 31.

Quote from Truett is taken from John Naisbitt and Patricia Aburdene, *Megatrends 2000* (New York: Avon, 1990), p. 136.

The quote from Richard A. Gershon is from *The Transnational Media Corporation* (Mahwah, NJ: Lawrence Erlbaum Associates, 1997), p. 30.

The final quote is from Anne Wells Branscomb, "Megamedia Moguls and Multimedia Madness," pp. 163-172 in Nancy J. Woodhull and Robert W. Snyder (eds.), *Media Mergers* (New Brunswick: Transaction Publishers, 1998), pp. 170-171.

Chapter 6 — The Global Media Critics

Quotes are from the following sources, respectively:

Robert W. McChesney, "The Political Economy of Global Communication," pp. 1-26 in Robert W. McChesney, Ellen Meiksins Wood and John Bellamy Foster (eds.), *Capitalism and the Information Age: The Political Economy of the Global Communication Revolution* (New York: Monthly Review Press, 1998), pp. 15-16.

Norman Solomon, "Corporations Growing Threat to Media Diversity," *The* (Eugene, OR) *Register-Guard* (October 19, 1997), p. 4F.

Ben Bagdikian, "Lords of the Global Village," *The Nation* (June 12, 1989), p. 807.

Annabelle Sreberny-Mohammadi, Dwayne Winseck, Jim McKenna and Oliver Boyd-Barrett, *Media in Global Context: A Reader* (London: Arnold), pp. xx.

Edward S. Herman and Noam Chomsky, *Manufacturing Consent: The Political Economy of the Mass Media* (New York: Pantheon Books, 1988), p. 306.

Nicholas Garnham, *Capitalism and Communication: Global Culture and the Economics of Information* (London: Sage, 1990), p. 121.

Herbert I. Schiller, *Culture, Inc.* (New York: Oxford University Press, 1989), p. 128.

A formal definition of corporate structure is presented in the "Introduction" and in the "Appendix."

William Allen White, (Editorial), *Emporia* (Kansas) *Gazette* (December 23, 1925).

Oswald Garrison Villard, "The Press Today: The Chain Daily," *The Nation* (May 21, 1930), pp. 597-598.

George Seldes, *Lords of the Press* (New York: J. Messner, 1938).

Commission on Freedom of the Press, *A Free and Responsible Press* (Chicago: University of Chicago Press, 1947), pp. 67-68.

Robert W. McChesney, *Corporate Media and the Threat to Democracy* (New York: Seven Stories Press, 1997), pp. 6-7.

The Holmes quote is from *Abrams v. United States*, 250 U.S. 616 (1919).

Ben H. Bagdikian, *The Media Monopoly*, 2nd ed. (Boston: Beacon Press, 1987), p. x.

Anthony Smith, *The Age of Behemoths: The Globalization of Mass Media Firms* (New York: Priority Press Publications, 1991), p. 71.

In 1997, 43 percent of all Americans owned stock in U.S. companies either directly or indirectly through mutual funds. The figures are lower in other Western countries: 25 percent in Britain, 16 percent in France, 10 percent in Italy, and six percent in Germany. Source: John Tagliabue, "Selling Europe on the Stock Market," *New York Times* (March 1, 1998), Section 3, p. 1.

Todd Gitlin, "Eye on the Media: Publishing Deal Can't be Good for Readers," *Newsday* (March 27, 1998), p. A53.

Peter Golding, "Global Village or Cultural Pillage? The Unequal Inheritance of the Communications Revolution," pp. 69-86 in Robert W. McChesney, Ellen Meiksins Wood and John Bellamy Foster (eds.), *Capitalism and the Information Age: The Political Economy of the Global Communication Revolution* (New York: Monthly Review Press, 1998), pp. 84-85.

Edward Herman, "Media in the U.S. Political Economy," pp. 75-87 in John Downing, Ali Mohammadi and Annabelle Sreberny-Mohammadi (eds.), *Questioning the Media: A Critical Introduction* (Newbury Park, CA: Sage, 1990), p. 79.

Howard Kurtz, "ABC Kills Story Critical of Owner Disney: Official Denies Corporate Link Influenced Decision," *Washington Post* (October 14, 1998), p. C01.

Paul M. Hirsch and Tracy A. Thompson, "The Stock Market as Audience: The Impact of Public Ownership on Newspapers," pp. 142-58 in James S. Ettema and D. Charles Whitney (eds.), *Audiencemaking: How the Media Create the Audience* (Thousand Oaks, CA: Sage, 1994), pp. 145-150.

For a summary of the community involvement debate, see David Pearce Demers, *The Menace of the Corporate Newspaper: Fact or Fiction?* (Ames: Iowa State University Press, 1996), pp. 228-229.

The full citation of the book titles are as follows: Doug Underwood, *When MBAs Rule the Newsroom: How the Marketers and Managers Are Reshaping Today's Media* (New York: Columbia University Press, 1993); James D. Squires, *Read All About It! The Corporate Takeover of America's Newspapers* (New York: Times Books, 1994); Dennis W. Mazzocco, *Networks of Power: Corporate TV's Threat to Democracy* (Boston: South End Press, 1994); Andrew Kreig, *Spiked: How Chain Management Corrupted America's Oldest Newspaper* (Old Saybrook, CT: Peregrine Press, 1987); and Richard McCord, *The Chain Gang: One Newspaper Versus the Gannett Empire* (Columbia: University of Missouri Press, 1996).

Some additional examples of case studies or anecdotes that support the critical model can be found in Ben H. Bagdikian, "Conglomeration, Concentration, and the Media," *Journal of Communication*, 30(2):59-64 (1980); Ben H. Bagdikian, *The Media*

Monopoly, 2nd ed. (Boston: Beacon Press, 1987); Douglas Kellner, *Television and the Crisis of Democracy* (Boulder: Westview Press, 1990); John H. McManus, *Market-Driven Journalism: Let the Citizen Beware?* (Thousand Oaks, CA: Sage, 1994); John Soloski, "Economics and Management: The Real Influence of Newspaper Groups," *Newspaper Research Journal*, 1:19-28 (1979); and Herbert I. Schiller, *Culture Inc.: The Corporate Takeover of Public Expression* (New York: Oxford University Press, 1989).

Peter Golding, "The Missing Dimensions — News Media and the Management of Social Change," pp. 63-81 in Elihu Katz and Tamás Szecskö, *Mass Media and Social Change* (Beverly Hills, CA: Sage, 1981), p. 80.

Celeste Condit, "The Rhetorical Limits of Polysemy," *Critical Studies in Mass Communication*, 6:103-122 (1994), p. 116.

Marc Raboy and Bernard Dagenais, "Introduction: Media and the Politics of Crisis," pp. 1-15 in Marc Raboy and Bernard Dagenais (eds.), *Media, Crisis and Democracy: Mass Communication and the Disruption of Social Order* (London: Sage, 1992), pp. 3-4.

William A. Gamson, "Constructing Social Protest," pp. 228-244 in Steven M. Buechler and F. Kurt Cylke, Jr., *Social Movements: Perspectives and Issues*, (Mountain View, CA: Mayfield Publishing, 1997), p. 242.

Michael Parenti, "Methods of Media Manipulation," pp. 27-31 in Carl Jensen (ed.), *20 Years of Censored News* (New York: Seven Stories Press, 1997), pp. 27-28.

Theodore Adorno and Max Horkeimer, "The Culture Industry: Enlightenment as Mass Deception," pp. 349-383 in James Curran, Michael Gurevitch and Janet Woollacott, *Mass Communication and Society* (Beverly Hills, CA: Sage, 1977), p. 36.

Chin-Chuan Lee, *Media Imperialism Reconsidered* (Beverly Hills, CA: Sage, 1980), p. 176. The extended quote is from Lee, *Media Imperialism Reconsidered*, p. 178.

Ariel Dorfman and Armand Mattelart, *How To Read Donald Duck: Imperialist Ideology in the Disney Comic* (New York: International General, 1975), p. 95.

Kim Christian Schrøder and Michael Skovmand, "Introduction," pp. 1-14 in Michael Skovmand and Kim Christian Schrøder, *Media Cultures: Reappraising Transnational Media* (London: Routledge, 1992), pp. 5-6.

William A. Hachten, *The World News Prism*, 4th ed. (Ames: Iowa State University Press, 1996), p. 86.

Garrett W. Ray, "Concentration of Mass Media Ownership," pp. 189-205 in Wm. David Sloan and Emily Erickson Hoff (eds.), *Contemporary Media Issues* (Northport, AL: Vision Press, 1998).

Golding, "Global Village or Cultural Pillage?"

Dennis W. Mazzocco, *Networks of Power: Corporate TV's Threat to Democracy* (Boston: South End Press, 1994).

Edward S. Herman and Robert W. McChesney, *The Global Media: The New Missionaries of Corporate Capitalism* (London: Cassell, 1997), p. 205.

Chapter 7 — Are the Critics Right?

The incident described in the introduction to this chapter occurred in the mid-1990s. The quote from Mowlana is from his book, *Global Communication in Transition: The End of Diversity?* (Thousand Oaks, CA: Sage, 1996), pp. 212-213. Later, he follows it up with the statement: "We should not be deceived by an illusion of the diversity of the subject matter and the vastness of the literature. We need to concentrate on promoting the diversity of cultural views and our ability to make the field more interesting and challenging by exploring new avenues and voices of knowledge." He appears to be arguing that diversity is increasing in relative terms but that even more critical research is needed.

The theory of diversity offered here is based on sociological research and theory that extends back to the 19th century. For an extended discussion, see David Pearce Demers, *The Menace of the Corporate Newspaper: Fact or Fiction?* (Ames: Iowa State University Press, 1996).

Research by W. James Potter, Roger Cooper and Michel Dupagne, "The Three Paradigms of Mass Media Research in Mainstream Communication Journals," *Communication Theory, 3*:317-335 (1993), suggests mainstream social science research continues to dominate in the field of communication. However, neo-Marxist and cultural scholarship makes up about a third of the total amount of research published in major communication journals.

The finding that media in small communities tend to eschew conflict is documented in a number of studies, including Morris Janowitz, *Community Press in an Urban Setting,* 2nd ed. (Chicago: University of Chicago Press, 1967 [1952]); Phillip J. Tichenor, George A. Donohue and Clarice N. Olien, *Community Conflict and The Press* (Beverly Hills, CA: Sage, 1980); and Arthur J. Vidich and Joseph Bensman, *Small Town in Mass Society* (Princeton, NJ: Princeton University Press, 1968).

Lars Willnat, Zhou Hje and Hao Xiaoming, "Foreign Media Exposure and Perceptions of Americans in Hong Kong, Shenzhen, and Singapore," *Journalism & Mass Communication Quarterly, 74*:738-756 (1998), pp. 738-739.

Michael B. Salwen, "Cultural Imperialism: A Media Effects Approach," *Critical Studies in Mass Communication, 8*:29-38 (1991), p. 36.

Michel Elasmar and John Hunter, "The Impact of Foreign TV on a Domestic Audience: A Meta-Analysis," pp. 47-69 in *Communication Yearbook,* Vol. 20 (Thousand Oaks, CA: Sage, 1997), p. 64.

Alexis S. Tan, Gerdean K. Tan and Alma S. Tan, "American TV in the Philippines: A Test of Cultural Impact," *Journalism Quarterly, 64*:65-72, 144 (1987).

Gerald Stone, *Examining Newspapers: What Research Reveals About America's Newspapers* (Newbury Park, CA: Sage, 1987), pp. 103-104.

My research on the corporate newspaper is reported in the following sources: David Pearce Demers, *The Menace of the Corporate Newspaper: Fact or Fiction?* (Ames: Iowa State

University Press, 1996); David Demers, "Corporate Newspaper Structure, Social Control and Social Change," pp. 375-398 in David Demers and K. Viswanath (eds.), *Mass Media, Social Control and Social Change: A Macrosocial Perspective* (Ames: Iowa State University Press, 1999); David Demers, "Corporate Newspaper Bashing: Is It Justified?" *Newspaper Research Journal* (in press); David Demers, "Structural Pluralism, Corporate Newspaper Structure and News Source Perceptions: Another Test of the Editor Vigor Hypothesis," *Journalism & Mass Communication Quarterly, 75*:572-592 (1998); David Pearce Demers, "Corporate Newspaper Structure, Profits and Organizational Goals," *The Journal of Media Economics, 9*(2):1-23 (1996); David Demers, "Revisiting Corporate Newspaper Structure and Profit-Making," *Journal of Media Economics, 11*(2):19-35 (1998); David Pearce Demers, "Corporate Newspaper Structure, Editorial Page Vigor and Social Change. *Journalism & Mass Communication Quarterly, 73*:857-877 (1996); David Pearce Demers, "Use of Polls in Reporting Changes Slightly Since 1978," *Journalism Quarterly, 64*:839-842 (1987); David Pearce Demers, "Corporate Structure and Emphasis on Profits and Product Quality at U.S. Daily Newspapers," *Journalism Quarterly, 68*:15-26 (1991); David Pearce Demers, "Effect of Corporate Structure on Autonomy of Top Editors at U.S. Dailies," *Journalism Quarterly, 70*:499-508 (1993); David Pearce Demers, "The Relative Constancy Hypothesis, Structural Pluralism and National Advertising Expenditures," *Journal of Media Economics, 7*(4):31-48 (1994); David Pearce Demers, "Structural Pluralism, Intermedia Competition and the Growth of the Corporate Newspaper in the United States," *Journalism Monographs,* Vol. 145 (June 1994); David Pearce Demers, "Does Personal Experience in a Community Increase or Decrease Newspaper Reading?" *Journalism Quarterly, 73*:304-318 (1996); and David Pearce Demers and Daniel B. Wackman, "Effect of Chain Ownership on Newspaper Management Goals," *Newspaper Research Journal, 9*(2):59-68 (1988).

Research on job satisfaction can be found in David H. Weaver and G. Cleveland Wilhoit, *The American Journalists: A Portrait of U.S. News People and Their Work* (Bloomington: Indiana University Press, 1986) and G. Cleveland Wilhoit and David Weaver, "U.S. Journalists at Work, 1971-1992," paper presented to the Association for Education in Journalism and Mass Communication (Atlanta, August 1994).

Support for the claim that journalists are more satisfied with their jobs can be found in David Pearce Demers, "Effect of Organizational Size on Job Satisfaction of Top Editors at U.S. Dailies," *Journalism Quarterly, 71*:914-925 (1994) and David Pearce Demers, "Autonomy, Satisfaction High Among Corporate News Staffs," *Newspaper Research Journal, 16*(2), 91-111 (1995).

The Frank A. Munsey story is summarized in Jean Folkerts and Dwight L. Teeter, Jr., *Voices of a Nation: A History of the Media in the United States.* (New York: Macmillan, 1989).

James Lull, *Media, Communication Culture: A Global Approach* (New York: Columbia University Press, 1995). The first quote is from page 166 and the second from page 167.

The managerial revolution is discussed in a number of works, including Daniel Bell, *The Coming of the Post-Industrial Society* (New York: Basic Books, 1976 [1973]); Adolf A. Berle, Jr. and Gardiner C. Means, *The Modern Corporation and Private Property* (New York:

Macmillan, 1932); James Burnham, *The Managerial Revolution* (New York: John Day, 1941); and John Kenneth Galbraith, *The New Industrial State*, 3rd ed. (New York: Mentor, 1978). Also see David Demers and Debra Merskin, "Corporate Newspaper Structure and Control of Editorial Content: An Empirical Test of the Managerial Revolution Hypothesis," paper presented at the annual meeting of the Association for Education in Journalism and Mass Communication, Chicago (July/August 1997).

David Demers, "Media Executive Pay: It's Size, Not Performance, that Counts," *Global Media News*, *1*(1):3-6 (1999), p. 6.

William B. Blankenburg, "Newspaper Scale and Newspaper Expenditures," *Newspaper Research Journal*, *10*(2):97-103 (1989).

William B. Blankenburg and Gary W. Ozanich, "The Effect of Public Ownership on the Financial Performance of Newspaper Corporations," *Journalism Quarterly*, 70:68-75 (1993).

Chapter 8 — Global Media and Social Control

L. Brent Bozell III and Brent H. Baker (eds.), *And That's The Way It Is(n't): A Reference Guide to Media Bias* (Alexandria, VA: Media Research Center, 1990), quoted material is from the book's back cover.

Jeff Cohen and Norman Solomon, *Through the Media Looking Glass: Decoding Bias and Blather in the News* (Monroe, ME: Common Courage Press, 1995), p. 22.

Journalists often argue that they try to be "fair" rather than "objective," the former arising in part from problems in trying to define the latter. Presumably this means that one does not have to give all sides equal weight in a story, as would be required under the ethic of objectivity. However, journalists have never satisfactorily defined fairness and how it differs from objectivity. For more on this topic, see, e.g., The Freedom Forum Media Studies Center, "The Fairness Factor," *Media Studies Journal*, *6*(4), (Fall 1992).

Former ABC News President James Hagerty, quoted in Edith Efron, "Do the Networks Know What They Are Doing?" pp. 133-149 in David J. Leroy and Christopher H. Sterling (eds.), *Mass News: Practices, Controversies and Alternatives* (Englewood Cliffs, NJ: Prentice-Hall, 1973), p. 134.

Herbert J. Gans, "Deciding What's News," *Columbia Journalism Review* (January/February 1979), pp. 40-45.

The citations for the studies cited in this review of the literature on social control are in David Pearce Demers, *The Menace of the Corporate Newspaper: Fact or Fiction?* (Ames: Iowa State University Press, 1996), pp. 109-114. Evidence backing up the proposition that mass media support the dominant power groups and value systems can be found in numerous studies, including Karen E. Altman, "Consuming Ideology: The Better Homes in America Campaign," *Critical Studies in Mass Communication*, 7:286-307 (1990); J. Herbert Altschull, *Agents of Power* (New York: Longman, 1984); W. Lance Bennett, *News: The Politics of Illusion*, 2nd ed. (New York: Longman, 1988); Robert Cirino, *Power to Persuade*

(New York: Bantam Books, 1974); Stanley Cohen and Jock Young (eds.), *The Manufacture of News* (London: Constable, 1981); Edward Jay Epstein, *News From Nowhere* (New York: Random House, 1973); Stuart Ewin, *Captains of Consciousness: Advertising and the Social Roots of the Consumer Culture* (New York: McGraw Hill, 1976); Mark Fishman, *Manufacturing the News* (Austin: University of Texas Press, 1980); Edward S. Herman and Noam Chomsky, *Manufacturing Consent: The Political Economy of the Mass Media* (New York: Pantheon, 1988); Doris A. Graber, *Mass Media and American Politics*, 3rd ed. (Washington, D.C.: Congressional Quarterly Press, 1989); Herbert J. Gans, *Deciding What's News* (New York: Vintage, 1979); Todd Gitlin, *The Whole World Is Watching* (Berkeley: University of California Press, 1980); Harvey Molotch and Marilyn Lester, "Accidental News: The Great Oil Spill as Local Occurrence and National Event," *American Journal of Sociology*, *81*:235-260 (1975); Harvey Molotch and Marilyn Lester, "News as Purposive Behavior," *American Sociological Review*, *81*:235-260 (1974); David L. Paletz and Robert M. Entman, *Media Power Politics* (New York: The Free Press, 1981); David L. Paletz, Peggy Reichert and Barbara McIntyre, "How the Media Support Local Government Authority," *Public Opinion Quarterly*, *35*:80-92 (1971); Fred Powledge, *The Engineering of Restraint* (Washington, D.C.: Public Affairs Press, 1971); Leon Sigal, *Reporters and Officials* (Lexington, MA: Heath, 1973); Lawrence C. Soley, "Pundits in Print: 'Experts' and Their Use in Newspaper Stories," *Newspaper Research Journal*, *15*(2):65-75 (1994); Phillip J. Tichenor, George A. Donohue and Clarice N. Olien, *Community Conflict and the Press* (Beverly Hills, CA: Sage, 1980); and Jeremy Tunstall, *Journalists at Work* (London: The Anchor Press, 1971).

Dan Schiller, "An Historical Approach to Objectivity and Professionalism in American News Reporting," *Journal of Communication*, *29*(4):46-57 (1979), p. 47.

Michael Schudson, *Discovering the News* (New York: Basic Books, 1978).

A good early history of the newspaper can be found in Sidney Kobre, "The First American Newspaper: A Product of Environment," *Journalism Quarterly*, *17*:335-345 (1940), p. 335.

Chapter 9 — Global Media and Social Change

Bob Woodward and Carl Bernstein of *The Washington Post*, the two reporters who played the most important role in digging out the Watergate story, helped the *Post* win a Pulitzer Prize for investigative reporting.

George A. Donohue, Phillip J. Tichenor and Clarice N. Olien, "A Guard Dog Perspective on the Role of Media," *Journal of Communication*, *45*(2):115-132 (1995).

Quoted material is from James S. Ettema and Theodore L. Glasser, "Narrative Form and Moral Force: The Realization of Innocence and Guilt Through Investigative Journalism," *Journal of Communication*, *38*(3):8-26 (Summer 1988), p. 11. Also see James S. Ettema and Theodore L. Glasser, *Custodians of Conscience: Investigative Journalism and Public Virtue* (New York: Columbia University Press, 1998), and Theodore L. Glasser and James S. Ettema, "Investigative Journalism and the Legitimation of Moral Order," paper

333333333333333333

NOTES 191

presented to the Association for Education in Journalism and Mass Communication, San Antonio, Texas (August 1987).

A very readable and entertaining history of the muckraking era can be found in Fred J. Cook, *The Muckrakers: Crusading Journalists Who Changed America* (Garden City, NY: Doubleday & Company, 1972).

The quote is from Dolores Flamiano, "The Birth of a Notion: Media Coverage of Contraception, 1915-1917," *Journalism & Mass Communication Quarterly*, 75:560-571 (1998), p. 567.

The role of the press in promoting civil rights is documented in David Halberstam, "The Education of a Journalist," *Columbia Journalism Review* (November/December 1994).

Sandra C. Taylor, "Vietnam," *New Grolier Multimedia Encyclopedia* (1993).

Lou Kilzer and Chris Ison, "A Culture of Arson," reprinted on pp. 149-189 in Kendall J. Wills (ed.), *The Pulitzer Prizes 1990* (New York: Simon & Schuster, 1990), p. 154. The first story in the report appeared in the *Star Tribune* on Oct. 29, 1989.

Thimios Zaharopoulos and Ronald E. McIntosh, "Newspaper Pulitzer Prizes and Their Relationship to Circulation," paper presented to the Association for Education in Journalism and Mass Communication (Kansas City, MO, August 1993).

Philip Meyer and David Arant, "A Test of the Neuharth Conjecture: Searching an Electronic Database to Evaluate Newspaper Quality," paper presented to the Association for Education in Journalism and Mass Communication (Kansas City, MO, August 1993).

For a review of the literature on social change, see David Pearce Demers, *The Menace of the Corporate Newspaper: Fact or Fiction?* (Ames: Iowa State University Press, 1996), pp. 109-114.

For a discussion of social changes that have taken place in the United States during the 20th century, see L. W. Banner, *Women in Modern America: A Brief History*, 2nd ed. (Orlando, FL: Harcourt Brace Jovanovich, 1984); R. Blauner, "The Ambiguities of Racial Change," pp. 54-64 in M. L. Andersen and P. H. Collins (eds), *Race, Class, and Gender* (Belmont, CA: Wadsworth, 1992); Celeste M. Condit, "Hegemony in a Mass-Mediated Society: Concordance about Reproductive Technologies," *Critical Studies in Mass Communication*, 11:205-230 (1994); J. R. Howard, *The Cutting Edge: Social Movements and Social Change in America* (Philadelphia: J. B. Lippincott, 1974); R. H. Lauer (ed.), *Social Movements and Social Change* (Carbondale: Southern Illinois University Press, 1976); D. McAdam, J. D. McCarthy, and N. Z. Mayer, "Social Movements," pp. 695-737 in N. J. Smelser (ed.), *Handbook of Sociology* (Newbury Park, CA: Sage, 1988).

For additional evidence of the media's role in social change see Donald L. Barlett and James B. Steele, *America: What Went Wrong?* (Kansas City: Andrew and McMeel, 1992); Leonard Downie, Jr., *The New Muckrakers* (New York: Mentor, 1976); Mark Neuzil and William Kovarik, *Mass Media and Environmental Conflict: America's Green Crusades* (Thousand Oaks, CA: Sage, 1996); David L. Protess, Fay Lomax Cook, Jack C. Doppelt, James S. Ettema, Margaret T. Gordon, Donna R. Leff and Peter Miller, *The Journalism of Outrage: Investigative Reporting and Agenda-Building in America* (New York: Guilford Press,

1991); and Leonard Sellers, *Investigative Reporting: Methods and Barriers* (Ph.D. Diss., Stanford, 1977).

Jesse Jackson's remarks were made in a speech he gave July 30, 1997, at the annual meeting of the Association for Education in Journalism and Mass Communication, Chicago.

David L. Protess, Fay Lomax Cook, Jack C. Doppelt, James S. Ettema, Margaret T. Gordon, Donna R. Leff, and Peter Miller, *The Journalism of Outrage: Investigative Reporting and Agenda-Building in America* (New York: Guilford Press, 1991), p. 246.

Rachael Carson, *Silent Spring* (New York: Houghton Mifflin, 1962).

Herbert J. Gans, *Deciding What's News* (New York: Vintage, 1979), pp. 68-69.

Jeffrey Alexander, "The Mass News Media in Systemic, Historical and Comparative Perspective," pp. 17-51 in Elihu Katz and Tomás Szecskö (eds.), *Mass Media and Social Change* (Beverly Hills, CA: Sage, 1981).

This history of corporate organizations is drawn from a number of sources, including Emile Durkheim, *The Division of Labor in Society*, trans. W. D. Halls (New York: Free Press, 1984 [1933]), see especially preface to the second edition; Daniel Bell, *The Coming of the Post-Industrial Society* (New York: Basic Books, 1973), pp. 269-298; S. Prakash Sethi, "Corporation," in *Academic American Encyclopedia*, electronic version (Danbury, CT: Grolier, 1992); and William H. McNeill, *History of Western Civilization*, 6th ed. (Chicago: The University of Chicago Press, 1986). There is no historical record of whether ancient Greece had corporate groups.

Statistical data are from U.S. Department of Commerce, *Historical Statistics of the United States, 1789-1945* (Washington, D.C.: U.S. Government Printing Office, 1949) and *Editor & Publisher International Yearbook* (various years).

Robert E. Park, "The Natural History of the Newspaper," *The American Journal of Sociology, 29*:273-289 (1923), p. 274.

My summary of the 18 studies is contained in David Pearce Demers, *The Menace of the Corporate Newspaper: Fact or Fiction?* (Ames: Iowa State University Press, 1996), p. 234-236.

The Jim Upshaw quote is from a personal e-mail message, May 2, 1999.

George A. Gladney, "Newspaper Excellence: How Editors of Small and Large Papers Judge Quality," *Newspaper Research Journal, 11*(2):58-72 (1990).

Roya Akhavan-Majid, Anita Rife and Sheila Gopinath, "Chain Ownership and Editorial Independence: A Case Study of Gannett Newspapers," *Journalism Quarterly, 68*:59-66 (1991).

Randall A. Beam, "The Impact of Group Ownership Variables on Organizational Professionalism at Daily Newspapers," *Journalism Quarterly, 70*:907-918 (1993).

Chapter 10 — The Global Managerial Revolution

For purposes of empirical research, corporate control is usually defined as "the power to determine the broad policies guiding the corporation, although it does not necessarily imply active leadership or specific influence on the day-to-day operations of the enterprise." See Robert J. Larner, *Management Control in the Large Corporation* (Cambridge, MA: Dunellen, 1970), p. 2. For a similar definition, see Neil Fligstein and Peter Brantley, "Bank Control, Owner Control, or Organizational Dynamics: Who Controls the Large Modern Corporation," *American Journal of Sociology*, 98:280-330 (1992). These definitions are much too limiting, however, as professional managers often control the day-to-day decision-making in most corporations.

Some of the scholars who have presented arguments in support of the managerial revolution hypothesis: Daniel Bell, *The Coming of the Post-Industrial Society* (New York: Basic Books, 1976); Adolf A. Berle, Jr. and Gardiner C. Means, *The Modern Corporation and Private Property* (New York: Macmillan, 1932); James Burnham, *The Managerial Revolution* (New York: John Day, 1941); Ralf Dahrendorf, *Class and Class Conflict in Industrial Society* (Stanford, CA: Stanford University Press, 1959 [1957 German version]); John Kenneth Galbraith, *The New Industrial State* (New York: Mentor, 1971); and Talcott Parsons, "A Revised Analytical Approach to the Theory of Social Stratification," in Richard Bendix and Seymour Martin Lipset (eds.), *Class, Status, and Power* (Glencoe, IL: Free Press, 1953).

Adam Smith, *An Inquiry Into the Nature and Causes of the Wealth of Nations* (Chicago: William Benton, Encyclopedia Britannica, Inc., 1952 [1776]), p. 324.

Max Weber, *The Theory of Social and Economic Organization*, trans. A. M. Henderson and Talcott Parsons (New York: The Free Press, 1964 [1947]), p. 338.

Adolf A. Berle, Jr. and Gardiner C. Means, *The Modern Corporation and Private Property* (New York: Macmillan, 1932).

James Burnham, *The Managerial Revolution* (New York: John Day, 1941).

Joseph A. Schumpeter, *The Theory of Economic Development* (Cambridge, MA: Harvard University Press, 1949).

John Kenneth Galbraith, *The New Industrial State*, 3rd ed. (New York: Mentor, 1978), pp. 107-108.

Daniel Bell, *The Coming of the Post-Industrial Society* (New York: Basic Books, 1976).

U.S. Temporary National Economic Committee, *The Distribution of Ownership in the 200 Largest Nonfinancial Corporations*, Monograph 29 (Washington, D.C.: U.S. Government Printing Office, 1940).

Robert Aaron Gordon, *Business Leadership in the Large Corporation* (Berkeley, CA: University of California Press, 1961 [1945]).

Robert Sheehan, "There's Plenty of Privacy Left in Private Enterprise," *Fortune* (July 15, 1966).

Robert J. Larner, *Management Control in the Large Corporation* (Cambridge, MA: Dunellen, 1970).

Philip H. Burch, *The Managerial Revolution Reassessed* (Lexington, MA: D.C. Heath and Company, 1972).

Joseph R. Monsen, Jr., John S. Chiu and David E. Cooley, "The Effect of Separation of Ownership and Control on the Performance of the Large Firm," *Quarterly Journal of Economics, 82*:435-451 (1968).

John Palmer, "The Profit-Performance Effect of the Separation of Ownership from Control in Large U.S. Industrial Corporations," *Bell Journal of Economics and Management Science, 4*:299-303 (1973).

Neil Fligstein and Peter Brantley, "Bank Control, Owner Control, or Organizational Dynamics: Who Controls the Large Modern Corporation," *American Journal of Sociology 98*:280-330 (1992).

David R. James and Michael Soref, "Profit Constraints on Managerial Autonomy: Managerial Theory and the Unmaking of the Corporate President," *American Sociological Review, 46*:1-18 (February 1981).

David R. Kamerschen, "The Influence of Ownership and Control on Profit Rates," *American Economic Review, 58*:432-447 (1968), and Brian V. Hindley, "Separation of Ownership and Control in the Modern Corporation," *The Journal of Law and Economics 13*:185-221 (1970).

See Chapter 7 for citations to my research on the corporate newspaper.

Chapter 11 — Global Media in the 21st Century

Bagdikian's quote is from Ben H. Bagdikian, *The Media Monopoly,* 2nd ed. (Boston: Beacon Press, 1987), p. 3. The quote from the fifth edition is also on page 3.

An extensive discussion of and additional references about structural differentiation and structural pluralism are contained Chapters 3-6 in David Pearce Demers, *The Menace of the Corporate Newspaper: Fact or Fiction?* (Ames: Iowa State University Press, 1996).

Thomas S. Kuhn, *The Structure of Scientific Revolutions,* 3rd ed. (Chicago: The University of Chicago Press, 1996).

Nicholas Abercrombie, Stephen Hill and Bryan S. Turner, *The Dominant Ideology Thesis* (London: Allen & Unwin, 1980).

Quote is from Stephen Hill, "The Dominant Ideology Thesis after a Decade, pp. 1-37 in Nicholas Abercrombie, Stephen Hill and Bryan S. Turner (eds.), *Dominant Ideologies* (London: Unwin Hyman, 1990), p. 2.

Phillip J. Tichenor, George A. Donohue and Clarice N. Olien, "Mass Media Flow and Differential Growth in Knowledge," *Public Opinion Quarterly, 34*:159-170 (1970).

Cecilie Gaziano, "The Knowledge Gap: An Analytical Review of Media Effects," *Communication Research, 10*:447-486 (1983) and Cecilie Gaziano, "Forecast 2000: Widening Knowledge Gaps," *Journalism & Mass Communication Quarterly, 74*:237-264 (1997).

Kasisomayajula Viswanath and John R. Finnegan Jr., "The Knowledge Gap Hypothesis: Twenty-Five Years Later," pp. 187-227 in B. R. Burleson (ed.), *Communication Yearbook*, Vol. 19 (Thousand Oaks, CA: Sage).

Chin-Chuan Lee, *Media Imperialism Reconsidered* (Beverly Hills, CA: Sage, 1980), p. 200.

Federico Mayor, "Preface," pp. 5-6 in *World Communication Report: The Media and the Challenge of the New Technologies* (Paris: UNESCO Publishing, 1997).

Appendix

For an introductory treatment of Max Weber's concept of bureaucracy, see Peter M. Blau and Marshall W. Meyer, *Bureaucracy in Modern Society*, 3rd ed. (New York: Random House, 1987). For the original work, see H. H. Gerth and C. Wright Mills (eds.), *From Max Weber: Essays in Sociology* (New York: Oxford University Press, 1946) and Max Weber, *The Theory of Social and Economic Organization*, trans. A. M. Henderson and Talcott Parsons (New York: The Free Press, 1964 [1947]).

For criticisms of bureaucratic organization, see Robert K. Merton (ed.), *Social Theory and Social Structure* (London: The Free Press, 1957 [1949]); Michael Crozier, *The Bureaucratic Phenomenon* (Chicago: The University of Chicago Press, 1964); and Robert Michels, "Oligarchy," pp. 48-67 in Frank Fischer and Carmen Sirianni, *Critical Studies in Organization and Bureaucracy* (Philadelphia: Temple University Press, 1984).

INDEX

200INDEX

Demers, David, xi-xiii, xv, xx, 179, 181, 183, 185, 187-189, 191, 192, 194
democracy, xii, xiii, xv, 3-5, 57, 63, 65-67, 73, 76, 79, 84, 106, 112, 114, 115, 119, 126, 138, 166, 169, 180, 185, 186
democratic ideals, xxii, 118
democratic principles, 4, 49, 79, 81, 176
democratic process, 66-68, 73
Democrats, 87, 102
Denmark, 13, 38
Dennis, Everette E., 181
deterministic, 133
differentiation (see *structural differentiation*)
diffusion, 69
Diller, Barry 31
discourse theory, 85
Disney (see *Walt Disney* and *Walt Disney Co.*)
diversity of ideas, xiii-xvi, 4-6, 8, 49, 59, 60, 62, 63, 67, 68, 70, 72, 73, 78, 79, 81-89, 91, 98, 124, 133, 138, 153, 157, 158, 160, 165, 166, 169, 173, 182-184, 187
division of labor, xxiv, 11, 16, 43-46, 78, 92, 107, 128, 143, 147, 148, 156, 158, 159, 168, 176, 177, 192
Dole, Robert, 103
Dominick, Joseph R., 181
Donohue, George A., 119, 170, 187, 190, 194
Doppelt, Jack C., 191, 192
Dorfman, Ariel, 76, 186
Doubleday, 37, 191
Downie, Leonard, 191
Downing, John, 180, 185
Duncan, Emma, 182
Dupagne, Michel, 187
Durkheim, Emile, xv, xvi, 128, 192

E

economic elites, 57, 62, 74, 76, 88, 94, 111, 115, 167, 172
economic institutions, 62
economies of scale, 8, 18, 45, 46, 48, 59, 71, 89, 91, 98, 131, 146, 162, 176

economy, 11, 22, 57, 68, 81, 82, 112, 143, 157, 161, 164, 179-185, 190
editorial vigor, 91
Efron, Edith, 189
Eisner, Michael 30
Elasmar, Michel, 90, 187
election(s), 103-106, 118, 121
elite(s), xxiii, 4, 13, 52, 57, 62, 74-76, 88, 94, 95, 102, 105, 109-112, 109, 111, 115, 123, 125, 126, 132, 133, 156, 161, 167, 168, 172, 173
Eltis, W. A., 183
Emery, Edwin, 181
Emery, Michael, 181
EMI, 40
empirical research, 53, 83, 93, 94, 109, 123, 143, 147, 166, 193
England, 13, 14, 43, 46, 51, 102, 107, 110, 115
Entman, Robert M., 190
entrepreneurial media, xxv, 5, 7, 48, 68, 70, 71, 91, 96, 177
environment, 64, 72, 88, 122, 125, 128, 130, 131, 158, 161, 173, 176, 190
environmentalists, 7, 73, 87, 94, 153
Epstein, Edward Jay, 190
ethics, 91, 96
ethnic conflict, 106
Ettema, James S., 120, 121, 185, 190-192
evolution, 79
Ewin, Stuart, 190
extremism, 106

F

family, 3, 15, 19, 31, 35-38, 46, 55, 56, 68, 84, 92, 96, 98, 109, 124, 128, 129, 140, 144-146, 149
fashion, 120
Federal Communications Commission (FCC), 33, 36, 42
Finnegan, John R., 171, 195
First Amendment, 104